RECOLLECTIONS

A JOURNEY OF COURAGE AND ABUSE

RECOLLECTIONS

A JOURNEY OF COURAGE AND ABUSE

CAROLYN BABER

COURTENAY BABER, MS LPC

KWE PUBLISHING, LLC

Baber, Carolyn, and Baber, Courtenay. *Recollections: A Journey of Courage and Abuse.*

Copyright © 2021 by Courtenay Baber

Published by KWE Publishing: www.kwepub.com

All rights reserved.

ISBNs: 978-1-950306-96-1 (paperback) 978-1-950306-97-8 (ebook)

Library of Congress Control Number: 2021905725

Note: With the exception of the authors, all names have been changed.

To all the survivors—and the people and animals who show them the way out of the darkness and into a more welcoming place.

FOREWORD

When I was asked to write this foreword I was told that this book was about horses helping a woman heal from sexual assault. Little did I know that this book would bring so much healing and pain with it while I read.

Horses have been a part of my life for as long as I can remember. My grandparents had a Quarter Horse gelding named Willy and a Thoroughbred mare named Paige. My aunt taught me how to ride in cabbage patches in Southern California. Some of my best and earliest memories include galloping with Willy through those fields. I never wanted to walk or trot, just run, as fast and as far as I could. I wasn't running from anything the way that Carolyn was in her book; however, I share in her healing through horses.

That is probably a gross understatement. Horses have served as such a powerful force of positive healing in my life that I dedicated my professional career as a therapist and executive business coach to partnering with these incredible beings and wise teachers. Although I never met Carolyn, we are kindred spirits in the aspect that I have found no better substitute for teaching people how to be better beings than a horse. Horses show us how to treat each other, how to support each other, how to take care of ourselves and our herds, and most importantly how to deal with pain and trauma.

Serving populations struggling with PTSD, addiction, eating disorders, and other mental illnesses through equine therapy has proven to me that the best therapists in the world have a beautiful coat, four hooves, a mane, and a tail. Horses bring healing to our lives that I never knew was possible and yet I have spent all my life benefiting from this majestic healing power.

Carolyn's bravery in sharing her story of sexual assault with such vivid imagery brought so much emotion to my life. I will admit to you as the reader, that I went to the barn and sat with my horses a few times while reading this book. My Clydesdale Paul sat with me through some of these chapters and held me while I leaned into Carolyn's life and inspiring journey with her mental health. Professionally I have so much respect for the decade-long dedication shared in this book to her recovery and struggles with depression. Personally, my heart empathizes with the pain that sexual assault can bring.

Although I had the benefit of an incredible childhood that my parents provided, I suffered an assault as a young adult and recall, as Carolyn describes, not having the words to share my pain with my family. Now having daughters of my own, I pray every day that they never know that terror and suffering.

Reading Courtenay's words explaining how she brought her mom's book to life was both incredibly beautiful and haunting as I can only imagine the strength that it takes to share this story on behalf of your mom. Knowing the truth that will be shared about your family, I can only thank you for that bravery and honesty.

This book is raw and real; however, one thing is absolutely certain. This book is filled with so much truth. The most powerful truth being the healing power of equines that bring light to the darkest of places and show us what quiet strength and loyal relationships truly look like. All the days that I could not stand in my life, I owe to my horse who carried me.

—Bunny Sumner Young, LPC
Founder of A Better Place Consulting, author of *Crossing the Line: Power Activities for Therapy and Learning*

INTRODUCTION

The world of human emotions is a complicated one, and the love between a child and parent is deep and intense at best. If things go smoothly, it will have moments of sadness that will stick with you that you will later laugh at and think about in simpler measure. However, it is when that relationship is rocked by inconsistency and cloaked in secrecy that problems begin to dance in the shadows of our minds, and they can dance from generation to generation.

This is what happened to my mother. This most sacred of bonds was broken between parent and child. It was instead replaced with lies, inconsistency, and secrecy. It created two worlds for my mother, and in those two worlds, she existed and found a way to move back and forth. She found a bridge between the two, a way to make sure she could stay connected and whole. That bridge for her was a horse. The quiet honesty of the horse allowed her to build trust in the world and to find courage in her strength. She was able to find hope and to build a relationship that did not let her down. This was a gift she gave to me. It was one of many she gave me in my life; however, the ability to be with horses, to love them deeply, and to feel their power and their gentleness in the same breath is the greatest gift.

I believe she wrote for a lot of reasons, reasons that changed over the time it took her to write her story. I believe at the end, she had come to learn that she had something important to say, and it needed to be said. I believe she wanted people to be able to learn from her story. She was a school teacher at heart, so I am not sure that teaching ever left her. Maybe more importantly, she truly recognized the distance she had come in healing during twenty plus years of therapy. She wanted people to know that healing was possible if work was done and commitment was made to the journey. She struggled with the journey. She sometimes had to be reminded to stay on it, and other times was so involved in it. She stayed on the journey till the end. She stayed, only wanting to learn more about herself and wanting to get better.

So, now you know why the book was important to my mother. Why is it important to me? It is important to me because this story is not only the story of my mother: it is the story of my family. It is the story of our struggles with her mental illness. She was the center of our family; she was larger than life. She would inspire and demand greatness, and she would also belittle and guilt. She was our mother, our caretaker; she was the one we ran to to get help and comfort from, and she was not always able to be there for us, in part because of what happened to her.

I was connected to my mother not only through my love of horses, the first gift she gave me, but also through the second gift she gave me, which was an interest in mental health. My interest in mental health began in fifth grade when I had to write a paper about the topic. I thought it was not right how people were treated in what were then called "insane asylums." I became fascinated, and I have not looked back. I have found recently a way to combine the two through equine assisted therapy, which is wonderful, and that is what all of us that spend time with horses know to be true.

I hope this story will be helpful to people who think or believe that there is no getting better or there is no hope in their situations. Things can always get better. There is always hope, and whenever you may think that something is not right, you should speak up. I think that people also get to a place where they are not able to go any further; they will not accept the negative conditions any longer. My mother reached that point that July day. She could not say it out loud to me in words, but she could say out loud to me in so many other ways. Her tears, her pain, her screams were for much more than just that day as I found out the next day when I finally confronted my sister. She did know one of the dark secrets of my family, and when I learned of this secret, I too refused to go one step further. I too said, "no more," and I made sure that my mother was sent to the hospital to get the help she and our family so desperately needed. So, our journey began and continued.

I am often told that I am just like my mother. At first, I thought that this was a bad thing. However, I now think that this is a good thing. I strive to have her optimism, her courage, her conviction, and her love. She loved so deeply and so completely despite her pain: that is a testament to her and her strength.

A few other things about this book that need to be noted. My mother changed the names of the people in the book when she wrote it, including her own. I believe that she changed the names because she wanted to give some cover to the characters in the book as they are real people. I think she wanted to offer some protection to them and to herself as she wrote her story and faced her past. So although the names are different, the characters are real. Some are living, some have since died, but the story will live as long as people continue to allow little girls to not be treated as little girls.

This is a book about love and a love story. There is a part of me that believes my mother wrote this book as a testament not only to love of horses but also to her love for her husband. The love they had for each other was the kind of love that not only breaks your heart it fixes it, too.

This book is not for the faint of heart; it will go to places that are not easy to read, so please consider your own comfort before diving in. It is a book of hope, and it does not leave you hanging for a resolution. It is a complex book about relationships, resilience, and a search for answers. You may not agree with the therapeutic techniques used in this book, and they may not be evidence-based currently. However, they were effective at the time for the client.

Finally, I hope this book will bring some enjoyment to the reader. This book explores a serious subject and goes to a dark place, but hopefully there can be something positive that will come from you reading this book. I hope it will give you strength, courage, and calm. I hope that you find the answers you need to your questions.

My mother had a saying that she would share all the time whenever anything good happened, and I think the end of my introduction and the beginning of her book is a good thing.

Now, isn't this nice...

—Courtenay Baber, MS LPC, 2021

1

MY JOURNEY BEGAN on a clear morning in July 1989. Linc, my husband, rolled over in bed and put his arm around me. I felt his breath on my neck and his body pressed hard against mine. I opened my eyes to the early morning sun. It was too early to be bright. There was still a softness to the mid-summer dawn.

"Lesley," he said softly.

I didn't move or speak. I didn't want to move. I lay there in limbo, waiting. What would he do next? I felt his hand move to my shoulder.

He shook me slightly. "Lesley, I have to tell you something, I can't stand to think of the shock to you."

I didn't care what he had to say. Nothing seemed to matter. I turned on my back and stared at the ceiling.

"What are you talking about? I have to get up and go over to the farm. The men will be there in a minute."

"I know, but I have to tell you this first." His voice was quiet but desperate. I could see him frowning out of the corner of my eye.

"What is it?" My voice had a monotone quality and sounded like someone sleepwalking. He gripped my shoulder and rose up a little, gently kissing my arm. His facial features were uneven and craggy with dark hair and skin that tanned easily. His build was stocky and thick, which made you know in an instant that he had great physical strength. Even with his strong build most people quickly knew he was easygoing and laid back. His eyes twinkled when he smiled, and most women loved him.

"They are coming this morning to put you in the hospital. They told me not to tell you, but I can't let you go over to the farm and be surprised like that."

The words sounded far away and hollow, but I knew what they meant. They were going to lock me up like they had done with Daddy, so long ago. So what? They were going to put me in a hospital. What difference did it make?

"Put me in the hospital, for what?" I asked the question, but I already knew. I knew, because I knew in my heart I couldn't go any further.

There was a huge timber above the bed in which was chiseled a shape resembling a car. I fixed my eyes on the car and imagined I was flying away. It was something I often did because I was desperate to leave—everything. "Put me in the hospital, like Daddy?"

"Yes."

"Where are they taking me?"

"St. Mary's, I think. Camille made the arrangements."

"Who are they?" I began to cry softly, the tears running down my cheeks, still raw from crying the day before. The day before was a Monday and the fourth of July. And, of course, the day before that had been Sunday, and then Saturday and Friday. Most people spent the weekend celebrating and enjoying the holiday. For me, it had been a deadly weekend of crying and depression. I remember actually saying out loud that nobody would help me. I had no idea that Lindsay was listening to me and she was going to help me. She and Rick had been here most of the weekend. Now, my deepest inner wish was coming true, even though I dreaded it and did not know what was going to happen to me.

I asked again, "Who are they?"

"Sarah and Lynn, Camille, Lindsay, Jimmy, and Kim; all of them are coming."

Sisters, daughters, son, and his wife. The whole family.

"I see." I wiped the tears on the edge of the sheet. "So, they're going to put me away like Daddy, lock me up. Anything to get rid of me, is that it?"

"No. They think you need help. I don't know. I am sorry, darling."

"Yes, I know you are sorry, but you're not sorry enough to help me, are you?" I sat up in bed. My head ached. My eyes were swollen almost shut.

"Camille called the doctor and is making the arrangements at the hospital."

"I see. When are they coming?"

"I don't know exactly, but early this morning."

Yes, I thought: Camille would be the one to make the arrangements. She's used to doing things. She has a business. A business I made possible, so she wouldn't have to relive my life doing something she didn't want to do like, teaching under the most difficult circumstances. Lindsay would help her because she has a master's degree in psychology and performed testing at a psychiatric hospital. But in my heart, I didn't care about anything, only that I knew at last someone was going to help me.

It was so scary. I didn't know what it was going to be like. I was going to have to tell this doctor all these horrible things and I didn't want to face it. I was going to have to tell them about the nightmares, the things that kept flashing in my mind. Worst of all, the thing that had happened when I was little, and which I had not told to anyone but Linc. No matter, I wanted someone to help me. A dog barked outside. Our bedroom was almost like being outdoors. There were two double windows on the east, French doors facing the north that looked out into a pecan tree which had been planted around 1750, and another set of French doors looking to the west and the horse barns. The bedroom had been a solace to me in so many ways, but now it was a reminder of what I wished for and felt I could never have.

I looked down at my feet, and my eyes began to brim with tears. My feet were long and thin. They were an immediate reminder of my mother's voice in the shoe store when I was a little girl. The voice came rushing from my childhood with the image of a shoe store in the forties. I was in a chair with one foot on a slanted footstool and the clerk was trying to slip my foot into the high top, lace-up shoe.

My mother sat beside me, frowning. "What size is that?"

The clerk looked up, his face, anxious. He picked up the box lid and quickly said,"

"It's a seven, Ma'am."

My mother's reply was instant. "Good gracious, I wore size nought until I was two years old. I never saw such big feet on a five-year-old child."

I squirmed in the chair, trying to make myself and my feet smaller or just to disappear. Would she never stop talking about my big feet? I hated going to the shoe store; I never wanted another pair of shoes. I knew everyone who saw me looked at my feet first and rejected the whole of me. Who could like a child with such huge feet? And it wasn't over yet.

"And these corrective shoes are so expensive. Between the doctor and the shoes, it's a fortune."

"Yes, Ma'am, but they will correct her fallen arches and prevent all that pain when she is older."

I am sure the shoe salesman felt for me, but I was a child and he needed to make a sale. Parents had complete control of their children then. There may have been sympathy, but there was no support.

My mother's answer was, "Well, I hope so."

"Come over here, young lady, and let's look through this machine and see how these shoes fit."

This was the only part of the trip to the shoe store that was bearable. I could stand in front of what looked like a drab jukebox, stick my feet inside, look down through the top, and see the bones in my feet. They looked black against the green background. The salesman would look to see how close the bones came to the edge of the shoe. It was awesome to think the machine could see through the shoes and into my feet. One look was never enough.

My mother's voice again. "Don't stand there too long, it's not good for your feet. It may cause something else and cost another fortune."

I flexed my toes. That humiliation in the shoe store stayed with me all my life. I learned to buy shoes, but I had gray hair before I learned to say with confidence to the salesman that I wore a size ten.

Like Mama said, my feet were big and ugly. I wore a size ten, and she wore a size nought until she was two years old. Those tiny feet were a great source of pride throughout her life.

I got up and went into my dressing room. My jeans were still on the floor from last night. I pulled out a clean tank top and sat down to put on my paddock boots.

Linc came in. "Don't go to the farm. Stay here and rest until they come."

"No. I'm not crazy, and if I am going to the hospital, the men have to know what to do."

"Jimmy can take care of that."

"No."

"Don't tell anyone I told you they are coming."

"Don't worry. I'll be surprised when they show up. Are you getting the sheriff, a judge, a lawyer, like you did for Daddy?"

"No, darling, of course not. You are not like your daddy."

"Oh! Yes, I am. I'm just not an alcoholic. That's the only difference."

"Yes, I suppose so. Just try to realize they're trying to help you."

"And I know something is wrong with me. Daddy thought he was perfect."

"The alcohol brought him to his knees, and he never really recovered. You are not an alcoholic and you won't have shock treatments, I'm sure. That's a big consolation isn't it?"

I pushed by him and left, ignoring his answer.

Since my mother's death, I had been managing the farm for the family. I knew every inch of the 1350 acres because I had grown up there, lived in the county all my life, and looked on Greenfield as the home I would eventually inherit. Now, as the manager, it was totally my responsibility. At least, that is the way I perceived the situation.

We–that is, Jimmy, my son and foreman, and I–had planned to move cattle that morning, so I went to the barn, saddled my horse first, and loaded him on the trailer. Snip was a thoroughbred gelding ex-racehorse, then show horse. He was older now, but like many horses, he naturally loved to chase cows and had learned the fundamentals quickly. I went through all the motions of saddling, loading, and driving without any thought of what I was actually doing. My mind could only think of what was supposed to happen later that morning.

I stopped in the yard at Greenfield and opened the ramp for Snip. Jimmy and the men were waiting. Neither Jimmy nor I mentioned the fact that his sisters were coming. In fact, I was denying at this point any need to be hospitalized, and Jimmy saw no need to arouse the lion before it was necessary. I rode, wrapped in my thoughts. Everything around me reminded me of my child-hood. There were the places I had played Cowboys and Indians with my cousins, places I had come to lick my wounds as a teenager, places that I had ridden with Daddy on his horse before I was old enough to ride the trails alone.

I had fallen off my first horse, Billy, galloping down this hill. This was the first thicket that held the big red fox we chased on Thanksgiving Day when Camille and Lindsay went on their first fox hunt. That was a favorite path Daddy liked to take on our Sunday afternoon rides. My nostalgia brought more tears to my eyes because I could see only a few happy moments in this reverie. These should have been happy times. What was wrong with me?

We finished with the cattle and were coming through the yard when my sisters, Sarah and Lynne, walked around the corner of the house. I would have been startled to see them if Linc had not warned me earlier. The sisters almost never came to see me or the farm. Linc said he felt so guilty about deceiving me about their coming. The thought even made me smile to myself because what I really thought was that Linc was trying to avert a very loud clash between my sisters and me about going to the hospital. He probably just couldn't stand another fight. But as I had told them all many times before, they didn't know what a good fight was. I had seen real fights between my mother and father. What little hell I could raise was nothing compared to what they had done. It was disgusting to me to see what little fighting my family could now stand.

Sarah stopped. "Lesley, we need to talk to you a minute. Can you come in the house?"

I forced back the tears. "Sure," just like I had no idea what they wanted. I gave Jimmy the reins and followed them into the house. I followed them into the very same room where we had met to put Daddy away some twenty years before. Even Jimmy and Kim came. I remember feeling so sorry for all of them, for having to go through this with me. I remembered the pain and humiliation in dealing with Daddy. My sisters were not there when Daddy was committed, so I felt really bad for them, too. Now they were going to know the pain and embarrassment of having a sister in a mental hospital when she wasn't even an alcoholic. She had just always been kind of crazy at times. She would yell and scream about something that seemed so insignificant to everyone else. Like Daddy often said about me, "She will blow up, but she doesn't mean anything by it." I looked around the room. They all seemed so young, and I felt so old. The tears began to roll down my cheeks; there was no holding them back any longer.

Even before they had uttered a word, I knew I had to go, knew I needed to go, and I wanted to make it as easy for them as possible. I knew they were all suffering that morning because of me.

Camille said. "Mom, we all think you need to go to the hospital. I have called the doctor and made the arrangements for you to go to St. Mary's." They sort of stood around and looked at me as if they hoped the whole thing would go away. It seemed so strange to me that no one was sitting down.

Lindsay said, "Mom, we know this is best and we will go with you."

Jimmy looked at me in his calm way and said "Mom, I think so too."

There was no arguing or wisecracks or crazy things happening like with Daddy. I was a woman, first of all, and a mother. Women are never allowed liberties of any kind that men are in similar circumstances.

For this reason, our meeting didn't last long. It was very short and quick. I agreed to go. Lynne went home. Sarah and Camille went with me back to my home at Raven Roost farm to pack. That didn't take long either. It was very solemn and there was little need to talk. I guessed they were waiting for me to explode and turn the whole day into another nightmare. But I had had enough of that, enough to last a lifetime. They would never believe it if I told them that deep in my heart, I really wanted to go.

Linc, Lindsay, and Camille took me to Richmond. I remember watching the familiar landscape go by and wondering when I would be able to be myself again. How long would I have to stay? When would the family trust me again? At that point, I really didn't care. I was going to get some kind of help, although I had no idea how anybody could help me then, doctor or otherwise. When you are depressed, as I was then, there is no hope.

I had seen Daddy depressed just as I was, but depression turns all the lights out and you are no longer able to see yourself or anyone around you. It is all dark and you want to stay there and hide. I was going to the hospital to hide. I remember thinking I wouldn't have to worry about the farm, the sisters, or Daddy. They were putting me away for good. It was all over.

I thought about Daddy most of the way to the hospital. I had put him away and now my children were putting me away. But I had not forced my family to have me committed as Daddy had. I was going as agreeably as I possibly could. I hadn't argued with them at all when they came that morning to get me from the farm.

I didn't know that finally, that fourth of July weekend, 1989, was to be a new beginning for me. The fifth of July was a new day. That day was the beginning of a whole new life for me. It was as though I had been dead all my life. My new life would unfold as my therapy progressed. But that's getting ahead of my story.

We pulled into the parking lot at St. Mary's and, as always

happens when you don't want to see anyone you know, there the person is right in front of you. A friend from the Hunt Club, someone I knew really well, and someone who knew everyone in the Richmond area, was crossing the parking lot heading straight for us. What to do? Everyone, including me, put on another face quickly so she wouldn't know what we were really doing there. We were all out of the car, suitcase in hand.

"Why, Lesley and Linc, what are you doing here?"

Linc smiled, the girls smiled, but no one said anything.

But I was up to it. I had had much more training than they have. I had had a lifetime of experience in knowing how to handle a situation like this. "Hi, Sue, how are you? What are you doing here?"

"I just came down to see a friend and I have to hurry back now to see what Henry is up to." She was laughing and smiling and gay.

"Oh, Sue," I said. "They're going to lock me up. Can you believe that? Will you come to see me?"

"Oh, right, they're going to lock you up. I know better."

She waved. "Bye, you all. Good to see you."

To this day, I don't know how I pulled that one off. It seemed so obvious to me that everyone could see that they really were going to lock me up.

Once inside the lobby of the hospital, my reserve was gone and the tears came again. The lady at the computer in admissions was very calm as she shoved a box of tissues at me and offered the trash can to catch the wet ones. I discarded the soggy ball and wiped my eyes again. She began asking the usual questions,

Name: Lesley Owens
Address: Derbyshire, Virginia
Date of Birth: May 15, 1936
Marital status: Married
Sex: Female
Father: Burton Henderson Jacobs, deceased
Mother: Esther Trimball Jacobs, deceased
Children: Three
Employer: Self-employed

Religion: Episcopalian
Do you wish a hospital minister to visit you? No

I answered the questions between sobs. I didn't know why I was crying. I just felt so sad. I didn't want to be crying. I couldn't help myself. The lady looked at me. She had a gentle face, framed with soft white hair. Her voice was low.

"Reason for admission?"

"Depression."

"That happens to us sometimes," she said.

"I don't know what's wrong with me," I moaned.

"That's why you're here. Let's see, who is your doctor? Oh! Dr. Maxfield. He's one of our best. I know you'll like him. Who recommended him?"

"My daughter recommended him. She works at Westbrook and does psychological testing there."

"That's nice. I know you're proud of her. Now, let's put this armband on you, and I'll ring upstairs to the sixth floor and let them know you're coming. Would you like a nurse to come down to meet you?"

Lindsay was standing behind the little cubby-hole. "No. We can take her up. I know the way."

The lady at the desk spoke evenly. She reached for my hand with the armband. I had not moved my arm from the desk. "I am sure you'll feel better soon. Take care and don't worry about crying here. We want to help you."

I looked at her and thought how nice of her to say that to me. It seemed so long since I had thought anyone really cared about me. She didn't even know me. But she sounded sincere.

"Thank you." It was all I could manage.

Linc picked up my bags, and we went out to the hall and up the escalator to the main lobby and the elevators.

The main lobby in St. Mary's has wooden paneling, high ceilings, and marble floors. There is a strong presence of strength and power. The doctors and staff walking around in white coats add to that impression, but it's really the height and grandeur of the walls and floor that make the difference. There is one other thing about the lobby. A small alcove shelters a white statue of the Virgin. I looked at it that day and said to myself, "I don't think even the Holy Mother can help me." And I know she was a good mother.

The elevator doors opened, and we walked in. Lindsay pushed the button for six and the doors closed. A doctor and another couple also got on and pushed their numbers. They didn't seem to notice me, but I knew they had to see the light on six. And I thought: they know, they're being polite and not staring, but they know. The doors opened and shut twice. I kept my eyes on the numbers at the top as the elevator progressed. The light went on six, the doors opened, and we faced a white wall with glistening tile floors.

To the left at the end of the hall was a large sign in legible block letters painted blue. Psychiatry. An arrow pointed the way. We walked slowly. No one said a word. The arrow pointed to large doors with glass at the top reinforced with wire. Lindsay walked up to the door and pushed a button. A voice answered, "Yes."

Lindsay replied, "Lesley Owens for admission."

My heart sank. I was near the end, there was no turning back, and I had to face whatever was on the other side of those doors. There was a clanking noise and Lindsay reached for the handle and pulled the door open. A nurse was standing there, but she didn't have on a white uniform. She was dressed in street clothes, with her identification clipped to her lapel.

The door closed and clanked again. Camille was standing closest to me, and I said, "See, I really am locked up. I can only leave now if you all and the doctor say so."

The nurse turned to me. "Now, let me show you around a bit as we go to your room. We try to make this as much like home as possible. This is our dining room."

It was a long room with windows looking towards the river and the best section of the city.

"This is our TV room. You can come in here any time you like. Across the hall is the nurse's station, and these adjoining rooms are conference rooms for group meetings and meetings with your doctor. Now we'll go down this hall to your room."

Linc and the girls were following without any comment. We came to my room and stopped. The door was already open. As I walked in, I realized it was small, a private room with a bath and place to hang my clothes, but no closet. There was a single bed, a nightstand, a bench with pillows, a chair, and some shelves with nothing on them. The room was painted a pale green and the furnishings were pleasant, but there were no curtains at the window. Then I noticed the lower window. The glass was very thick and there were scars everywhere. It had deep gashes in the glass and rough, jagged-looking scratches, but no chipped glass. I knew someone had tried to escape this room many times.

Linc put my bags on the bed and the girls made several comments about the nice room. I wasn't crying then, just exhausted. I was there and there was nothing else to do. I sat down on the bed and looked out the window. My window looked to the north across the hospital grounds and Patterson Avenue, a busy east-west thoroughfare to downtown. I watched the cars zip by, not in the least interested in where they were going.

Lindsay's voice interrupted my thoughts. It was a voice of authority. She was in charge now, not me. "Mama, we're going now to get some lunch and we're going to get you a few things you need, too. Do you want anything to read?"

"No. I don't need anything." I couldn't imagine having the energy to read. And just a few hours ago I had been on a horse getting up cows.

"Okay. Take care and we'll be back in a little while." They all kissed me on the cheek and left.

I lay down on the bed, put my head on the pillow, and began to cry again. I wiped my eyes on the bedspread and let my mind float away to all the bad things that had happened to me recently. It was all I had been able to think about for months. But that's why I was here. The hospital was going to help. I had to believe that. Another tear ran down my face as I closed my eyes and tried to hold back more tears.

2

———————

A FEW MINUTES later a nurse came by. This was one thing I learned very quickly. You were never left alone for more than a few minutes, night or day.

"Mrs. Owens, it is almost lunchtime, would you like to go to the dining room for lunch?"

"No, I am not hungry," I answered her quietly.

"All right, it won't be too long before dinner, and I am sure it has been a difficult morning for you. I will get you a snack in a few minutes."

I didn't ask any questions about anything. It just seemed useless. I would do what they said and try to be good. I didn't want to do anything to make them think I was any worse than I was. I knew I had to be bad to be there, or my family wouldn't have put me here. I had always tried to be good, but I never seemed to be good enough.

She went out to get me something for a snack. I could hear sounds in the hallway and people talking, but it didn't matter. I had no curiosity about them or their conversations.

The nurse returned with juice, crackers, and another woman with an identity badge and a notebook. She introduced herself and pulled up a chair to the bed. There wasn't any small talk and I don't remember the questions specifically, but they were all to the point and about my family life. I later found out she was a social worker. I remember thinking distinctly, "I can't hedge on any of the questions, and I have to answer the exact truth because the doctor will read them and say I didn't tell the truth."

Her first question was something like, "Why are you here?"

"I am depressed."

"Why are you depressed?"

"My husband had an affair."

"When did you find out about this?"

"I found out in March."

"Are you still living together?"

"Yes."

"Has he had other affairs that you know of?"

"I thought he had. I accused him, but it wasn't true."

"I see, so the first time you thought he was having an affair, but he wasn't, and this time you didn't think so, but he was."

"Yes."

"What does your husband do?"

"He's a lawyer."

"Does he practice in Staunton?"

"Yes."

"You have three children?"

"Yes."

"And your daughters had you admitted here. Why do you think they did that?"

"Because I was fighting with Linc and they thought one of us would get hurt, I guess."

"Does your husband fight with you?"

"No, he never fights back; I am the one who hits him."

"Have you ever abused alcohol, been arrested, or been in any other trouble involved with the court system?"

"No." I was embarrassed to be asked these questions and ashamed to be in a mental ward, but I answered them honestly. I was at the end of my rope. The damage was already done. I would never be the same again in the eyes of the world.

She closed her book and left. I lay down again.

As I have said, you are never alone very long in a mental hospital, and a few minutes later another nurse came in and asked me to unpack my clothes.

"Lesley, you can hang your dresses up here, and put your undergarments in the drawers, and your toiletries in the bathroom. But bring any mirrors, compacts, fingernail files, tweezers, and anything with glass or a sharp point to the nurse's station outside. We don't want you to hurt yourself while you are here."

My God, I thought. They think I may attempt suicide. I wouldn't do it with those things. I opened my suitcase and methodically began unpacking. It was slow and tedious because I really wasn't interested, and the events of the day had been so overwhelming. I was amused at the suicidal reference because suicide had been in my thoughts lots of times over the years, really since high school. I had planned it carefully many times.

It was always the same plan because it seemed a good, logical, clean plan that would result in sure death. My plan was to drive to Richmond and jump off the Huguenot Bridge. The only detail I had not fixed in my mind was the car. Should I stop right before I got to the bridge and run to the middle or stop on the bridge and leave the car? I couldn't decide which would be the most likely to succeed without someone intervening. The thought of the cold water on my body was always soothing. And I knew there were enough rocks under the surface to end my pain forever. It would be clean and quick. It wouldn't be messy for anyone.

Maybe some people think about what it will be like without them on earth. How their friends and family will react. Maybe they contemplate their funeral. I don't know. My thoughts and plans for suicide were before the fact; I didn't think about the funeral and what would happen afterward. I knew everyone would be glad I was gone, and I certainly would be, so there was nothing else to think about.

I smiled as the thoughts ran through my head. Maybe the reason I had never made the trip to the bridge was that my suicidal thoughts had most often been at night, but I knew, in the final analysis, there was a survival instinct that had forced me to live one more day. But I never drove over the Huguenot Bridge without thinking about my plans. It would be so easy. The cement railing was low and the bridge was high enough.

I finished unpacking, then gathered up the glass and metal objects in both hands and walked to the nurse's station. A nurse was writing on a chart. "Excuse me; I have these things for you."

She looked up. "Yes, this is just a precaution and you can have them all back when you leave. If you need anything in particular, just ask and one of us will help you."

"Thank you." I turned and started back to my room. She was really nice, but it was so obvious what they were doing. They didn't think I was capable of taking care of myself. Maybe I wasn't. Maybe I would try to kill myself with some of those things. Maybe I would try to beat the window out with a chair as others before had tried to do. I had only been here for a few hours. I didn't know what it was really going to be like.

As I walked into my room, I noticed another door beside the bathroom. I hadn't noticed it before. It was small, like a closet door. The knob turned easily. There was another door behind it with a half glass top and a light switch beside it. I clicked the switch and stared into a small box-like room with nothing but the walls and a floor. I caught my breath. This was solitary confinement, or as close as I had ever been to it. I leaned my head against the glass and the tears streamed down my cheeks for the forty-eleventh time that day.

They had put me in this room to prepare for anything. They took away everything that I might hurt myself with, and they had this little room to put me in if I became violent. What else was there that I didn't know about yet? I wept for a while, feeling sorry for myself and hating myself, and then I cut the light off and closed the door. And I waited for the next nurse, social worker, maybe even a preacher. They always came around in the hospital.

At dinner, we sat down at tables of six. A hospital tray was set before us with everything we needed. Nobody said anything to me, and I didn't bother to talk to them. I just ate a little and watched.

There wasn't much conversation. Some people were not eating, some were picking at their food, and every once in a while someone would yell. But it didn't seem too unusual or frightening. I wasn't afraid anyway. It all seemed natural to me. We were just a bunch of very sad people.

A nurse came in pushing a cart with lots of small medicine bottles on it. This was to become a routine. After meals, the meds nurse came in with her bottles, cups, pitcher, and chart. As she called out the names, each person came up and took his or her meds. The nurse had to watch you take it, swallow and drink. Sometimes someone refused. Then a small group of nurses came in and quietly went out with the patient. Later I learned the patient was escorted back to the ICU unit and was given the medicine, one way or another. After mine, I went back to my room and lay down.

It wasn't long before a man knocked on my door. It was open. They said the doors had to stay open. I sat up.

"Mrs. Owens," he said, as he walked toward me with his hand extended. "I am Dr. Maxfield."

My heart did another flip-flop in panic. How could Camille do this to me? This man was handsome, tall, imposing, dashing, well-dressed, and had a wonderful voice. And I was supposed to tell him all my secrets? How could I? He was so intimidating. I knew I looked a wreck; my life was a wreck. How was I going to talk to him? And he had another quality that I couldn't name at the time and certainly didn't consciously see, but it was the real reason I felt intimidated. The man reminded me of my father. There was something about his mannerisms and body language, besides the fact he was tall and muscular.

"May I sit down?" He sat on the bench and crossed his leg. He had on gray pants, black loafers, a blue vest with a red tie, and a navy blazer. His shirt was blue striped with a white collar and cuffs. He looked very dapper. He was totally at ease, as he should be, and I was totally ill at ease. The more I took in about him, the less I felt I could talk to him. He talked easily while reaching in his pocket for something.

"How do you feel?"

"Not good."

"So, you are depressed."

"Yes." For some reason, I wasn't crying then. I just looked at him and thought how much I dreaded telling him all the things I had to say.

He was fiddling with something in his hand.

"Do you mind taking pills to help you feel better?"

"No, I'll do anything."

"I'll leave instructions for something and I will be back to see you tomorrow."

He got up and left. I hated myself for being afraid of him because he was very nice and had certainly said nothing to upset me. He was just too handsome, too confident, too tall, too big. I was not aware of the significance of this at the moment. My morbid feeling was much worse after he left. I just couldn't imagine being open with him. And the worst thing was I knew I was not pretty, not smart, I was from the country, and I had nothing that could possibly make him think I was worth anything. The fact that he was a doctor and was supposed to help me never entered my mind. I was seeing him only as a man and I was afraid.

I looked out the window for a long time. Watching the cars stop and go at the light on Patterson Avenue. Where were those people going? How many of them were as unhappy as I? How many were going to a meeting of some kind? Maybe some were going to the mall, to a movie, to their home, to play tennis. There were so many options. I soon realized I didn't have to go anywhere or see anyone. I could just watch these people. I was safe in this mental hospital. I wouldn't have to face anyone or be anybody else. I could just sit and watch the world go by.

I didn't even think about the farm. What difference did it make? There was nothing I could do.

The cars kept going by. It was so easy to sit and watch, so easy and safe. Twilight came and the cars all had headlights now. Two bright beams on each car, like bugs or ants in a line, going, going - - - - - - a never-ending line. I watched the lights on the trees, making shadows, shapes, contortions of all kinds. Yet the leaves were a feathery background making a soft playground for the shadows.

A nurse came in and announced bedtime and more medication. I left my reverie and undressed. The pills came with juice. I didn't even ask what they were. I took them and lay down. The nurse said she would leave the door open a crack because they would be checking on me during the night. If I awoke I was not to worry, they were just looking in on me. I thought this was a little odd and certainly unnecessary, but lots of things had been that day so why bother, just let them do whatever.

Sometime during the night, I awoke to a great commotion. There were lots of people in the hallway and they were making lots of noise. A man's voice shouted, loud and clear above the rest. "Just call me snake. There is not a goddamn thing wrong with me except my goddamn boat ran ashore. Just call me snake, that's what I am, a goddamn snake."

I sat up in bed listening. People were opening doors, scuffling. And this man kept on. "There is nothing wrong with me except my goddamn boat ran ashore. Just call me snake." I felt groggy, but I could tell the nurses were having a hard time with this guy, whoever he was. There was more noise, then quiet. I went back to sleep.

Several times during the night, I awoke to a flashlight in my eyes and a nurse would say to me, just checking. It all seemed so funny, but the sleeping pill was working.

There were other times I awoke to hear doors open and shut. Each time there was lots of talk wherever these doors were. It sounded like double doors shutting against each other. Sometimes I could hear people hollering. What was going on behind those doors? I had no idea what it was or why these people were so wide awake.

The next morning, I could hardly drag myself out of bed. My head weighed a ton and all I wanted to do was stay in bed and sleep, but I knew I couldn't do that.

All my life, no matter the circumstances, from going to school after an all-night fight between my parents, to worrying myself to sleep as a teenager that I might be pregnant when my conscious mind knew I wasn't having sex, I had always done what I had to do. I thought getting up and going to breakfast was one of them.

The sleeping pill had worked, but the antidepressant was slower. My depression that morning was abominable. If the floor could have swallowed me walking to breakfast, I would never have known it. My thoughts were deep and dark, black images crossing a gray landscape rutted in gullies with jagged edges no one could cross, yet I was making my way. I felt hopeless, but I kept going on a natural instinct of determination and courage. I kept going on, not knowing or caring what was on the other side, only what was before me had to be crossed. The truly depressed person cannot see beyond the landscape before them. There is no tomorrow that is distinct from today.

I remember watching my feet mark the black and white tiles. Each step was two tiles; it was my way of going forward. I sat down at a table with a tray before me, semiconscious of what was around me. There were other people, some in bathrobes, some dressed, some staring at their food, some talking, some even eating. I ate something because that was what I was told to do. I spoke to no one and no one bothered me.

Then I heard the voice again. "Just call me snake; I am just a goddamn snake." The voice got closer. The words were the same I had heard before. A few minutes later, the voice sounded through the door. A heavy-set blond man, about forty years old, came in with a bedspread wrapped around him as if it were a Roman toga and he was Caesar. At any other time in my life, the scene would have been hilarious, but I didn't laugh. I watched him parade around the room, preaching his same sermon. He didn't see anyone, and he didn't sit down. Obviously, he had been told to go to the dining room.

A woman at my table elbowed the woman next to her and said, "Suppose you were married to that."

Her answer, "He's a macho bastard, isn't he?"

They both laughed.

Soon, a group of men nurses came in and gently pushed him

out the door. The women smiled. "They will fix him, he won't be preaching for a while."

I wondered what "fix him" meant, but I didn't ask.

After breakfast, I took my tray up, took the meds, and started back to my room.

On the way, I discovered what "take care of him" meant for Mr. Snake. He was sprawled out on the couch in the dayroom. His head resting on the back, both arms extended, his legs straight out in front of him with his bedspread crunched under him. He had on a pair of shorts and no shoes. He was snoring. That was another hilarious sight that did not at the time strike me as funny. We all just walked past him, looking without seeing.

Back in my room, I threw myself across the bed again. It was so good to lie down. I must have been exhausted both physically and emotionally.

A few minutes later there was a soft knock at the door. I thought maybe I didn't hear someone knocking, as the door was already open, and whoever it was could just walk in. The knock came again. I rose up this time. Two women were standing there looking at me. One was tall, and thin with brown hair, the other short, and stout with graying hair. They looked at each other. The tall one spoke.

"Honey, we don't know who you are, but we saw you at breakfast and we saw you coming back to your room. We just wanted to tell you that you can't stay in your room during the day or you'll never get out of here. We know. You get up now and come on to the dayroom. If a nurse walks by and sees you on your bed, it's a black mark against you and means at least two or three more days added to your stay, every time they catch you."

"I see. All right, where is the dayroom?"

"It's right across from the nurses' station. There's a TV and magazines there, and other games too. Come on, we'll show you."

I got up and started toward the door. The tall one said, "I'm Jean, and this is my friend Vie. We're roommates and you can come to our room any time you want to. We can all sit around and talk, but you can't stay in your room by yourself."

Again, I said, "I see. I guess I need someone to tell me what's going on."

"Come on, we'll show you where the dayroom is."

I didn't care where the dayroom was, and I really didn't care if I never got out of the place. I just wanted to sleep and be left alone, to lick my wounds. I had plenty of them. My wounds in order were: my husband's affair of three years; the commercial landfill, which had been my idea to bring to the county; the dope case, as I called it; my husband's family; my family and my childhood; and in my estimation a generally failed life. In my mind, there was plenty of reason just to stay in the hospital. I was locked up, and as my family thought–meaning my sisters and children–could do nobody any harm. My husband only wanted me to forget the affair; the rest would work itself out.

We walked down the hall while they pointed out rooms I needed to be aware of, doctor-patient conference rooms, group meeting rooms, payphone. The doors on the phone booth were padlocked. They were only opened at certain times of the day.

Mr. Snake was still sprawled on the couch in the dayroom. My friends turned up their noses and walked around him in disgust. Jean said, "Isn't he something, I bet anything he's an alcoholic who beats his wife and children and anything else he can get his hands on." Vie nodded in agreement.

They turned their attention to me. "Let's sit down for a while before the meeting."

"What meeting?" I asked.

"Oh, you want to know about our hall meeting. One of the counselors will be here and tell you all about it. Don't worry."

The intercom came on a few minutes later and a gentle voice announced the weekly hall meeting. Everyone was to come to the dayroom.

The patients slowly drifted in. Jean and Vie didn't want me to miss anything important like who were the sickest patients.

"See that girl over by the window. She's been here for four years. Can you believe that, four years? She never talks to anyone and never has a visitor. Stay away from her. She is really odd. And see the man with the suit and tie. He's a preacher. He talks to himself all the time and twiddles his fingers." They laughed. I looked at the girl, maybe in her twenties. She seemed withdrawn and sullen. The little man in the suit looked like a preacher, which certainly didn't interest me. I had seen enough preachers to last a lifetime and could care if I never saw another one. Worst of all, it didn't seem strange that a preacher would be locked up like me.

A young-looking counselor came in with his clipboard.

"Good morning all. Let's go to the dining hall where we can all sit down and spread out more."

We obeyed, following him down the hall like a quiet bunch of zombies. At least that's how I felt. We left Mr. Snake on the couch. He wasn't able to join us yet. After we were all seated, the counselor introduced himself and then introduced the new patients, including me. As I raised my hand to be recognized everyone turned to look. It was at this moment that I realized I was truly one of them. All these sick, crazy people sitting around, and I was there too. Their looks were of acceptance. I looked to them like I belonged there. No one said anything or smiled. They just looked and turned back to the counselor.

The counselor went on. "The first order of business is work duties for the week. For those of you who are new, we assign certain areas of the hall for each patient to be responsible for during the week. Whatever job you choose, you must accept for the week. This is a serious responsibility and gives us an indication of how you are progressing." Pressure, I thought. They are putting more goddamn pressure on me than I can stand. Something else you have to do to get out of here. I don't care. I had just as soon stay. But that would mean failure and I could not let myself fail again. I listened carefully.

"Let's get down to business, shall we? First–there is the TV. Who wants to be responsible for the TV?" Hands shot up all around, but there was no waving like in school; everyone was very subdued. "Well, I know this is the choice job, so it can't be someone who has already had it. How about you, Neal, would you like this job?" The man smiled and put his hand down. "Neal, you know if the TV is left on and no one is watching it, you must turn it off. Also, you are the only one who can turn it on in the mornings, and it is your job to see that it's off at nine o'clock at night. If there are any problems, you report them to the nurse's station." He nodded. He understood and was very happy with the responsibility.

The counselor continued through his list until there were only a few of us left: the girl who stared out the window, the preacher, me, and several more who sat quietly waiting. The anticipation seemed to be enormous. We all wanted to show someone we could do something. I realized I had better volunteer for something, or I would be left out and that would definitely be a black mark against me. "Who would like to take care of the laundry area?" I raised my hand. "Good, Mrs. Owens. Okay, you check the personal laundry room each morning and night to see that nothing is left there.......no clothing, magazines, newspapers, and the like. If there is, turn it in at the nurses' station."

I hit a panic button. What had I done? I didn't even know where this laundry room was. Could I do this, would I make a mistake, what if someone was in there when I went to check? I didn't think I could confront anyone, not even to ask about their things. This panic was not new. My heart was pounding, and I was scared to death. I lowered my head and waited. When the meeting was over, I went up to the counselor and asked where the laundry room was and exactly what I was supposed to do again.

He was very gentle and patient and explained it once again. I said, "I'll do my best."

At ten-thirty, we had our first meeting to discuss getting along in a group. There were six of us and a counselor in a room all seated around a table. I was with the preacher again, but the girl who stared out the window was not there. The preacher was the only man and he refused to sit at the table. He sat in the corner alone, looking at us but not participating. This is bad, I thought. This preacher is definitely out of it and I am in the group with him.

The discussion proceeded, but I didn't say anything. I watched. The counselor was a very nice girl, soft voice, patient, and gentle. I began to feel more relaxed and drowsier. Finally, when I thought I could no longer sit up, I interrupted and told her. She immediately went to the door and called a nurse. They talked for a minute and she came back in. "Mrs. Owens, the nurse is going to call your doctor. She'll be right back." I couldn't believe the immediate response. This wasn't like most hospitals.

Then I was frightened. What was the doctor going to say?

Were they going to put me behind those double doors that they called the ICU? I wanted to sleep, but I didn't want to go behind those doors. There were terrible sounds back there. I didn't want to be put there. The discussion went on. A few minutes later a nurse came in and said, "Mrs. Owens, your doctor says this is a residue from the sleeping pill last night. It's nothing to worry about; you'll probably feel much better this afternoon. He will see you at rounds." She smiled, patted my shoulder, and left. I felt a sense of relief. Maybe I could stay awake until lunch.

Our next group meeting was at eleven fifteen, for handicrafts. This is really something, I thought. Talk about Mickey Mouse, this is me, and yet I didn't really feel that cocky. Could I do this? The counselor laid out kits of needlework to choose from. An embroidery kit with a picture of a pine tree struck my eye. Perfect. I picked the kit up and looked closer. It was a big pine tree on the bank of a pond with more pines on the hillside in the background.

I fingered the kit, thinking, How appropriate. My whole life has been involved with pine trees. My heritage, my livelihood, my identity is bound by pine trees and lumber. I did not know at the time that my illness was immersed in a dark amber slime–like what rotting pine bark produces. A slime that absorbs sounds and weather and shocks, and could tell tales of anguish and death and survival if it could talk. But, as Freud says, everyone has a conscious and a subconscious mind, and my subconscious mind did know the truth. In its simple way, it was saying, Here is your answer, in this little package of plastic, cloth, and thread, the answer to all your hysterics is in here. The amber slime would appear to me again in the ugliest way as I waded through the therapy. So, I fingered the plastic bag kit and told the counselor quite innocently, "This is what I want to do."

"Great, Mrs. Owens, there are needles in this basket. You pick one and if you need any help just let me know." I looked at the package a while longer, then tore open the top and pulled out the cloth. It was very small. My first thought was, Can I finish this in two days? I didn't realize how much I had slowed down. I looked at the design thinking, What should I do first? It seemed like a major decision. What part of this simple design can I do now? I looked carefully at the water, the grass, the background, the sun, and the pine tree. I was sure of only one thing. The last thing I would do was the tree itself. I chose a needle and decided it would be easiest to begin with the sand along the shore of the lake.

Lunch was uneventful. Now, it was rest time. Thank goodness. I could go to my room, lie down, and go to sleep. I didn't care what I dreamed or thought about, just to put my head down and rest. I was generally aware of the intercom the whole afternoon. There were announcements of all kinds: doctors on the floor, patients to the nurses' station, people walking up and down the halls. Who cared? I didn't. None of the announcements were for me and certainly no one was coming to see me. I didn't have to worry.

Rest time was over. I got up, went to the bathroom, looked at my face, and decided I might as well go to the dayroom and wait for supper. I would be out of my room. I sat down in the dayroom and tried to look as if I were watching TV, but I wasn't. I was watching the other patients. All like me, locked up for something.

Mr. Snake was no longer with us. I didn't know what had happened to him, but he had disappeared. Behind the double doors, I thought. At any rate, he was gone, and I didn't see or, I might add, hear him anymore.

Dinner was normal, then med time. Nothing unusual happened. My friends walked with me back to the room. "Your doctor will be around in a little while. Is everything okay? Try to appear relaxed if you can. Don't be nervous. That counts against you."

"Thank you," I said, without any emotion or outward sign that whatever happened mattered. The truth is...it didn't matter. How could things be any worse for me? I didn't want to talk to any doctor, let alone the one I had seen the night before. It was not going to be easy for me. Like everything else, it was going to be tough. I just had to brace myself for it.

It wasn't long before the doctor knocked on my door again and said, "Mrs. Owens, let's go up to one of the conference rooms so we'll have more privacy."

"I'll come." I followed him up the hall and watched as he took a great handful of keys from his pants pocket and began trying to unlock the door. After several tries, the door swung open to a little room with two overstuffed chairs, a lamp, and an end table. We went in and sat down.

"Well, tell me about yourself."

"You mean you don't know me from all the coverage on TV? I am a very famous bad person."

"Oh, really, well I'm sorry, I don't know you." He almost laughed.

"Well, you're the only person in the State of Virginia who doesn't know all the bad things I've tried to do in Derbyshire County. I'm going to poison the ground, the groundwater, the streams, even the Chesapeake Bay."

"Well, if you're going to do that, you are quite a person."

I looked at him. I don't care what you say. I know you know me, and I know what you think of me. Like all of those so-called friends I grew up with in Derbyshire County. Like my sisters, who haven't faced a bit of the heat. No one has sent them rubber snakes in the mail, called them up and said they were pigs, shot at their cars, or painted their husbands' office with bad words. They don't give a damn about me and never have. I don't understand why, but I know they don't.

"Why are you here?"

"I am worrying my family to death. They think I am going to kill my husband, myself, or someone else. They wanted to put me someplace where I would be cured fast."

"I see."

"Yes, my children, especially, think you can fix things overnight. Young people always think that."

"That's true."

"I was going to take a trip to Ireland next week, but I guess that's off now. I am locked up in here, that's for sure."

"You like Ireland."

"Yes. I've never been there, but I know a little about it."

"I'm Irish."

A spark of interest went through me. "Really? I thought I noticed a slight accent."

"No, I was born here."

An immediate feeling of rejection flashed over me. Now see, you idiot, I said to myself, made another fool of yourself, didn't you? I could kill myself, damn it. I can't do anything right. Now he knows not only all the bad things he can see, but I also am too tall, too ugly, my hair is awful, my feet stick out like a sore thumb, my skin is bad, and on top of that, I make silly mistakes. I twisted in my chair and tried to push my feet under the chair. There was no way to hide except be quiet.

"How long has this affair been going on?"

"Three years?"

"How did you find out about it?"

"I found some letters she had written in his briefcase."

"What does he say about it?"

I laughed. "He says he didn't have an affair. She chased him."

"So, he doesn't acknowledge it.?"

"Yes, I know she chased him. In fact, the first time I met her I told him she was after him, but he didn't believe me."

"Well, you were right, weren't you?"

"Yes. It doesn't do any good now."

"So, you're still together?"

"Yes, he says he never loved her, he only loves me. You know, the same old stuff."

"Do you trust him?"

I looked at him for a moment and waited. I wanted my next words to have an impact. I said very slowly. "I don't trust anybody now. When I married him, I didn't think he would hurt me." I shook my head, "But he did. I told him from the very beginning, when I first met this woman, that she was after him and he insisted I was wrong."

"Well, you were right." Again. It was a statement of fact. He believed me. It was surprising to have someone believe me so quickly, without questioning me, drilling me, or doubting me. I looked at him for a second and said quietly.

"Yes,"

"Have the two of you ever had any counseling?"

"We were going to a marriage counselor before I came here."

"Did it do any good?"

"Maybe some, I don't know. But he just won't tell me the truth."

"How do you mean?"

"Oh, he says it was just sex and it didn't mean anything. And I say you don't see someone for three years without feeling something. And during those three years, he lied like a dog about it and lying just sends me over the edge. I don't know why. I just can't stand a lie."

"Yes, sometimes a lie is hard to take. We'll stop now and I'll see you tomorrow. Is everything else all right here?"

"Yes."

He left, walking down the hall, tall, straight, confident, immaculate in his dress, his black hair neatly combed. But, I thought, he doesn't have those blue eyes like some of the Irish. Well, he knows what a wreck I am now, but I did get through it. I don't know how.

I walked back to my room. It must be almost time to go to bed. At least I can lie down and maybe go to sleep. In my room, I undressed and got ready for bed. I made it through the first day, a lot of mistakes I knew, but I made it. I just wish I didn't have to talk to that doctor. It is so hard to look at him. There is something so intimidating about him. He is very nice, but he scares me. I don't know why and there is nothing I can do about it.

That night I slept better. Maybe I was used to the noises by then and the checks by the nurses, maybe it was the medication, but I was feeling better too. At least I wasn't crying all the time; I was still morbidly sad, but not crying. There is something about a psychiatric hospital that makes you feel safe, free of the outside world.

Maybe I am the only one who feels this way, but I don't think so. Somehow you know your life has been taken out of your hands and the only thing you have to do is rest and get well.

I went to sleep that night, as I had every night since March, wondering how I had misjudged Linc so much in thinking he wouldn't hurt me. How had he allowed that woman to take over his life? What had happened to my life? I had believed he would never, ever hurt me and he had. The first time was in the "dope case" as everyone in the county called it. He, as the Commonwealth's Attorney, had signed the papers to let the defendants out of prison and not told me about it. I had read it in the Richmond Times-Dispatch on Easter Sunday. It was front-page news.

I knew as I held the paper in front of me and tried to take in what I was reading, that this would destroy his career as a prosecutor and make it impossible to practice anywhere else in the state, certainly not get a job in a firm. He had betrayed not only me but his friend, Denis, a Commonwealth's Attorney in Northern Virginia, whom he had asked to help him prosecute the case. The prosecutor was quoted in the same story saying, "I knew nothing of the deal to release the defendants." Linc had not told him what he was doing. Why had Linc succumbed to the pressure of the defense attorneys, I asked myself over and over. I felt so responsible because Denis had warned me in numerous calls from Fairfax: "Don't let Linc cave in." Why had Denis seen this coming, and I had not? I thought our support was all Linc needed. I never dreamed he would turn the defendants loose and not even tell me. And certainly, he would have told Denis what he was doing.

Then there was the landfill. Why was everyone against it? Why couldn't they see that the county needed the money desperately, and there were few places to get that kind of tax revenue?

That's when I found out about Linc's three-year affair. It was more than I could stand. I was so confused and totally depressed by it all. My thoughts went in circles and never came to any conclusion. I was trapped and beaten at every turn. I could no longer trust Linc. His family had never liked me, and the people whom I had known all my life were after my skin because my family was trying to bring a landfill to the county. There was nowhere to turn except to my children. I still believed in their love and support. As the worries revolved in my mind, the sleeping pill took over and my problems were buried in dreams I did not at that time remember.

A new day started as usual. Routine is good for everyone's faith whether you are sick or not. Change is a shock. For the depressed person, routine can be counted on and is the best of all worlds, except to have all your problems solved like in a fairy tale. I did not know it as I dressed, but that very morning, what I perceived to be a major problem was about to be solved.

3

I sat with my friends for breakfast. We didn't talk because I was dreading the moment I would have to see the doctor again. They were talking, but I paid little attention. I didn't care what they said because I had my own troubles.

After meds, I noticed doctors were coming around and talking to patients or leaving with them. Oh, God, I thought, I am going to have to see him again this morning. Why can't they just leave me alone? I won't bother anybody ever again if they will just leave me alone and let me sleep. But it wasn't to be, and I knew it.

A young doctor walked up to my table and said, "Mrs. Owens."

I looked at him and a wave of apprehension spread over me.

What did he want? He wasn't Dr. Maxfield. Why was he here? What was going to happen now? I opened my mouth and a very quiet "Yes" came out.

"May I sit down? I am Dr. Thomas. Dr. Maxfield has to be away and, if it is all right with you, I will be taking over for him for the next few days."

"Yes." My vocabulary seemed very limited. I was so surprised to see another doctor and immediately felt relieved. I didn't understand why. Dr. Thomas seemed much smaller, his voice was quieter, he had a wonderful open face and he seemed much less imposing. I felt more comfortable talking to him. Why? He was even better looking than Dr. Maxfield, dressed just as well, had a beautiful understated gold watch, but his hands were smaller. What was it? There was nothing intimidating about him to me. I still dreaded talking to him, but I definitely felt more at ease.

He did not stay long, just went through my chart, marking things, making notes, and asking routine sorts of questions. He was closing my chart when I heard myself say, "Will you take over my case even when Dr. Maxfield comes back?" I couldn't believe what I had done. I had actually asserted myself. I couldn't believe it, but I was glad I had done it.

He looked up at me a little surprise in his smile and said, "Of course I will, if that is what you want."

"Yes, it is what I want." I could hear the relief in my voice as it spread over my body.

After he left, my friends came over.

"Who was that? We didn't recognize him, but he was good-looking."

"I don't know exactly what his name is, but he is taking over for Dr. Maxfield while he is away. He seemed real nice and I liked him."

"Oh! That's so good," they said. "He looks nice. We just haven't seen him around much. So, you don't know much about him?"

"No, I don't know a thing really."

"Well, that's good...we would know it if there was something bad about him."

"Oh, yes, I am sure you would."

We went to the dayroom and waited for the daily activities to begin. We always came to breakfast dressed. Not in bathrobes, as lots of the younger patients did. That would be very improper for us. We talked and whispered like college friends, or friends at work, women who had something to talk about; but more importantly, we trusted each other.

We had to be a funny sight: three middle-aged women in a psych ward whispering, talking in low voices as if we were teenagers talking about the latest heartthrob or movie or scandal.

We were bound together because we were women who had all learned individually that life is a bitch, as they say, and then she had puppies. To us it wasn't a joke, it was the truth, and we were in the psych ward as proof.

No one was going to look out for us. No one had. That's why we were here. If we were to survive and get out, we would have to do it on our own. We could help each other in small ways, but we all knew, in the end, it was up to us. We all knew too, we didn't want to end up alone like the other patients, keeping to ourselves, looking out the window, talking to the floor, pacing up and down the hall, sitting, holding our heads. Those patients were gone, they had slipped over the edge and only a miracle would get them out. We had to bind ourselves together and show this small closed world that we could make it outside because we were making it inside. We were normal human beings doing the things everyone does.

A preacher came to see me that afternoon. He was one of the new breed, casual, wearing a tee-shirt, a world traveler, carrying the word of God across his chest. I was civil to him, but I resented his coming. He had come from Linc's family church. The Methodist church I had left because I couldn't stand the criticism I felt every Sunday from Linc's family. No matter what I did, it was never enough. I wasn't Christian enough, and never could be because I wasn't blood kin; I would never be good enough for them, no matter how much I did for or in the church. Why did this man think he could console me? I had never even met him. He approached me as if I were a sinner. That was silly. Of course, I was a sinner; all of us were sinners just by being born. I knew I was a sinner, but I didn't want him pointing it out to me. I had had a lot of talks with God about that very thing, and I didn't think I needed this little arrogant man at the moment.

I am sure I kept my true feelings to myself, as I was accustomed to doing, because he came again before I left. I'm not going to accuse him of reporting on me to the community, or family, or church, because I don't know what he did or to whom he talked, but that's my suspicion because I know the nature of unsolicited help. There was no sincerity in his visit, but the couple who visited from the community I felt was sincere. He was representing the church. They were just representing themselves and I truly appreciated their visit. I was impressed that they would come to a psychiatric ward.

I would not say anything about why I was there to the preacher. I didn't want him to know anything about me, the real person. He talked to a woman with a mask that could be put on and taken off in a second. There were years of practice behind my skill.

It rained that night and I watched the water bead up on the window with all the scars of angry patients before me. It was peaceful to watch the raindrops slide down the glass. I staged races and made bets, outrageous bets, fantasy bets, about smashing the winner with my thumb and rubbing it out. The raindrops had the face of Linc's lover. It was satisfying to obliterate her with one swipe of my hand. It didn't matter that the raindrops were on the outside of the window and, in truth, each little drop escaped and ran down the wood facing.

I watched the lightning split the sky in jagged streaks. It was almost like fireworks, but better because there was more force. I imagined the streaks were switchblades and each streak was cutting her heart out. I wanted her heart like Salome wanted the head of John the Baptist. But I didn't have that power, except in my fantasy. And I didn't want her heart on a platter, I wanted it on the end of the spike still beating as it pumped the last drop of blood from her lifeless body.

As the storm ended, so did my fantasy of rage. And as always, the rage turned inward, and I began to cry at another defeat. I watched the rain slow down until there wasn't any and there were many more teardrops on the inside window facing me than on the outside.

The intercom announced nine o'clock, time for bed. No more reverie for me. A nurse would be by soon and I couldn't be sitting by the window watching the rain. It was much too close to solitude. I undressed, splashed water on my face, and brushed my teeth. I looked in the mirror. The likeness was close to someone I used to know, but I wasn't at all sure what was going to happen to the face that looked back at me.

Tomorrow was a new day, another chance. I had always hung onto that thought before. Never give up. It was never too late. To many people, these thoughts were just words strung together like beads to make a pretty necklace. To me, they were life-giving thoughts that had saved my life and sanity so many times, just the belief that every day was new and might be better.

A nurse came looking for me. "Mrs. Owens, Dr. Maxfield ordered a gynecology check on you. Did you know that?"

"Yes."

"Dr. Gomez is going to do it, and he has set it for ten o'clock tonight. I know this sounds strange, but he is very busy, and this was the only time he could do this. Anyway, if you will just keep your robe on, I will be back in a few minutes and take you downstairs to obstetrics."

"Thank you." It was all I could think to say. Inside it made me panic. What if he thought I was crazy? I was coming from the psychiatric ward, what else was there for him to think. The name Gomez was definitely Spanish. I didn't know him, and I didn't want to see another doctor, but there was nothing I could do. I sat on the side of the bed and waited.

The nurse took me through the hall. The lights were out, and everything was in a gray shadow from the light at the nurse's station. We walked past. Everything was quiet. There were a few sounds coming from the nursery. I remembered a nurse had once told me gynecology was the happy floor: new babies, new life. I wondered what they called psychiatry. The crazy unit. What else could they call it? That's where all the loonies like me were.

We went into a little room, still almost in the dark. The nurse closed the door and turned on the lights. It was a makeshift examining room. I lay on the table and waited. It wasn't long before the doctor came, a nice-looking Spanish type. I had always liked dark men. How could a woman who had three children possibly be embarrassed by a doctor? I was more afraid of what he was going to ask me than of the exam.

He was very soft-spoken and tried to put me at ease. "Mrs. Owens, you know we need to do this because if your hormones are not functioning correctly, you will be very depressed. We will do an exam and Pap smear because I understand you haven't had one in a while. Is that correct?"

"Yes."

"Then we will make a few lab tests to determine your hormone level."

"Yes, that's fine."

"Good, just relax, this won't take long."

After the exam, he said, "Everything looks fine, Mrs. Owens. Now, do you have any questions?"

All I could think was how much I wanted to leave. Then he startled me. "Mrs. Owens, do you have any problems with sex? Does intercourse hurt you?"

"No, no." I couldn't answer quickly enough. I didn't want to talk to him. I just wanted to leave. I looked at the nurse, but she didn't say anything. Maybe he sensed my panic. Maybe he was tired. He didn't pursue the subject any further. "All right, Mrs. Owens, I'll send the lab reports and my report to your doctor. Thank you for coming so late." He left quietly.

The nurse helped me with my robe, and we went back to the sixth floor. I was relieved after I heard the lock click behind me. It was like coming home, only better. There were no worries here other than talking to the doctor. The lights were out on our hall too, and there were no sounds coming from behind the big closed doors at the end of the hall. The nurse took me to my room, and I fell on the bed, exhausted. The night passed without incident.

In the afternoons each of us had a one-on-one session with a counselor. They weren't as bad as talking to the doctor, but I still had my reservations. What were they going to think? What would they say about my thoughts? Each time I talked to them I was putting myself on the line. Or maybe it was because over the years I had so trained myself to keep my problems to myself that I couldn't let anyone into my private world.

At the time I knew nothing about therapy and the relief it could bring. I had no sense of talking as a way of releasing anxiety. This particular counselor was a young man. We were talking about my problems when he said, "What does your husband say about his affair?"

I looked at him quizzically. "What do you mean what does he say? He says he didn't have an affair."

He looked at me for a few seconds. "You know that if he doesn't admit his responsibilities, there is no way you can reconcile your differences. Accepting his responsibility is the first step."

I shot back at him. "That's what I've told him over and over, but he says it isn't true. And that just makes me angry because I know he's lying. He saw this woman for three years and he says he didn't have an affair."

I lowered my head. I was agitated and practically in tears.

I couldn't believe this counselor was telling me something that I had said to Linc all along. Why did Linc's refusal to acknowledge what he had done make me so angry? But this counselor thought the same thing I did about this. I must not be wrong about everything. Why did Linc torment me with this? If he would just admit he had an affair, I would feel differently.

The counselor went on. "If you can't be honest with each other, you can't repair the damage. He has to accept what he has done."

"He admits meeting her at motels that she paid for, talking to her on the phone when she called, accepting her gifts, but he says he never called her in three years, never paid for a motel, everything was her idea."

"And you believe this?"

"No. You don't see someone for three years and not feel something."

"Think about what I have said and talk to him about it."

He got up to leave.

"I will." I watched him go. It was all so strange and out of kilter for me. I couldn't understand why Linc wouldn't admit he had an affair, but I knew in my heart he still loved me and didn't want to leave me. Why did I feel so betrayed when I was willing to take him back? Why was I trying desperately to hold on to a marriage when he had hurt me? What was wrong with me? I had trusted him not to hurt me and now he had. I would never trust anyone ever again, certainly not him.

The days passed until the night before I was to go home. We were going as a group down to the lobby to walk around for a little while. This seemed to me a strange thing to do. I was very uneasy about it. I would see strange people in the lobby. These were people who might not understand or know about the sixth floor.

It wasn't just me who was nervous. Vie and Jean, my new friends, were too. We went down after dinner. The lobby was full, but there were still some places to sit. I went over to a window seat and sat down. It was strange to look out at the ground and see it so very close. All I could think about was what it would be like the next day to walk out of the hospital and go home.

Was I ready? I didn't know, but I was very ready to go on our trip to Ireland. Dr. Thomas had given me permission. It was my one bright spot. Nothing had been resolved with Linc, but I was so looking forward to this trip. I was feeling better, no longer crying all the time, but I had had no stress either. The hospital stay had helped. I had medicine, a doctor that I liked, and I was going on a two-week trip. It was going to get better.

Vie came over and sat in a chair near me. She seemed at ease, unlike me.

"You bought something," I said, eyeing the brown paper bag in her hand.

"Yes, I picked up something in the gift shop for my grandniece. She's a sweet little thing. Don't you want to go and look around at least?"

"No, I'll just sit here for a while."

"It's hard to get used to being out, isn't it?"

"Yes, I just feel very self-conscious, I guess, like everyone knows where we all came from." My new friends always came right to the point.

Vie smiled her most knowing smile. "Don't worry, honey, I don't think anybody much is paying attention to us. But I know how you feel. It was like that for me, the first time I came to the hospital on the psychiatric floor, but now it doesn't bother me. I just hope I can go back to my old job. That doctor had better give me a letter."

This letter was the biggest thing on Vie's mind. "I am sure he will. Try not to worry." I hoped I sounded convincing, but I really didn't know.

Jean came up then. "Guess what? I just saw an old friend. She was telling me all about her children and her husband. I haven't seen her in years. She wanted to know what I was doing here. I told her I just had a little setback and had to come to the hospital for a little while."

I looked at them, so relaxed and talking freely about coming to the hospital. I didn't want to look around because I might see someone I recognized, and I wasn't sure I could handle it just yet.

The nurse was standing by the elevator, our signal to go. I walked toward her thinking, I have made it this far, the real test will be going home tomorrow.

The next morning came early for me. It was hard to tell my friends, the nurses, the counselors, and everyone goodbye. I had been there for about two weeks, but in some ways, it seemed I had been there all my life. I couldn't have imagined I would so quickly become adapted to the hospital. But I had. I was both apprehensive and anxious for the last hour to arrive. There was so much to do to get ready for the trip.

4

THE TRIP EXCEEDED ALL my expectations for a good time. The weather was perfect, no rain, not one day. The people on the tour were very congenial and the guide exceptionally helpful and knowledgeable. Linc was more than attentive. I tried not to think about our troubles and just enjoyed fifteen days in Ireland, England, and Scotland. I am a great traveler anyway and, having never been to Ireland and Scotland, I could focus on what we were seeing. As one of my best friends liked to say, "We had a grand time."

One point of interest that we visited was Hampton Court, the main residence of Henry VIII. Linc and I had been there before with friends on another trip. We were revisiting the gardens and the palace itself. There are many types of gardens, but one that we were interested in was the formal Tudor Knot and Topiary Garden.

Each Tudor Knot is laid out in prescribed dimensions with pebble walkways between each row. The topiaries are scattered throughout the walkways with benches here and there. Tudor Knots have fascinated me since seeing them in Colonial Williamsburg even before the restoration began in the late forties. Linc and I were walking separately, each analyzing the patterns and colors. I was intrigued by the minute details attended to in the coat of arms, flags, and insignias of royal families, all done in vivid summer flower colors.

I made several trips down a certain pathway and back not realizing that I was tracking my steps. I seemed to be drawn to one of the Tudor Knots. The pattern and colors were mesmerizing. A horrible memory from my early childhood shot across my mind. A memory I had tried to forget because of the guilt and shame I associated with it. Suddenly, the momentary pictures out of my dark past were as real as the landscape in front of me, the memory drained every ounce of energy from my body, and I staggered, weak-kneed, to a bench. When I could get my breath, I called to Linc.

He was a good distance away, but there were few people in the gardens at the time so he could hear me. He came quickly.

"What is it?" His voice was anxious, and he looked worried.

He had been so attentive since I came home from the hospital, and especially on the trip. I knew he felt responsible for everything even though he admitted little. He was just that kind of guy. I had been, and still was, so mad with him, but at this moment I needed him terribly. There was no bitterness in my voice, only desperation. He bent over me in order to hear me better. I was sitting down and could hardly speak. My hands gripped the bench until the veins rose in my arms. My heart pounded. The roses on the blouse across my chest seemed to pulsate. My breath came in gulps as if there was not enough air in the early morning English countryside. Slowly my breathing subsided enough for me to look at Linc, but my voice was strained and deep.

"If I live to get back home to see Dr. Thomas again, the first thing I'm going to tell him is what happened to me a long time ago."

He sat down beside me and put one arm around me, and held my hand with the other. "What do you mean? I don't understand." His face was creased with worry and his eyes were searching for answers.

"Linc, you know. I told you years ago."

"You mean about Cooper and the whipping." He squeezed my shoulders.

"Yes, that's what I mean."

"Why did you think about that now?"

"I don't know, I just did, and I feel terrible. I'm so afraid."

"Don't be. It's all right." He tried to be reassuring.

I covered my face in his arms and tried to ease the awful fear and guilt I felt from the horrible scene forty-two years earlier. I was so little then and seemed so pitiful. A little girl being punished for an act she could not help.

We sat there together in the morning sun trying to understand why the worst of all memories had come back to me this morning, in a garden in England. Neither of us had any idea. But much later in my therapy, I understood so clearly how the Tudor Knot in England triggered the memory. That morning, we could only deal with the moment at hand. Memory is like a cue ball that bounces off a trigger ball on the way to making a long shot. Each ball in the game of memory has to be sunk before the whole memory is out. My first shot was in England, but the game was to be long and tedious.

That morning I shivered in what seemed to be cold air, but it couldn't be. The sun was shining, bright and golden, and my skin felt warm. But I continued to shake. The cold seeped through my body and into my legs, leaving my toes curled. I was sure I was going to vomit.

What was the matter with me? I felt totally frightened and unnerved. Was I going to make it through the rest of the trip or was I going to have to go to a hospital in London? The prospect was unthinkable. Was Linc thinking the same thing at this moment? Was he trying to recall where he had seen a telephone so he could call Dr. Thomas? Was he too worried that I would have to go to the hospital? I had to get control of myself. I had to get away from this garden and the memories. I tugged at Linc's arm. "Let's go to the gift shop. I don't want to be here any longer, please."

"It's O.K., we can leave. I just don't understand what's happening. Are you sure you're alright?"

"Yes, yes," I blurted. "I'll be fine. I just want to leave. Help me up, I feel so weak."

He held my hand and pulled me to my feet. His hand was warm and strong. He quickly put his arm around me, and we started back to the palace.

His voice was low and calm as he began to speak. "I've been so worried about you since you left the hospital, and I thought everything was going fine. You seemed bright and almost happy during the day and I was so grateful to have this trip to help you adjust to being out of the hospital. It's been a godsend and now this. I can't tell you how sorry I am, and I'll try to help you get past it. Please try to hang on today and tomorrow we'll be somewhere else. I don't know why you had to think about a bad memory today."

"I don't either. These memories just seem to follow me and pop out at the worst times."

He squeezed me again and I could feel his desire to help. I needed his understanding so much and I was so grateful for this moment, but I knew it could change so quickly because my thoughts and emotions were out of my control.

A sign nearby directed us to the gift shop, located behind the house and gardens. We turned down the path and soon came to an inviting white clapboard building. Inside, the aisles were filled with souvenirs, cards, and statues. The room was warm and cozy. A little man with white hair and steel-rimmed glasses greeted us in crisp English.

I squeezed Linc's hand and nudged him toward the man. "Just let me look around a little bit and I'll be fine."

He gave me a troubled look but didn't argue. A few minutes later, he was engaged in a conversation about the differences between the city of Richmond, England, which is Hampton Court's address, and our home city of Richmond, Virginia.

I listened as I walked quietly down the rows of merchandise. My mind wandered as I gazed at the trinkets, but the question remained. Why had I remembered that horrible day so long ago? A day I had tried so hard to bury, to forget, to not be reminded of again. I had never told anyone but Linc, and I only told him after we had been married several years. Even then I glossed over it as best I could.

Now, I wondered if I really could tell Dr. Thomas or if I would back out. No, that was impossible. I had said I was going to; there could be no backing down. Somehow, giving my word was very important to me, and once committed I tried never to back out of anything. But the question remained. How would I ever tell a doctor about that morning in June?

I remembered how desperately I had tried–and succeeded–in not telling my psychiatrist, Dr. Brooks. Before each session with him, I had prayed that I would not make the mistake of revealing something that would lead back to that event in my childhood. The therapy was only for six months, and it took place during the time Daddy was hospitalized for alcoholism and had decided to sell the lumber business. My stamina was stretched to the limit, but the six months with Dr. Brooks had restored my mental state enough to last another twenty years.

My eyes roamed the gifts in their neat rows. I thumbed through the postcards, not really seeing them. My mind was locked on the events of that Saturday morning in June when I was eight years old. They were so vivid, the pictures of memory slipping across my mind like a silent movie screen. I felt my cheeks flame as if the gift shop man could see the pictures with me. I was both paranoid and delusional at that moment. I tucked my head to look towards him out of the corner of my eye. He was still talking to Linc and seemed oblivious of me, but I couldn't trust that. I had to stop thinking about that day. "Please, God, give me the calm to last until I get home, and I will tell Dr. Thomas the whole thing, I promise."

I picked up a handful of cards and walked toward the cash register. Linc came toward me. "Feeling better?" he asked quietly.

"Yes, let's just go to the bus. It must be time."

He paid for the cards and we left the little man in the shop. I couldn't be absolutely sure that he had not been able to read my mind. I didn't want to give him a second chance.

That night after dinner Linc and I took a walk by the Thames. The river flowed gently, but it looked so dirty and muddy. Not a trashy look, but one that gave you the feeling of dirty things lurking below the surface, things unseen and smelly. Slimy things that made your skin crawl.

The street lights were on even though the sky remained bright. I squeezed Linc's hand. "What do you think of the river?"

"Oh, I don't know. It seems a little dirty. Does that bother you?"

"Yes, it does. The dirt reminds me of myself and that awful thing I remembered this morning."

Linc's eyes swept my face, and all the concern I had seen this morning returned.

He spoke gently. "I hope this doesn't affect you too much. It's pretty heavy-duty stuff and I would hate for something that happened forty years ago to mess up this trip."

I smiled and touched his cheek. "Don't worry. I have wanted to see Ireland too long to let it go now." His cheek was warm and soft. For a moment the feelings of our youth returned, and I leaned to kiss him full on the mouth. It was a passionate kiss that begged for a return. I felt my body lighten and I knew he was feeling the surge of hunger for my body as well as my spirit. We held each other for a moment as the sound of footsteps came nearer. We turned away from each other and began walking slowly again. His hand was firmly locked in mine. In an instant, all the sweetness of the moment before was wiped away by his next comment.

"You have had a rough time for quite a while and I worry about you,"

There it was again, the affair. Why had he reminded me of this now? Why had he ruined a beautiful moment by bringing the affair back? I couldn't see that he had meant to be kind. I said, "You should have worried before now and maybe I wouldn't have had such a bad time." It was the first time I had cut back at him on the trip, but the damage was done. His face fell and his jaw twitched. He raised his hands with palms facing me; not to hit me, but to plead. His voice was quiet, but there were lines on his forehead and his words were pointed.

"I am sorry. I would give anything if I could take it all back, if I could change my life or if I could make it right again."

"You could if you wanted to."

"That's not true. I do want to. I have tried to change myself all my life, but I don't know how. I have always misjudged what you were thinking and have never been able to second guess what you really want from me."

"That's easy. All I have ever wanted is to be loved and taken care of."

"But I do love you and I have tried to take care of you."

"Do you call jumping in bed with that woman, betraying me and your family in the dope case, loving me?"

"No, I don't. I have made terrible mistakes. And I am sorry. I just don't know how to change myself."

Tears came to my eyes as I remembered bad things that had happened much later in my childhood and as an adult. I didn't pursue our argument. I simply turned away and began the short trip back to the hotel. I just didn't have the strength to go on with the argument any further, but I could think.

Linc had always blundered through life making mistakes and not learning from them. And I blamed his family, that's for sure. His mother, his grandmother, and everyone in his family–almost–had patted him on the head and told him what a good boy he was. He had been raised as if he were a little king who could do no wrong. But if you are a little king you are expected to take care of your citizens, which he did in his law practice. He thought his queen could take care of herself. He had only to answer to his own needs and those of his citizens. He was a true aristocrat, with the best of intentions and the least know-how. He neither believed in good and evil nor did he have the street smarts to do anything about them.

By the time we reached the hotel, my anger was subsiding, but I wasn't going to risk another word and the possibility of upsetting him or myself further. An already bad day ended on a less than happy note. As hard as we both tried, there would be others. I knew in my gut I would never be able to change this, and I would have to learn to live with it if I stayed with him.

We slept in each other's arms that night hoping to ward off any bad dreams or bad memories, either from the present or from long ago. The warmth of his body and his even breathing always soothed my nerves. I tried to control my thoughts.

As often happens, the next day was better. A lot better. Linc was even more attentive than usual, and I could see the worry in his eyes and hear his asking for forgiveness each time he spoke. There was no way to tell if he was thinking about my past or my present, but my reaction to the flashbacks had struck a nerve in him.

The days–filled with new sights, sounds, and impressions– passed quickly, but the memory lingered in my mind, and every day I promised myself to end the secrecy once we arrived home. I now had a mission that had to be accomplished.

On the last night of our trip, there was a lavish banquet in an old castle. Everyone was in high spirits, especially Linc. The entertainment was an Irish tenor with a silky voice that stroked his words into ribbons of feeling that bound everyone's yearnings. The band was equally sensuous, and Linc and I were caught up in the blinding euphoria of the evening as we flowed with the dance and music.

Linc pulled me close and whispered just above my ear. "God, you are beautiful tonight."

I leaned my head back and looked into his eyes. "I am glad you think so."

"Have you had a good time?" His eyes were alive with questions and his face mirrored tenderness.

I smiled back at him answering all of his questions. "Yes. Definitely."

His lips brushed my neck and I could feel his hand tighten just below my waist. My heart began to beat faster. I wanted his advances, but I was afraid. My body shuddered and my hand gripped his neck. What was happening? I had never had this reaction to thoughts of sex, but suddenly I heard myself thinking: it will hurt and I am scared. That was ridiculous. I had had three children, for God's sake. I certainly knew what sex was. Where did that thought come from?

Linc leaned back, looking at me. "What's wrong? I thought you were enjoying this."

"I was. I am. I don't know what happened." I did know my body had grown tense and my mind had shut down. Again, a moment had been ruined, and I had no idea why.

"It's O.K. You don't have to worry." He laid his cheek against my hair and held me close. For a moment I was transported back to our first years together and recalled the magic that had brought us close. We were young and in love and I trusted him with my heart and my life. We believed then nothing could happen to us, no one could tear us apart, but they did. We believed we could overcome anything. The future was here, and this test was real. In that instant, I forgot his betrayal, all the betrayals, and remembered only the goodness of the man I had married. But the instant passed and we were left with only hope.

Later in our bed, we listened to the sounds of the night and waited for a new time. The old bitter memories had to be forgotten and forgiven. Then I could face a new life as a whole person. I had no notion of where confession of the secret would lead me. I just knew my suffering had to end. I knew I wanted my old life back. I wanted my family, and I wanted to be rid of the darkness that was always around no matter what I did. The next day would bring us home, and somehow Dr. Thomas and I would have to find the answer.

5

I DIDN'T TELL anyone what had happened on the trip after I got home. It was a subject I had never approached with my family and certainly did not want to now. It was going to take everything in me to tell Dr. Thomas. Linc and I told everyone what a great time we had had, without a whisper of what had really happened.

One night, soon after we had arrived home, I overheard Linc and Camille talking. She was asking about me.

"How do you think Mom made out on the trip? We were all so worried about her being away so soon after she left the hospital. Was it good for you both?"

"Oh, I think she did great. It was definitely good for her and for us. She had one really bad day, but she seemed to adjust to it."

"What caused the bad day?"

"She remembered something from long ago and it really shocked her. I know what it was, but her reaction was alarming, I thought."

"What did she remember? Did she lose control?"

"I can't tell you because that would be another betrayal and I can't make another mistake this soon. It was what the remembering did to her that upset me. I have no understanding of emotions but this one was at the core of her psyche. She only lost control once and that was a tongue lashing."

"Daddy, how can you make such light of it? You know it's serious and you should take up for yourself."

"I do take it seriously and I know your mother doesn't mean to lose her temper."

"Lindsay says she's really sick, but I don't know what's wrong. I just hope Dr. Thomas will help. A lot of people in the community are talking about her, but that doesn't really matter."

"What does Jimmy say?"

"I know he's missed her on the farm, and he thinks he could cure her in two hours with the Bible."

"I wish he could. That'd be great, wouldn't it? Jimmy is a good guy."

"Dad, he's almost a fanatic. You know that."

"No, I don't think he is a fanatic. He's just more religious than I want to be. I don't think he is a fanatic, because he isn't a firebrand who believes he can convert anyone and everyone. He's quiet, very quiet about his beliefs, and he's very sincere."

"I guess so, but I don't trust his religion, and I certainly don't want him talking to me."

"I can understand that, but you have to remember he's very close to your mother and if he could cure her, I know he would. Now listen, you go on home now and try not to worry. It's going to be alright."

She got up and left. I was shaken by the conversation and by their concern. I must really not have any idea about what was wrong with me. I went to bed that night not sure of how I would deal with my family or friends in this matter.

I have always known that I am lucky to have all my family close by. Then, however, something happens like the hospital and suddenly everyone is telling me what to do. Although I always wanted Linc to take care of me, being the object of such concern and attention has never been my strength. This was another contradiction in my life.

The next morning Lindsay came by to have coffee with me. I

had just made the coffee when she came in. We sat at the kitchen table and watched the birds in the feeder. I could spend hours watching them and let my mind wander through my problems. Theirs seemed so different; their concern was purely the here and now. Where was the best piece of grain? A bird has to keep an eye out for a predator, or for another bird that may steal the fattest of all the morsels.

Lindsay broke the silence. "How did you really get along on the trip? I thought about you a lot and I hope it was as good as you and Dad say." She sat her cup down and looked at me, the same questioning look I had gotten used to since sometime before the hospital. It always reminded me that she was a psychologist and knew what she was talking about with me. It was unnerving in a way because it seemed to put me on the defensive. I had to give her the right answer even though I didn't always know what the right answer was. This morning I was going to try harder than ever.

"The trip was wonderful. It was great for me and your Dad. It was great for us."

"There weren't any bad days? Did you go into a rage like you do sometimes and hit Dad?"

I always felt this question was unfair, a hit below the belt, but I didn't flinch. It reminded me that my children knew nothing of a real fight. As I often told them, they had never seen what a real domestic fight was like. I had lived through fistfights, knives, furniture throwing, scratching the blood out, and catfights. I was ashamed of it, but it was the truth. And now Lindsay's question cut as it habitually did. "Yes, there was one bad day and no, I never hit your Dad once on the trip."

"That's good. What was the bad day about?"

"We were at Hampton Court walking through the gardens and I remembered something I would give anything to have forgotten forever. It made me weak, sick to my stomach, and completely unnerved. For a while, I was a basket case."

"I see. It must've been very traumatic when it happened and almost equally so again when you remembered it."

I nodded my head to say 'yes'. "It was totally debilitating. It was hard for your Dad to understand but he was very supportive of the way I felt."

"I can imagine. Dad isn't good at hearing or dealing with bad things. Did it affect the rest of the trip?"

"Actually, I thought I recovered pretty quickly. That is, I was much better the next day."

"So, what was the memory?"

"I don't want to talk about it now, but it's the first thing I'm going to tell Dr. Thomas. I don't know when I'll be able to tell you."

"You don't have to tell me now, I am just glad you're going to tell him. I'm really proud of you for the way you're handling this. Are you taking the medication regularly?"

"Yes, I am." I was so glad to hear the praise. It seemed praise was one thing I couldn't hear enough.

"Good. You know it won't do any good if you don't. And the therapy won't help either if you aren't honest with him and really work on your problems."

"I know that too. Can't we change the subject? I feel like I'm already in the doctor's office."

"Sure, I just want you to know I'm concerned about you and care a great deal."

"I do too, and I love you all more than you know, or I wouldn't be putting myself through this. It wasn't easy going to the hospital and it's not going to be easy the rest of the way, I don't think. Anyway, tell me about the horses."

"They're doing well. I'm working on the grey mare, but she's a tough one. I want to show her next year."

We finished our coffee and Lindsay seemed satisfied with my answers. I watched her for a moment, poised, confident, lovely to look at with her regular features, fair skin, and blue eyes. I could be so proud of her. If I thought about it long enough I had so much to make me proud and happy. Why was I depressed and miserable?

After Lindsay left, I put the dishes in the sink and went to the bedroom. My eye caught my handbag sitting on the desk. It held my appointment card tucked safely away. It told the day and the hour I would finally tell my story. I found myself slipping my hand in the handbag to rub my fingers across the card. I couldn't feel the writing, but I had memorized what it said.

The day arrived in late July. It was hot, as it should be, but the heat in Virginia is different. It swelters and steams, and rises and falls as the mist on a mountain, but it never goes away. It follows you and, like a cloak, wraps its wet mass around you until every part of your body is wet and slick and hot to the touch. The heat had followed me to Richmond that afternoon. I could see it rising off the hood of the car and turning to fog on the corners of the windshield where the air-conditioned cool air spread across the glass.

I pulled the car into the parking space and braced myself for the blast of heat that hit me as I opened the door to get out. I felt the hot cement through my shoes. I could even feel the heat on my ankles. My appointment was at four-thirty. I was seeing Dr. Thomas at a drug treatment center. There were offices downstairs; the hospital was upstairs. I had never been to this hospital, but I knew a lot about it. Not particulars, just that it was another alcohol and drug treatment center. It was better than most by reputation, but I knew enough about alcohol to know that sometimes nothing worked. It all depended on the attitude of the patient. I had seen enough drunks not to be the least bit interested or sympathetic to their cries of pain and persecution. My father had cured me of that. My theory was that an alcoholic was totally useless to himself and to everyone else until he decided to do something about it. An alcoholic would lie, cheat, steal, and commit the most horrific deeds just to get a drink. And keeping a promise? There was no such thing.

I entered the building with a chip on my shoulder. I didn't mean to have one, but the sight of patients in their bathrobes wandering through the waiting room, smoking cigarettes, their flushed red faces drawn in worry, made me want to yell at them and chase them all away. I was sick to death of self-pity. I had always had a love/hate regard for men, and most of these patients were men. Today was not the day to test my compassion. I bit my lip and looked away from them.

I gave my name at the desk and picked up a magazine. The waiting room was small but pleasant, and the furniture was comfortable. I flipped through a magazine hardly seeing the pages. My mind was on my mission for the day. I had to tell Dr. Thomas. I had promised myself that morning at Hampton Court. I couldn't carry it around with me anymore. It was vile and filthy, and I was so ashamed. I had never identified the source of it, but I felt the anger at myself and maybe at the whole world. I had no idea what was wrong except I felt this was my last chance with myself to get this leprosy out of my system.

I put the magazine down and began staring at the wall. What was Dr. Thomas going to think? What would he say? Could I make myself get it all out? I didn't know, but I had to try. My thoughts were jarred by the receptionist's voice.

"Mrs. Owens, Dr. Thomas will see you now."

I jerked my head up, startled. I stood up and followed her to the doorway.

"You can have a seat. He will be here in a moment."

The door closed behind her leaving me alone in a cool semi-dark office. The blinds were almost closed. My eyes had to adjust, but I could see the big pieces of furniture. There was a nice wooden desk, with a dark red leather chair behind it. There were two green upholstered Queen Anne-style chairs in front of the desk. The soft green walls were decorated with rows of degrees and licenses. The room gave me a feeling of security and safety. I sat in one of the chairs beside the wall, not one of the big ones, but one of the lesser ones. I didn't want to draw attention to myself. It was a pattern developed over the years.

Moments later Dr. Thomas came in and turned his full attention to me. All I could think about was telling him. The thoughts rang in my ears. I did not want to tell him–or anyone–anything. Waves of shame, humiliation, dread, fright swept through me, leaving me weak and dry-mouthed.

He looked at me. "Well, how was your trip?"

"It was fine."

Silence.

He sat back a little, eyeing me. "Did you have any problems? This is the first time I've seen you since you left the hospital."

Another silence.

Finally, "Something happened that I want to tell you about."

"By all means, please. I want to hear it."

6

"WE WERE in the gardens at Hampton Court and all of a sudden, I felt as if I was going to faint because I remembered something that happened a long time ago. The thoughts ran through me like a convulsion and left me weak and light-headed. I managed to find a bench a few feet away. I collapsed on the cement slab and clutched myself. I was sick to my stomach and panicked. I tried to find my voice and call for Linc. He had gone a short way up the path unaware that I was sick. When I found my voice, he turned and ran back. He knew something was terribly wrong."

Dr. Thomas listened intently. He had not taken his eyes off me.

I paused for a minute trying to find the nerve to continue. He sensed my hesitation and waited, but the tension was in the air. I wet my lips and moved on. "Linc sat down beside me and put his arms around me."

Another pause.

"I told Linc I remembered something."

"What did you remember?"

"Something awful that I don't want to talk about, but I promised myself if I lived to get back home it was going to be the first thing I told you at my first appointment. I can't stand this any longer. It has haunted me all my life and I just can't live with it anymore. Linc was afraid I was going to fall apart. I asked him to stay close to me for a while. I really needed his support."

Dr. Thomas spoke softly. "Does he know what happened?"

"Yes, but he is the only one."

"You have never told anyone else."

"No."

"How old were you when it happened?"

"About eight."

"Why don't you tell me and take your time." He seemed to lean back in his chair.

I gripped the arms of the chair I was sitting in and drew a deep breath and began slowly.

"It was to be a special morning for me. Cooper had promised to help me hook Daisy to the buggy and we were going to pick up apples for Mama. The apple orchard was laid out in rows, just beyond the garden. The buggy creaked and strained as the iron-rimmed wheels crossed the ruts making the turn through the gate. The horse stumbled a bit on the hard rim of ground, but she was old and paid little attention to small ruts. I held the lines up like a real driver, feeling the importance of my position. Cooper sat beside me, his wooden leg stretched out in front of him. Driving Daisy was fun; I could even tolerate Cooper because of it.

"My voice was young but firm. 'Let's go this way O.K.? We'll go all the way to the end of this row and turn down the next row and start at that end.' I wanted to twist and turn to show Daisy I was really driving. 'I don't know why Mama wants these ole June apples anyway. I think they are sour and too small. We should just feed them to the pigs. I'm going to save some for Daisy and Billy.' I was talking more to myself than to Cooper. He was too slow, and besides I always had to wait for him to spit the tobacco juice before he could answer.

"I pulled Daisy up at the first tree and hopped out of the buggy, not waiting to see if Cooper could swing his wooden leg out and somehow let himself to the ground on his good leg. Just about everything about him repulsed me, especially the fact that he was the only one on the farm who would hook up the buggy for me. It was the spring I turned eight years old. I couldn't hook Daisy up because I was too small to get the harness over her. I was tall enough to reach up and hook the traces, but not tall enough to put the lines through the hooks on the back band.

"'Cooper, you get the basket out the back of the buggy and I'll fill it up.' I didn't wait for him because it would have taken too long. I just started sorting through the apples on the ground, kicking them first with my toe to roll them over to see if there was a hidden rotten spot underneath. The ground was thick with the apples, some totally rotten, some mostly green with a little brown spot near the stem. That little brown spot usually meant the apple was rotten to the core and it would take at least four cuts with the paring knife to get a little of the white meat. I quickly skirted the whole ground floor under the tree, picking up only the good apples.

"In the sun, away from the tree, it was hot, but the grass felt good to my bare feet. I worked feverishly. The quicker I could fill the basket and the floorboard of the buggy, the quicker I could drive Daisy back to the house, and Cooper would not say anything if I drove around a bit on the way.

"We had covered half the row when I heard Aunt Pearl, the cook, calling, 'Lesley, Lesley, where are you, Baby?' I couldn't believe it. What was wrong? Why would Aunt Pearl be calling now? I was doing exactly what Mama wanted. I dropped the apples in my hand into Cooper's basket and turned toward the sound of Aunt Pearl's voice. I could see her coming down the lane from the house. Her big frame seemed to glide along, her head with the brown stocking pulled over her hair and knotted at the top hair moved evenly above the board fence. The only sense of motion was in her swinging arms with each stride. Cooper stood motionless, waiting as Aunt Pearl opened the gate and started up the row toward us. She was almost running now, if you can imagine that a woman of her immense size could run, she was running. I stood my ground. I couldn't imagine what Aunt Pearl wanted and I wasn't leaving without good reason.

"She spoke. 'Lesley, your mama wants you to come to the house right now, honey. I don't know what she wants, but she is awful upset about something.'

"I looked up at Aunt Pearl; she was so much bigger than me. 'But, Aunt Pearl, I can't come now. We haven't finished getting the apples. You tell Mama, I will be there as soon as we get the buggy loaded. There are lots more apples to get. See they are all over the place.'

"Aunt Pearl shook her head. 'No child, you come with me right now. Your Mama is terrible upset. I can tell by the way she told me to come and get you. So now, you come on and you can come back in a little while.' She reached for my hand, closing it firmly in hers. 'Now, you come on, honey, so she won't be any more upset. Let's go now, so you can come back in a little while.'

"I turned to Cooper. 'You be sure and wait until I get back so I can drive Daisy to the house. O.K.? Don't leave. Promise!'

"Cooper leaned on his cane. 'I'll rest until you come back.' He looked toward the buggy. I thought he would wait if it didn't take too long.

"Aunt Pearl held my hand all the way back to the house. Neither of us spoke. I was trying to hold back the tears because it had been such a struggle to catch Daisy. I had to do that because Cooper couldn't run. And now I had to go back to the house and hadn't gotten to drive hardly at all. Aunt Pearl pressed my hand every few steps. Mama was standing by the back steps with her hands on her hips. She looked so mad.

"'Mama, I was doing just what you wanted, and I have to go back so I can finish loading the buggy. Cooper is waiting for me.'

"Mama's voice was sharp. 'Forget about that, you come with me right now.'

"'But, Mama, please let me go back. I have to finish getting the apples and unhook Daisy.'

"'No, Mr. Cooper will do that, you come with me.'

"She was pushing me through the house now, towards her bedroom. She gave an extra hard push through the door and slammed it shut behind her, then turned to lock it. I stumbled toward the bed and caught myself on the high oak post. Mama rushed over to the chair by the stove and swooped up a white cloth. She fumbled with it for a few minutes then turned around. The cloth was stretched between her fists and she held it close to my face. 'What's this?' she said, and I could feel the fierceness in her voice. I had never, never seen her so mad at me. At Daddy, yes, but never like this at me. I hugged the bedpost trying to figure out what I had done.

"Mama stood still holding the cloth under my nose. Her eyes were cutting through me and I didn't know why. She made me feel naked and small and afraid, and I wanted to run to her and say, 'What's wrong, Mama, what's wrong?' but I couldn't. The force of her anger kept me quiet and still. My grip on the bedpost tightened to hold my weight. I waited for her next move, for anything to break the awful silence, but she held the cloth and the silence demanded an answer from me.

"I tore my eyes away from her face and managed to look at the cloth. It was my underpants that I had dropped by my bed this morning. Suddenly, Mama stepped closer to me and I almost fell backward. Her body didn't touch me, but I could feel it scorning, accusing, and demanding an explanation. The panties with the milky, pasty spot were inches from my face. I lost my grip on the bedpost and slipped to the floor. My hair fell over my face. Strands of it fell in my mouth. I tried to speak, but my throat ached, and my mouth was dry from fear.

"I tried again and again and finally a wail came from the pit of my stomach, 'I don't know.'

"Mama stepped over me and from behind she yelled in my ear, 'You do know, you do know.'

"But I didn't know. I could hear her words. I could feel her fury, but I didn't know. I didn't know. I only knew I wanted her to stop being mad at me. I wanted her to stop screaming and tell me what had happened. I didn't know. I wanted her to put her arms around me and hold me and tell me it was all right. I wanted her to listen when I said I didn't know. I had dropped the panties there that morning because they were wet and sticky, and I didn't want to wear them.

"Instead, Mama leaned closer and hissed 'Get up, get up, I'm going to call your Daddy. You'll tell him what you did.' She was moving toward the door.

"I raised my head and crawled towards her. 'Oh! Mama, No! Don't bother Daddy please, don't, please, don't, I don't know what happened. I woke up this morning and my panties were wet, and I don't know how they got that way. I don't know. I wanted to tell you, Mama, but I was afraid. I should have told you, but I didn't think it was important and I didn't want to bother you. Oh! Mama, please! Don't bother Daddy. Please!'

"I was crying now, huge convulsive sobs on Mama's knees, my arms around her thighs, my head buried in her full skirt. I clung for dear life. 'Oh! Mama! Please don't call Daddy. Don't tell him I have done something bad - please!'

"Mama reached down and pulled my arms away. 'Yes, I'm going to call him now and he's going to whip you good. You'll tell him. Get up and make that bed while I'm gone. Get up and make that bed without a wrinkle in it. You don't know how to do a thing in the house, do you?'

"'Oh! Yes, Mama, I'll show you. I can make the bed.' I ran to the bed and began to smooth the bottom sheet. 'See, Mama, I'll show you, I do know how to make the bed. I'll do whatever you want.'

"Mama seemed pleased for a moment. 'All right, I'm going to call your Daddy. See if you can make the bed right.' She paused at the door for a moment, brushing her hair back into place and smoothing her skirt as if none of the events of the last five minutes had ever taken place. She opened the door and was gone.

"I folded the top sheet back as I had seen Aunt Pearl do. The tears were still falling in big splotches on the sheets and it was hard to get all the wrinkles out because I had to lean on the bed to reach the middle. I raced around the bed several times to try and get the sheets just right, then the blanket, and finally the heavy bedspread. I kept checking the hemline of the bedspread to make sure it was even on both sides of the bed. Mama always wanted everything just right. I had stopped crying by the time I finished making the bed, but I knew Mama had gone to call

Daddy and it was just a matter of time before she would come back.

"I looked around for something else to do. There must be something I could do to please her. She was so mad. I remember I wasn't worried about why I didn't know what she wanted from me, just that I had done something bad, obviously, and I was going to be punished for it. Mama had whipped me before with Daddy's belt. I knew what a whipping meant. Her dresser looked messy, so I began to straighten the comb and brush and hairpins and blow the powder off the top. I rubbed my hand across the pale spot and brushed it on my clothes. Then I realized Mama would be mad about dirtying my clothes, so I tried to brush out the wrinkles I had made in them. I had on a shirt with shorts. A pillow had fallen off the daybed by the window and I picked that up to fluff it up and put it exactly in the corner of the bed, so the embroidered butterfly and flowers showed just right.

"The windows were up in the room and I could hear the swing moving on the front porch. Mama and Daddy were sitting there, talking. My heart was beating so fast. What was Mama telling Daddy? I went closer to the window to try and listen, but I couldn't make out the words for the screeching of the swing. I could tell though that they were arguing.

"I did hear Mama say, 'I know it was Edwards. You know how Lesley's always out in the fields or in the barns with the horses. I know it was him and she'll tell you if you whip her.'

"My heart sank. What were they talking about; I didn't know anything about Mr. Edwards and me. He was the farm boss and I never saw him except in the mornings or at night. And he never said anything to me. He was big and rough, and I never got in his way.

"Daddy was talking then, but I couldn't understand what he said except I didn't think he wanted to do what Mama wanted. He got up from the swing and walked down the porch. 'Let me go out here and see Edwards for a minute. I'll be right back.' Edwards was cutting alfalfa hay in the field next to the yard. I could hear the tractor running.

"Mama's voice was piercing. 'You ask him. You hear.'

"Daddy didn't turn around or stop walking, which was usual when Mama yelled at him. I watched him go. What was he going to ask Edwards? What would Edwards say? Soon the tractor stopped, but it didn't cut off. A few minutes later it started again, and I knew Daddy was coming back.

"Mama met him at the steps. 'You didn't ask him, did you?'

"'Yes, I did, Esther.'

"'What did he say?'

"'He said he hadn't seen her.'

"'What does that mean? That doesn't mean a thing.' Then I heard Mama's voice again, 'Maybe so, but if you whip her, I know she'll tell us.' I was frantic. I watched Daddy get out of the swing.

"'All right, all right, I'll do it.' He walked across the porch, down the steps, and out to the big maple tree. I watched him reach in his pocket and take out his pocket knife, unfold it and cut two long thick branches off the tree. He trimmed the smaller branches off, then ran his fingers down the ends of the single branches to take off the leaves. He folded the knife, slipped it back in his pocket, and walked back toward the house with the switches in his hand.

"I listened as he and Mama came in the front door, then the bedroom door opened and suddenly he looked bigger than the house. Mama was right behind him. I moved back away from the window toward the stove, then, to the opposite corner of the room. I couldn't speak, but I could move away.

"I felt his grip around my wrist, and he began to lift me off the floor. I heard the switches scrape the ceiling and sing through the air as they came down on my thighs. The burning took my breath away and I tried to leap behind Daddy to escape the fire. The air ripped apart again, this time on the small of my back. Then his voice came out of the inferno of my pain.

"'Who did it? Who did it?'

"And my own voice strangled with sobs, 'I don't know.'

"Around, around I struggled to get away from the burning whip, from the sounds and the grip on my wrist that held me like a vice.

Through it all I could see my mother's face, frowning, set, waiting for me to confess.

"Five swoops of the arm, then ten, fifteen.... I don't know, but finally, the voice said, 'I can't do this anymore.' And my wrist was free. I fell headlong on the bare floor away from the rug. The room was spinning, meshed together, but the sound was still there. Daddy left the room with Mama at his heels and the door slammed shut.

"They were gone. My only thought was to leave, too. Get up and open the door. Go upstairs even though each time I bent my knees it sent pain shooting up my legs. I stumbled up the stairs, blind with fright. There was the landing — four more steps, then across the hallway to the bedroom. Shut the door and fall on the bed in a heap and cry. My heart was breaking.

"I lay there all afternoon, my consciousness wavering between the nightmare of the whipping and the pain in my legs and back. My cheeks burned from the tears and sweat. My legs and back burned from the red welts that laced my lower body, thighs, and calves. The hot June sun streamed in the west window and covered the bed, making the coverlet soak up its rays and wring the last bit of energy from my body. Sweat soaked the covers and the under bedding so that when the evening breeze billowed through the curtains it made me cold. I lay listening to the activity in the house and outside, but nobody came to call me to supper. Nobody came to soothe me or say they were sorry or ask for any more explanation.

"I thought about Daisy. Had Cooper brought the buggy back? Had he turned her loose and hung up the harness? I thought about Daddy and my heart was both broken and terrified. I couldn't admit to myself that he had whipped me. I could only remember his face. Each time his face caused the tears to come again and I cried to myself. 'Daddy, I told you the truth. I have never lied, and I don't know what happened.'

"I thought about Aunt Pearl, how she had kept squeezing my hand as we walked to the house. I knew Aunt Pearl wouldn't come because of Mama. I knew she couldn't come.

"Each time I thought of Mama I cried too because I knew she wouldn't come. I had to be better. Mama had made Daddy whip me. She had the power to do anything. I had to be better, I had to do better. Whatever it was couldn't happen again.

"The thought that it must never happen again brought me back to the real world. It was dark now and the whippoorwills were out. I didn't get up to turn the lights on but lay curled up trying to know what had happened the night before.

"I remembered waking up with a pillow over my head and not being able to turn over because of this weight. I was so scared, the weight was somebody, a man, and he had done something to me. That's why Mama was mad. He must have had something to do with the pasty stuff. The man had come into my room, but I didn't remember it. I didn't remember anything but the weight and the pillow over my face. Then, I remembered feeling like I was going to smother because I couldn't get my breath. The next thing I remembered was waking up in the morning and feeling the wet, cold panties. I had sat up and looked down at them and then pulled them off. I didn't know what to do with them. Should I show them to Mama? No, I would just leave them by the bed and she would find them. I got up and went into the bathroom and washed myself, then got dressed. That was all that happened. I didn't know anything else except Mama was furious with me and Daddy had whipped me. A man had done this. So, I must always keep my door locked. Every night I would keep my door locked and I would never, never be alone with a man again.

"Sometime later I fell asleep after I had locked the door and hidden my panties under the bed. My last thought was nobody must know. I will never talk about this again and maybe Mama will love me. I must protect myself. I'll be good so the bad man won't come again."

By the time I had finished my story, I was gripping the arms of the chair so hard I had half raised myself out of the chair. My feet were stretched in front of me; toes pointed straight ahead, legs ridged.

Dr. Thomas's face was strained but compassionate. I could tell he thought it was a horror story. He didn't say anything for a few minutes; then he said in his quiet voice, "Is there anything else you want to tell me?"

"No."

Dr. Thomas gave me an appointment card for the next week. I turned and stumbled out the door. I had done what I came to do. That gave me hope.

7

THE HEAT HIT me as I opened the outside door. It wasn't a fancy storm door as you might expect, but an ordinary aluminum two-paned house door. It even dragged a little as it opened across the small stoop. I managed the two steps down to the walkway then walked like a zombie to the car. I certainly wasn't immobile, but the emotional drag of the last hour had taken a toll on my steadiness.

The car was an oven. I tossed my bag into the front seat and waited a few minutes for the intense heat to leave. By then it was nearly six o'clock and there was some relief from the burning sun to the west. I eased the car along the tree-lined drive basking in the shade of the long branched old oaks. I don't remember anything about the drive home except the silent calm of having accomplished my mission and the thoughts around it.

It has been fifty-four years since that night in June. It has been thirty-six years since I first told Linc about it, and it has been seventeen years since I had six months of intense psychotherapy when I was in my thirties. During that period of psychotherapy, I dreaded the possibility that my psychiatrist would somehow wrench this abominable happening from me. That dread was behind me now. I had, at last, brought the truth out into the open, at least to my doctor. I had no idea where I would go from here. I just knew that somehow I had to climb out of this hole that my life had fallen into. Truthfully, I had thought Linc's affair, the dope case, and the land-fill attacks had more to do with my present depression. It really didn't occur to me that this horror in my childhood had anything to do with my going to the hospital. It was just a nightmare that kept recurring. That old nightmare I had over and over of the big brown bear chasing me up the loft steps in the red barn. Both the whip-ping and the bear haunted me. I drove home in the present leaving the old horrors in the doctor's office. Maybe they would stay there.

During the following week, I tried to concentrate on things in the present. It wasn't hard. There was so much going on in my life. My biggest goal was to feel better. I was taking Prozac at the time and it was helping, but I didn't trust it to keep the depression away. Those black holes were ghosts I wanted to avoid at all costs.

I seemed to be walking in a maze during the day. Always think-ing, trying to unravel the turn of events that had brought me to this point–the affair, the landfill, and that damned dope case–which I thought were the causes of all my troubles now. I knew they were all three burdens for me. That awful dark, dark past of my child-hood was gone. I had dealt with that in Dr. Thomas's office and there was no reason to dig that up again. Besides, now that I had told my doctor maybe it wouldn't come up again.

Now I only had to deal with those things in my adult life in the immediate past that I wanted so much to forget, especially the affair. Why couldn't I just will myself to forget it? Other people seemed to be able to forget and go on as if nothing had happened. When I was with Linc something would always come up that reminded me of "that woman" as I called her. Then the rage would sweep over my whole body and overcome anything that my mind could control. I became, in a matter of minutes, totally out of control. No matter how much I wanted to avoid the confrontation or walk away, the power to do so was never there. I simply could not forget. And always depression followed those outbursts of rage.

I didn't understand about anger. I certainly knew that I got mad, so mad that I wanted to tear that woman apart with my bare hands if I could get to her. Somehow my bare hands and my own strength were most important to me. I never wanted to shoot her or cut her to ribbons, I just literally wanted to tear her apart with my own strength. So, the anger was directed outwardly at her; then, because I was frustrated by my inability to reach her, it turned in on me. The result was another fall into depression. I didn't realize then that depression is anger turned on the self, or that the real root of anger is often beyond the awareness of the conscious mind. All I was able to comprehend was that this woman had taken away from me my peace of mind, and sent my thoughts into the outer realms of space which was full of black holes.

A week passed with as few black holes as I could manage. I stayed at home as much as I could and had as little contact with people outside my immediate family as possible. I was afraid of people. I imagined they knew everything about the affair, and that they knew I had been in a mental hospital. I felt certain that because of the dope case they hated me already. I was a woman rejected by her husband, hated by the community where I had grown up, I was mentally ill, and had been locked up in a mental ward.

My immediate family tried to be supportive, but I am sure it was very difficult to be around me, maybe like tiptoeing through a minefield. The saving grace for Linc was that he was in therapy, too. He had many issues to deal with besides the affair. His group pointed out things about him that helped him know what was going on with me. It was a great source of assurance to me that he went to group every week because I had confidence in what I was trying to do, and I thought Linc needed a doctor too.

When I was in the hospital, Dr. Thomas had said "Mrs. Owens, I realize you can't conceive of this being true at the moment, but just remember, 'The sanest one in a family is always the one who ends up in the hospital.'"

What in the world did he mean? Anybody could see I was the sickest one in my family. I was the only one who ever got angry with Linc. Everybody thought he was the sweetest, most wonderful man in the universe. My children certainly weren't sick. They were bright, healthy, responsible adults. My mother and father were dead, and my sisters had never had any problems that I knew about. There was something missing here, something I had no inkling about. I was totally blind to my own situation.

Every time I thought like this, my mind went around in circles. There was no answer.

The week passed. Thursday afternoon at 4:30 came for my second appointment. There had been a break in the heatwave. The drive to Richmond was pleasant. The afternoon traffic had not begun. The car glided over the roads almost by itself. I guided it and kept my foot on the gas pedal, but my mind was on what was going to happen when I faced Dr. Thomas.

I thought the doctor could see through me the moment I walked into his office, and therapy seemed to be the process of extracting a confession from me. Once I had confessed that was all that was needed. I had confessed my most horrific secret, so what else was there to talk about?

The image of that woman reared before me like pictures in an album as I was driving. Yes, that was it. There were endless things to talk about her, the bitch. My hands gripped the steering wheel. I wanted to wipe her image, her name, everything about her out of my mind forever. I struggled with pictures in my mind of her and Linc. I had to maintain control until I got to the doctor's office. I didn't want to go in with my face tear-stained. The session was going to be hard enough anyway.

His office appeared the same. Thank God. I always studied any new surroundings. This habit learned in childhood kept me alert, or so I thought. I didn't know that for me, it was a matter of safety. Finding the room, the sameness gave me some sense of relief. I began to try to relax, hoping to keep my fears under wraps. I sat in the same leather chair and waited. The minutes ticked by. I tried to take deep breaths and let the air escape quietly from my chest. My heart thumped away as if I were running to catch a train. I focused on his desk. Everything was placed neatly and in its place. I liked that. Several lamps burned to give a soft glow instead of real light in the semidarkness. Closed blinds kept out the harsh sunlight and offered blessed privacy from the rest of the world. The quietness of the room gave me a sense of seclusion, a place where no one would know my secrets.

Dr. Thomas came in. "Well, how was your week?"

"It was fine." Of course, it wasn't fine, but that was my practiced response. I must never, never let my true feelings show. I had learned that early in childhood. No one had ever told me why, it was just something I knew. Like never, ever talk to anyone else about what happened at home. I must never, ever talk about Daddy drinking, or Mama and Daddy fighting all the time.

"Oh, that's good. I didn't expect you to say you were fine after our meeting last week."

I didn't want to hear anything about last week or talk about it. Didn't he know I had told him everything I knew? "I guess I am not fine, but maybe O.K." I had to say something. I didn't want him mad at me since trying to please everyone was one of the goals in my life.

"I hope so. Are you taking the Prozac?"

"Yes, every day."

"Are you having any problems with the Prozac?

"I seem to get sleepy driving."

He looked up. "Be careful of that. Sleepiness is one of the side effects of the drug."

"I will."

There was a short silence that seemed very long to me. He had closed his file and laid it on the desk. Each of us waited for the other to speak first. I didn't want to. My heart had slowed down a bit, but I was not anxious to begin this trip into darkness.

His face was relaxed as he spoke. "Have you had any more thoughts on our discussion last week?"

"No, I told you everything last week. Except who it was."

"Oh, so you know who it was."

"I figured it out, later."

"Who was it?"

"It was that awful old man, Mr. Cooper, as Mama made us call him. He lived in the house with us, in fact, his room was right next door to mine. I don't know why he was there. He couldn't do anything because he had a wooden leg and he was really old. He would putter around feeding the chickens and ducks. He would harness up Daisy, but I did all the work, even at eight. I couldn't stand him. And after that night I kept my door locked every night and I tried to stay away from him. Worst of all, I was so afraid for my sisters. They always wanted to follow him around in the yard to watch him feed the chickens, cats, and dogs, or whatever. I would follow them to make sure he didn't bother them too. I worried about them all the time."

"I see. So, you felt you had to look after them."

"Yes. I had to protect them from Cooper, and when Mama and Daddy were fighting I would try to protect them by taking them upstairs or putting them in bed with me."

"Your mother and father fought a lot."

"Yes, always about Daddy's drinking."

"So, let's get back to that night. What made you think it was this house guest?"

I fidgeted in the chair and shot back at him, "He wasn't a house guest. I don't know what you would call him, because he didn't do any work and he stayed there all the time, but he certainly wasn't a house guest."

"I see. But I still want to know why you thought it was him."

"Because his room was right next to mine and there wasn't anybody else in the house that could have done it."

"Did he ever try to molest you again?"

"No. But once later he grabbed me. There was a backstairs going up to his room from the kitchen. One night I forgot and went up the backstairs to go to my room. He was sitting on the bed as I went by and he grabbed me and pulled up my dress and started to fondle me. He tried to pull me down on the bed, but I was stronger than him and I got away. He said 'I just want to rub you a little bit, I won't hurt you. And don't tell your Mama.' I got away and ran into my room and slammed the door. I was really scared. I certainly didn't want another whipping."

"Did you tell your mother or father what had happened?"

"No, I knew better than that. By then, I knew what Cooper did wasn't right, but I had gotten one horrible whipping and I wasn't ever going to tell them anything else about sex. I still don't know how that night happened. All I remember is waking up and feeling this very heavy weight over me and a pillow over my head. I couldn't move. Then I blacked out."

"You didn't see or hear the man come into your room?"

"No, I don't remember a thing." I was crying then. I had lost control. I was so embarrassed to be crying in front of Dr. Thomas. It always made me feel terrible to cry and especially in front of a man. He handed me a box of tissues.

"He probably ejaculated on you."

"Yes, I guess that's what happened." I would have agreed to anything at that point just to stop talking about it. I didn't want to think about that night, about Cooper, or anything else to do with sex. The word gave me the shivers. In my life, it had always been something nice girls avoided. It was something bad girls did before and after marriage.

I took more deep breaths, sighed heavily, and dabbed at my eyes. I knew I looked a wreck by now, but who cared. I was doing the best I could to maintain my appearance, but that usually included trying to keep clean, washing my hair, putting on a little make-up, and wearing something I had found in my closet. Shopping for clothes was a thing of the past. It had been so long since I had bought a new dress, much less read fashion trends in the paper or magazines. It didn't interest me in the least. After all, I couldn't think of a single reason for dressing up.

Shopping and dressing up had been one of my mother's greatest joys. I almost smiled at the thought. There had been so many times in my life when my mother was ashamed of the way I looked. I wondered what she would think of me now. I had on a straight khaki skirt, plain white shirt, and leather sandals. She would have said I was much too masculine looking. I looked too 'plain Jane', not enough color, and of course, I had ruined my naturally curly hair by cutting it so short.

I sighed once more and said. "I have been thinking about that woman a lot."

"By that woman, you mean the woman in Linc's affair?'

"Yes. I have been thinking about her a lot." Was he going to let me change the subject? I held my breath.

"Is there any particular reason that you have been thinking of her?"

Thank God. He was letting me change the subject. I sighed a deep sigh of relief and turned my full attention to that woman.

"No, it's just hard not to think about her when I am reminded of her so much."

"What reminds you of her?"

"There are lots of things. Like when I go to the farm and I go in the house. I think of when my mother died, and she came to see me with another friend. At least, it was someone I thought was my friend. But we all know how that goes. Anyway, she came and sat in the library with my friend, and they both pretended to be so interested in me and my family. Can you imagine the nerve? Why would she bother to come other than to see Linc?"

"I can think of lots of reasons. She was curious to see your mother's house. And she was curious to see you. Check out the competition. Size you up so to speak. I know it's painful to be reminded, but that is the way people are."

I cried in the tissue again. "It just hurts so badly and there is nothing I can do to her except fantasize. And you don't want to hear my fantasies."

He smiled. "Fantasies are healthy as long as you don't act on them."

"I see. Well, if that's the case I'll tell you I visualize myself tearing her limb from limb. And I mean tearing." My voice rose a little.

"Don't you think it would be better if we called her by name, instead of that woman? I am sure she has a name."

"Oh, she does, but I don't want to call her name, but I will if you insist."

"I think it would be better."

I looked at him a moment then said her name as if it were fire on my tongue.

"Why don't you tell me something about her?"

"What do you want to know? She is a first-class bitch."

"Let's start with what she looks like? Where does she live? How did Linc meet her?"

I looked at him thinking. Is this for real? Why does he need to know this? But I answered the questions.

"She was, is, I hope she's dead. But she's tall, thin, black hair, black eyes, talks all the time. She is pushy beyond anything you have ever met. She lives in New Jersey, but she has a place in Staunton too. She has a nice husband with a good job in New York and two or three children. She has a raucous voice and she thinks she runs the world."

"You know her pretty well then."

"No, I don't know her that well and I wish I had never heard of her."

"So, how did Linc get involved? These things usually get started when both parties are in close proximity for a while."

"That's true. Linc had been the family lawyer for a time, and then an older aunt died and Linc was helping with the estate. The family was bickering, and Linc being the good shepherd to everyone, was trying to make everyone happy–especially her. It didn't take her long to move in on him either, even though at the time I knew nothing about it."

"How do you mean?"

"Well, I told Linc after the aunt's funeral that this woman was making a play for him. Of course, he denied it, but at least he admitted it later."

"So, you think she was pursuing him."

"Oh, yes. I believe that, because of Linc's nature. She made the first moves. As a matter of fact, he says he never called her, paid for any motel rooms, wrote her letters, or anything. I love that part of it."

"It's interesting, but women often make the first move unless the man is a real womanizer or addicted to sex. We are speaking of married people now."

"You know, if she had not invaded my territory so many times maybe it wouldn't have hurt so much."

"How did she do that?"

"She gave a big party and invited Linc and me. There I was eating her food, being a proper guest, and she was whispering sweet nothings to my husband. I mean, that is a cheap shot. Then she would call the house all the time, supposedly about business. Once she even came down from New Jersey and spent the night in Linc's office because there was a snowstorm and she didn't think she could drive home. I just wish I had known about them then. But, dummy me. I guess the worst thing she did to make a fool of me was to persuade Linc to meet her in a motel in Richmond when my mother was dying in the hospital.

He told me all the reasons she gave him for meeting her. Then he left her and came to the hospital to be with me at ten o'clock at night...said he had a lot of work to do. Boy, I was so gullible, and he was such a damn cheat."

"Tell me a little more about how she invaded your territory."

"Well, she kept trying to be around me. She got another friend to bring her to our house. Then she wanted to see pictures of our daughter's wedding, talk about our horses, anything to find out more about us. She got another friend to invite us out to dinner when she was down here alone. She arranged to sit by Linc. They were probably playing footsie under the table for all I know. And each time I disliked her more and more.

"She did another thing that was really strange. She wore black all the time. I never saw her when she didn't have on black. There is something they call New York Black, and she was it. Apparently, people in the city wear lots of black because it shows less dirt or something. She even sent us Christmas cards with a black background every year. And she gave Linc all these drawings of black crows and buzzards with what she thought were funny inscriptions. They were nothing but pornographic trash. I mean she was weird from the word go."

"So how long did this last?"

"About three years. I think."

"And when did you find out about it?"

"I found out this past February. Linc was so depressed for a long time and I couldn't figure out what was wrong. I mean he looked like he had lost his best friend, couldn't sleep, wouldn't say anything much. Then when I found out about them, he said he had wanted to get out of the affair for a long time but didn't know how. I said that's a lot of baloney, all you have to do is say you are leaving. But he is like that. He can't say no to anybody. "

"I think you knew about this long before you found out anything for sure. You may not have known what was happening, but you knew at some level that he was having an affair and for some reason, you chose not to believe it or pursue it. I don't think it's true that the spouse is the last one to know."

"Maybe so. I knew something was wrong with him for a long time, but I didn't know what."

"No, I think you did know. I think you knew and for some reason chose not to say anything. Remember, you have been mad with Linc for a long time."

That's certainly true, I thought. I was a little irritated that he had called my hand on this, but at least we had gotten away from the sex issue.

"This is maybe a good place to stop today. Keep taking your medication. Remember it is vital that you take it every day. Don't skip a day or two; it doesn't work that way. You have to keep a steady dose to make it work."

"I'll do my best."

"Good. Now, if you have any problems at all, call me. O.K.?"

"Yes." I managed a weak smile and left.

At last, I was out of there. I felt totally drained and exhausted. It was a feeling I would learn to expect after a session. The walk from the office to the car was short, but it felt like I was walking a tightrope. If each foot wasn't placed in front of the other precisely, I would fall off this wire that my mind had set up in the past hour. It had taken an hour to mark my path this far. I had no idea then the hours ahead it would take to find the final turn.

8

OVER THE NEXT several months my therapy was concentrated on that woman. I felt I needed to talk about her because it was the most recent thing that had happened to me. Looking back, I am sure Dr. Thomas felt he had to gain my confidence first by letting me choose the way. I am sure he had no idea at the beginning whether I was serious about wanting to get to the root of my problems. Would I stay the course? Come each time, be on time, take the medication, and most importantly, really work on the problems. I am just as sure he recognized the root of the problem after my first visit. But I had to get rid of all the dust and cobwebs before I could work on the real dirt.

Did he think I was a spoiled brat who had grown into a spoiled adult? I don't know. I only know I was serious, and I did everything he suggested. My psyche had reached its limits and I wanted relief from the depression, the anxiety, the insecurity, the lack of self-confidence, and all the things that make sane people miserable. I had tried every way possible to help myself, but I ended up crying, having a fit over minor incidents, yelling at everyone around me. I had thoughts of suicide, planning it in detail as I had from high school on. I tried to be with other people constantly so that I couldn't think about the things that really bothered me. I had already tried everything. It was in a way like being an alcoholic. I had reached, what I thought, was the bottom of the well and there was nowhere to go but up. I didn't know it would be so hard to face myself or to look at myself in a mirror and see who was really there.

I have to say here that one of my greatest problems was one that developed over the years. It was much harder for me to talk to my doctor because I trusted no one.

It was one of the first questions Dr. Maxfield had asked me in the hospital.

"Do you trust your husband?"

"No!"

"Do you trust your mother?"

"Absolutely not."

Did I trust Dr. Thomas, now? Somewhat. I trusted him enough to talk about the things in the present, but not the things in the past that haunted me in the early hours of the morning. I had told him about the whipping, but there were other things that I didn't want to tell anyone. They had happened as a child, some as a teenager, and some as an adult. They all had to do with sex. They made me ashamed, uncomfortable, and embarrassed. They would have to wait until I felt more comfortable with him. And at this point, I saw no need because I had told him about the whipping, and we hadn't discussed it since. Of course, I had not mentioned it. I thought just telling him was enough.

One day at the beginning of a session, I said to Dr. Thomas, "That happened before the dope case."

He looked up. "You've mentioned this dope case before. Why don't you tell me more about it?"

"It's another thing I would like to forget."

"Why?"

"It makes me remember bad things. I think it was the beginning of all the trouble Linc and I have had recently."

"Oh, in what way was it the beginning of all your troubles?"

"I will have to tell you the whole thing to make it make sense."

"Good."

"Well, I don't know if you want to hear all of this or not, but it began back in 1978. In fact, it was the night of our Christmas party. We always had a big Christmas party every year and invited friends from all over. Anyway, it was December the twenty-second, 1978, about eleven-thirty at night. The party was in full swing. The sheriff's office called and said they needed Linc at the Courthouse. He was the Commonwealth's Attorney then. They sent a state trooper to pick him up. Nobody knew what was happening, not even Linc, except that they were making a raid in the county and needed him to give advice on how to make the charges. He left. And that put an end to the party almost.

"It was quite a scene though, everyone standing around in their holiday finery with Christmas in the air and a patrol car with lights flashing, showing up literally at the front door. We have a circular drive that comes within a few feet of the front door. Linc ran out in his white ice cream suit with a red vest, handkerchief, and Santa Claus tie. We called it his ice-cream suit because it was white wool and one of the children had made the comment that 'Daddy has on his ice-cream suit.' He loved to dress dashingly as he called it and the ice-cream suit with Christmas accessories was one of his best.

"Linc made a quick exit and got in the car with the Deputy and off they went, lights flashing and siren blasting. Everyone was left gasping in disbelief that something like this would happen in Derbyshire County. They probably thought it was some sort of joke until they realized I was not laughing, and Linc didn't come back.

"It was hours later when Linc got home. I was wide awake as soon as he walked into the house. 'What in the world happened? Where have you been?'

"'You won't believe it,' he said, trying to get out of his rumpled ice cream suit and stay coherent at the same time. 'The State Police made a raid tonight, last night, near the lake. It was a tractor-trailer load of marijuana. They arrested four or five people and they're going to Richmond this morning to raid a motel and make more arrests.'

"I stared at him and laughed. 'A trailer load of marijuana in the State Forest.' Serves it right, I thought. I have a special interest in that state forest.

"'Yes, a tractor-trailer load of marijuana was found in the Derbyshire State Forest. This is going to be a damn mess for me. I know that.' He dropped his last shoe on the floor and stumbled toward the bed.

"I lay in the gray light of a winter morning for a moment, trying to comprehend what he had said. There was no basis for knowing what was going to happen. Derbyshire people knew nothing of marijuana. Drugs were in the city. The drug war was still in the mind of its makers. Still, I knew this was big. I had no idea how big or how ominous the night would prove for us.

"I wondered about the children. How would they be affected? Jimmy was married and had his own life now. And he was level headed. He had never gone off the deep end about anything, even in high school. He would probably not even notice except when he was drawn into a conversation. Jimmy had his own interests and was usually undisturbed by things outside his world, other than the church, his family, the farm, and his Army Reserve Unit. But the girls were teenagers, both in high school. Camille was away at boarding school. Lindsay was home with us. How would they be affected by all this? I knew they had solid backgrounds, but we were on unknown turf now and it worried me.

"I knew Linc would be the focus of the community for a while, I didn't know how long or in what way.

"Later that morning Linc went to Richmond. Another raid had taken place at the Stratton House on Bloom Street. More people arrested, a suitcase filled with a million dollars in cash confiscated. Nothing like this had ever happened in Derbyshire, a poor county in Piedmont Virginia, south of the James River.

"By the next day, the grapevine in the county was alive and growing. Tales and facts were mixed to suit the teller. For me, it was a time to be proud of my husband. I was excited with the prospects of my husband involved with the biggest drug bust of all time. That's what the Richmond Times-Dispatch reported. Then the raid was billed on the news as the biggest drug bust in the United States, ever. The authorities had followed the marijuana trail from Florida and were ready to press charges, on what they hoped would be a major catch. Calls began coming from lawyers in Florida, New York, New Jersey, Colorado, and North Carolina. It didn't matter that this was just a few days before Christmas. In fact, the Richmond arrests were made on the twenty-third of December. It is needless to say that I remember nothing of the Christmas of 1978. It lingers in my mind as the beginning of the Dope Case.

"The girls were home from school and ready for Christmas. They were irritated at the countless phone calls and the constant tension in the house about the dope case. They yelled at me for paying more attention to Linc than to them and yelled at Linc for staying at the office. Everywhere we went that Christmas we faced a storm of questions about the arrests. Linc and I found ourselves sitting at the kitchen table every night drinking coffee at one o'clock in the morning and eating fruit cake. The conversation was always about the office that day. The girls would come in and joke about the latest gossip of the case or fret about what we couldn't do together.

"From the very first, Linc realized this was going to be a major trial, and he knew he had to have some help. As the prosecuting attorney in a rural county he had almost no experience in prosecuting drug cases. But he had a Commonwealth Attorney friend in northern Virginia who had experience and was recognized as one of the best prosecuting attorneys in the State. Denis was young, aggressive, self-confident. An Irish Catholic who believed in all the virtues of the home, family, and a society which drugs were poised to destroy. He was glad to help a friend and be part of a big trial. He was not afraid of the lawyers from the big cities or the money behind them.

"A hearing date was set in January. Every ear was tuned to the court case for news, not only about what happened inside the courthouse but the parade of lawyers and press that swarmed over the village. Each defendant had to be represented by a Virginia Bar member. This brought out the finest the state had to offer from Richmond, Charlottesville, and the biggest politicians in Southside, Virginia. These lawyers drove big cars, carried soft leather briefcases, and dressed in subdued pin-striped suits with two-hundred-dollar white shirts and cuffs. No one in the county who went to the courthouse during this time was disappointed.

"The press had a field day. Not since the Ferguson trial in the thirties was there so much news in this little poverty-stricken county of Derbyshire. In the Ferguson trial, two brothers went to prison for shooting a preacher at high noon on his front porch with his wife and children looking on. It was a love triangle. In that trial the citizens of the county were about equally divided; in this one, it was unified against the evil of drugs.

"The local paper, the Richmond paper, Charlottesville paper, and other regional papers found newsworthy stories under every rock in the county. As the case progressed into the spring, the Washington Post did a two-page spread with pictures. But the publicity was not good. Linc was pictured in his ice-cream suit going to the raid. The picture made him look like a character out of a Dukes of Hazzard show. Local residents were quoted as saying they had never seen lawyers in the county carrying briefcases before.

"The Post billed the county as a sleepy, forgotten village, whose residents lived in the nineteenth century and had little notion of the modern world or the threat of drugs. I agreed with every word, but it hurt to see my husband shown in that bad light. I had always believed in his ability as a lawyer. He graduated from The University of Virginia Law School in 1963. Most of all I believed in his character. The drug of choice in the county was alcohol and white lightning which was still distilled in the countryside. The Post understood why the county had been chosen as a place to hide a trailer load of marijuana. It was a perfect hideout and close to a big city.

"My hopes for Linc and the case were fast fading in light of the bad publicity. Also, Denis called me often to say, 'Don't let Linc cave in, Lesley, whatever you do.' I knew what he meant. I just didn't know how prophetic his words of warning were to become. My answer would be, 'Don't worry Denis, it's going to be all right. I talk to him all the time about not letting someone talk him into something.' I would hang up thinking how great it was that Denis put so much trust in me, not realizing what I really had to fear in Linc. I was totally confident that I could keep Linc from caving in to pressure. I really thought Linc would do the right thing anyway.

"Everyone talked about the case in one light or another. Some laughed, some were serious, but it was on everyone's mind and found its way into all the local conversations. Along in April, Linc received a letter from a lawyer in North Carolina offering the county a million dollars if the Commonwealth's Attorney would release the defendants. There was also an article stuffed in the envelope from a North Carolina paper telling how this had been done in North Carolina and had been used for so much good: school budget, recreational facilities, and welfare. The Richmond paper picked up the story and referred to it as a bribe, which it was, but to the county, not to Linc.

"The county could certainly have used the money. The only source of business revenue to speak of was the pipeline from Texas carrying crude oil to New York, and that agreement from the fifties was fast running out.

"Linc did not accept the million dollars for the county because it was, in fact, a bribe and he referred to it as such. But, the damage to his name had still been done. A local lawyer had gotten out of the case soon after Christmas with the words. 'It's just too dirty for me. I don't like all those Mafia types calling to make offers. It just smells too bad for me.' The case was looking more and more like a big sum of money up for grabs.

"It was whispered everywhere. How much do you think they are all getting? The Commonwealth's Attorney, the judge, the lawyers, all of them. Which one is really on the take? I couldn't believe people were saying that about Linc, but they were. I knew his character was flawless, I believed in his integrity and I knew without any doubt he would not lie, cheat or steal.

"This is when I really began to worry about our daughters. I couldn't stand the fact that people were joking about their father behind their backs or worse yet to their face. Camille was in boarding school, and I knew she had access to the Post and the other newspapers in the state. She was steadfast for her father, but I knew it had to hurt, even if she knew it wasn't true. She called me often and always tried to cheer me up.

"Lindsay was in school at home and heard everything. I didn't know what was being said in school, but I could guess. I realized the pressure she was under when one night at dinner she screamed at me, 'Mom, I can't take this anymore. All you and Dad talk about is this damned dope case. It's driving me nuts. You don't care a thing about what I am doing or what happens to me.'

"'Lindsay! That isn't so. I do care. I care more than you know.'

"I pushed my chair back and reached out to her. She was sobbing then, and my own heart wanted to break as I cradled her head in my arms. A child is never too big or too old to hold. Lindsay was sixteen: a soft, cuddly, sometimes a needy, but endearing girl.

"'I am so sorry, honey, I know it is hard, but we will get through this. You know and I know your Daddy didn't take any money from these drug people. We will just have to be strong.'

"Linc spoke up. 'Your Mom is right, Lindsay, I haven't taken any money and I won't, but that isn't going to stop people from talking.'

"'I know, Dad. I just worry about you and Mom so much because people are being so mean. I just don't want anything to happen.'

"I realized then just how hard the whole episode had been on all of us. I still had faith in Linc, but I was wearing thin. It seemed all the gods were against us. And I had never wanted to leave Derbyshire more.

"I soothed Lindsay's feelings for the time being, but I knew there would be more outbursts like this one. I did promise her and myself to pay more attention to what she was doing.

"The case for me was looking worse and worse. I no longer thought of how it could help Linc. Instead, I just wanted it to be over. The summer came and went, finally the fall and the real trials."

9

_____

"IT SEEMED STRANGE TO ME, but I was called for jury duty for the very first trial of the defendants. I had never before been called for jury duty or even been to court. I was surely going to be struck from the jury because of Linc, but at least I would be able to see what was going on. To me it was an honor to be called for jury duty.

"The panel of jurors was endless as the clerk read out the names. I answered clearly when my name was read. I had chosen a seat near the window on the left side with a direct view of the podium. The judge looked up and nodded to me as my name was read. It was a sign of recognition. One I needed.

"The morning had dawned a cold, crisp autumn day, typical of the middle of October. I sat quietly looking out the window feeling secure and hopeful. Maybe today was the day something good would come out of this whole nightmare for Linc. Just then I saw the first big snowflake float slowly to the ground. In a few seconds, another, turning silently as it made its way past my view. The snow began as slowly and harmoniously as a church choir began its chant for the preacher's final amen. The big flakes soon covered the ground and clung to the trees, branches, and trunks. It was as though I could hear the humming of the voices in the background. The snowflakes that brought stillness and beauty on the outside, just as silently and quickly blanketed the courtroom in a death shroud for me. The harmony of the choir turned to a death chant and my blood ran cold.

"A shiver went up my arms to my neck as I realized this was a very bad omen. I didn't know of any witch's tales, old wives' tales, or superstitions to make it a bad omen. The pit of my stomach told me. It was nature talking to me as surely as the spring rains bring the new grass. The great outdoors was telling me something. Something I should listen to, just as all those times when I was a child and I found myself outdoors with no one to talk to, no one to hear my prayers, no one to listen to me except all of nature, the great outdoors itself. It was way too early to snow, but the snow fell silently, and the courtroom droned on in a dull half-noise. There seemed to be no correlation between the glorious crystal white of the outside and the morbid dark colors and mood of the inside.

"The outdoors soon turned to what we call a postcard snow, a fairyland. Snow piled on the window sills, on the cars moving slowly on Route 60. The sky was gray, and a slight breeze was blowing. But it was too early to snow. We never had a real snow before November. My heart pounded under my sweater because I felt the dark pangs of wrongdoing settling over me. I resettled on the hard, wooden benches that matched the colonial building in style but hurt my back. Maybe that was a good thing for a courtroom, I thought. No one should be comfortable in court. My mood was changing from excitement at being in the courtroom, witnessing a trial, and my husband as the prosecuting attorney, to apprehension. There was something very wrong. The snow was a warning, but I couldn't put my finger on the problem.

"The big doors opened, and Jimmy came in as a spectator. He made his way to the back. I heard the chair scrape as he sat down. I was so glad he was there. Even though we could not sit together I felt comfort and support from his being there. Jimmy had been solid throughout the ordeal. But he was staunch about everything. He was strong, quiet, determined, and sure of himself. I was proud of him as a son, and even though he no longer lived in the house he was very much a part of the family. He and his wife were always with us in spirit.

"I turned my attention to the front of the courtroom and began to watch the proceedings. Linc was speaking but I couldn't really make out what he was saying. Then I heard the judge say, 'How do you plead?'

"'Guilty, Your Honor.'

"I was stunned. Linc had said they were pleading not guilty. What kind of deal had Linc agreed to in order for the lawyers to let them plead guilty? What had happened behind closed doors before court? Linc had spent a lot of time writing up instructions, memorandums preparing for a trial. Why were they changing at the last minute? Now, what was going to happen?

"I looked at the defendant who was standing, hands held together in front of him. His stature did not suit the voice. He was about 6 ft. 2 inches, 250 lbs. He had our son, Jimmy's, red hair, light complexion with freckles, and a ruddy face. His hair was short, a crew cut in fact. The lawyers had probably made him cut it. His voice was soft. A sissy voice is what it would have been called in the fifties. He had on a navy blue, wide pinstripe suit, subdued, with a white button-down collar, and shiny loafers. The shoes were certainly not the business look the lawyers prepped him for. They must have overlooked his feet.

"I shook my head at his appearance and thought about what I knew he had done. What a slime ball. He had come to this county, where almost no one made thirty thousand dollars a year, with a trailer load of marijuana and over a million dollars in cash. To think he could hide out here and distribute his weed, worth more than half the county. My stomach turned. I wanted something awful to happen to him at that very moment. But nothing did. He was facing the judge and his voice was meekness itself.

"'Do you have anything to say?' asked the judge.

"'Yes, your Honor. I wish to apologize to the court and to this county especially, for what I have done. I know there are a lot of people here who are very angry at me. The money made me forget what I was doing and the harm it could bring so many people. I just want to say I am sorry and ask the court's forgiveness. And I promise never to be involved with this kind of thing ever again.'

"How can they all stand there and listen to this, I thought. Who told him to say that? He was a joke. I bet he had never worked a day in his life and had made his living suckering other people. I twisted in my seat, crossing my legs and arms.

"I looked at his lawyer standing beside him. He was alert, confident, and he was one of the best trial lawyers in Richmond. He enjoyed a reputation as a legitimate, hardworking lawyer. I couldn't be mad at him, no matter how hard I tried. He was a classmate of my brother-in-law. I knew he had worked very hard for everything he had. Everyone thought of him as a bright, hard fighter for his clients. The local heavy artillery stood next to him. This was a seasoned lawyer, a retired congressman, a good friend of the judge, and a friend of Linc's. I had never liked him or trusted him. I didn't know why. It was just the way I felt. Half the courtroom owed him a big debt, one way or another. The big guns were out, and they were out for the bait–money. My throat was dry, and my eyes were burning. I didn't know what was going on, but now the judge would hand down the sentence on Linc's recommendation. What kind of a deal had Linc agreed to with the defense lawyers? Would Linc hold up? I didn't want to think about this. If Linc didn't hold up under the pressure to make the sentence light, Denis would be there, he would hold the line.

"The judge spoke again. 'Members of the jury, your services will no longer be needed. The court wishes to thank you for your time in coming out this morning and your willingness to help see that justice is done. You are free to go at your convenience.'

"Most everyone got up to leave. I sat there waiting to see what would happen next and why the last-minute change in the plea. A cold burst of air came through the large double doors as the jurors left. The few flakes of snow that had blown in past the jurors lay against the dark gray carpet and slowly melted away, taking my last hopes for the trial and Linc with them. What had Linc agreed to for them to plead guilty?

"There was little to see or hear in the courtroom. The question remained. Why did the defendants change their pleas at the last minute?

"Jimmy appeared beside me and took my arm. 'Well what do you think of that?' His voice was low, but there were questions on his face.

"'I don't know Jimmy, but I am afraid. It looks bad to me. But the real question is, why did your Daddy let them plead guilty?'

"'I don't know. Let's go home and maybe Dad will be along before too long.'

"There were no answers that day or in the weeks that followed, but speculation was rampant. What kind of deal had been made? There was no limit to the money available, everyone knew that. As the cases came and went, it became more and more apparent to many that something was terribly amiss. All seven defendants pled guilty. The judge would sentence the defendants to 25 years in prison and suspend all but 2 and ½ years. With good behavior, they would be eligible for parole in five months."

"What did the community think of this?" Dr. Thomas asked.

"That was just the point. Most of them couldn't believe it. I certainly couldn't, after all the work and aggravation everyone had been through in law enforcement because of the case. Believe me, that was all it took for people to believe that everyone in the Court House had taken a bribe of some sort. I knew that Linc hadn't, or if he had, I hadn't seen any of it. But, no one else knew that."

"What about his family and your family? How did they react?"

"My family was very supportive of Linc publicly and privately. They stuck by him. His family didn't even acknowledge that the case was happening. This was typical of the way they thought. I would later call it denial mechanisms. But their thought was no one would dare think anything bad about Linc anyway. His family was above reproach. Even after all the publicity my mother and sisters defended Linc. They said he had a reason for what he had done, and wouldn't listen to anything else. Linc's family never mentioned it to us. There were no questions and no support either. We were just in a vacuum."

"That must have been hard on you."

"Yes, it was. But I am sure it was harder on Lindsay and Camille. They couldn't believe their father could be accused of doing something which seemed so opposite of what everyone else thought was right. Jimmy was surprised that the community had turned against his father like they did, but he adjusted to the rumors better than any of us.

"There were some difficult times in our house after that. Each of us tried to find something to hang onto. The girls turned to their horses and the upcoming summer. But they were crushed by the whispers and giggles and stares. They were not prepared for the people they had grown up with turning on their father. The county people thought the defendants should have been given twenty-five years, as I did. They didn't understand anything that had happened.

"Some of the lawyers had told me that Linc had done a great job on the memorandums for the case and had complimented his work in other ways. So, I tried to get him to try to get another job. I wanted to leave Derbyshire. I had wanted to leave all my life."

"So, did he try to get a job?"

"No, he didn't want to, and he never tried. I didn't understand why."

"And this was hard for you?"

"Yes, I had tried ever since we were married to leave Derbyshire. I even gave him the money when he finished law school to go to Denver to get a job. And he had a perfect opening. He went with a friend of ours who knew lawyers out there and he introduced him. He went, but he didn't get a job. He just didn't want to leave Derbyshire."

"You've always wanted to leave home."

"Yes, and I thought this was a good chance."

"So, you were disappointed in Linc after the dope case."

"Disappointment does not really explain my feelings. I was angry that he had spent so much time on the trial and tried to get nothing from it. I was humiliated by his 'no care' attitude, and I felt cheated and abandoned. I felt doubly bad for the girls. They deserved to live somewhere else. They were young and needed a larger world. Lindsay went to boarding school for just that reason."

Dr. Thomas had a look I had not seen before. "If you felt this strongly, why didn't you push him harder?"

I felt a rush of anger. "You don't understand. I did. I did everything I could. He is stubborn." With that, the tears began to flow and I sank deeper in the chair. "And besides I didn't feel nearly as bad then as I did a year later."

"What do you mean?"

I sniffled in a tissue and continued. "It was a Sunday in early April, Easter Sunday in fact. We were having my sisters, their families, and my mother to dinner. I didn't go to church that day. I stayed home from church to fix dinner. We always had leg of lamb, lots of salads, vegetables, hot rolls, and fresh coconut cake to celebrate Easter. This particular Sunday was a beautiful warm day in April. I remember feeling happy and content that morning. I loved to fix the table with flowers, my best china, and things had not gone too bad in the kitchen. My sisters and mother got there first. Everyone was talking and crowding around in the kitchen.

"When Linc and the children came in, he had the Sunday paper with him. He handed me the paper and didn't say anything. I didn't understand until I unfolded the paper, and staring back at me from the middle of the front page of the Richmond Times-Dispatch was a picture of Linc with the headlines *Derbyshire Commonwealth's Attorney Turns Drug Dealers Loose Early*.

"Cold chills ran down my spine. I couldn't speak. I couldn't believe what my eyes were telling me. I sat down at the kitchen table and read. In the end, my worst fears could not match the present truth. The reporter outlined the events of the last week. In fact, on the recommendation of the Commonwealth's Attorney, the Judge of the Fourth Circuit Court had indeed signed the order to release three of the defendants. They were released, not serving lighter sentences, not paroled. They were free.

"There was a quote from Linc's friend Denis, the Commonwealth's Attorney in Northern Virginia. 'I am astounded. I knew nothing of the release. This is the first I have heard about it. No one has informed me or asked me anything.'

"More importantly there were references to the Attorney General of Virginia looking into the legality of what had happened. Could the judge do this merely on the recommendation of the Commonwealth's Attorney? It was a question he intended to pursue.

"I don't remember much about the dinner except that I couldn't eat, and I wanted to cry. More than anything I wanted some explanation from Linc. He had betrayed me, his friend Denis, and his job–for what? I couldn't understand. Had he heard anything that had happened the last two years? Had he heard any of my pleas to leave the county, to get another job?

"Dinner was over. Everyone had left. 'Why did you do this?'

"Hadn't he heard what the village people thought about the whole case? Did he know what this would do to his career? Did he realize what had happened?

"'What do you mean?'

"'I mean just what I said. Why did you recommend the release of those drug dealers?'

"'Because, they asked me to, and I didn't see anything wrong with it?'

"'Who are they?'

"'You know. The congressman came by and asked me if I would consider it and I said sure, why not. The judge indicated what he wanted. They have served enough time. I don't know what all the fuss is about.'

"'Linc, don't you know what is going to happen. You are taking the blame for the whole thing. It's going to look like you made a deal. And how could you do this to Denis? You asked him to help you, then you didn't even tell him what you are doing? Why didn't you at least tell me before I read it in the paper?'

"'You're right. I didn't want to tell you. I knew you would be against me signing the release and I didn't want to tell you.'

"'Do you see what you've done?'

"'No, I don't. I am sorry you're upset, but I wasn't going against the judge.'

"'Don't you see that he is using you and the other lawyers too, especially the local ones. You are going to be hung with this. You could tell the reporters the truth and fight this. Why are you taking the blame for the judge, the lawyers, the congressman? Why are you doing this?'

"'Because I don't think it matters.'

"'It does matter. It matters to me, the children, all of us. You'll see. This is going to blow up in your face. Those damn people don't care a thing about you, and you shouldn't cover for them.'

"'Maybe you're right, I don't know.'

"The next night the judge, all the local lawyers and politicians had a party at a private hideaway in the county. Of course, Linc was there too. These men controlled politics in Southside Virginia. They still drank homemade Moonshine liquor, ate hog chitlins and traded favors. It was a good ole boy party–no women allowed. I wouldn't have gone anyway. I stayed home and answered the telephone. A TV News reporter called, among others.

"Linc came home in high spirits. The judge had bragged he didn't care what that damn little boy in Richmond, the Attorney General, was talking about, who swore he wasn't taking back any order. The judge had made the motion at the time of the trial on Linc's recommendation to reconsider the case at a later date and that was all there was to it. The judge said the Attorney General could take it to the Virginia Supreme Court for all he cared. The TV reporter called back, but Linc had no comment. That was noted in the eleven o'clock newscast

"The newscasters had a heyday at Linc's expense. The Attorney General did go to the Supreme Court and the order was rescinded. The defendants were put back in jail to serve the rest of their time which was all of six months. And Linc was not reelected Commonwealth's Attorney. He had served sixteen years."

Dr. Thomas looked at me for a few moments. "Is this the first time you had any hint of Linc's true nature? You must have seen this part of him before. Surely, this was not the first time he had done something similar. Maybe not as bad, for you, but something that showed his passive nature."

"Yes, I'm sure you are right. I guess I had just not wanted to believe it before. I didn't know enough to call it depression at the time, but my spirits sank. I felt betrayed, beaten, and abandoned. Linc didn't really care about the children or me. We were doomed. This was the first break in our marriage. I had supported him in every way before. I had believed in his integrity and counted on his love. I didn't believe he would hurt me. Now, I felt it was no use to struggle any longer. In effect, I gave up. I told him I would never again ask him to leave Derbyshire or get another job."

I paused. Neither Dr. Thomas nor I spoke for a minute.

"What about the children? You were concerned about what was happening to them?"

"Yes. I was concerned. I had tried to be more attentive to Lindsay, but I was so horrified at what Linc had done, it was hard to think about her. She seemed to be angry at both of us, and I thought she should only be angry at him."

"Do you know why you were so angry at him?'

"Yes, I have told you. He betrayed me. He betrayed me in the worst way because he ruined his career and threw away his reputation. The girls were devastated. Not only for what their father had done but what it had done to the family. There seemed to be no trust left for any of us."

"Do you know why trust is so important to you?"

"Yes," I shot back. "It's important for everyone."

"True, but you in particular."

"I don't know. I'll think about it."

The session was over, but my head was spinning. Why had Dr. Thomas been so hard on me? Linc had betrayed me and everyone. I was the victim.

Oh, to hell with all of them, I thought. I am going home.

10

Dr. Thomas and I spent many more sessions working and reworking the dope case. There was so much there I could not understand, about what and why it had happened. But there came a time when we had to move on.

By then, Dr. Thomas had moved his office to a hospital on the north side of town. The new office had big double windows that faced the back of another building, so it wasn't always necessary to have the curtains drawn for privacy. I could sit for a few minutes sometimes while I waited and watch the sun rays on the roof next door, or watch the rain beat down and make little rivers on the plate glass window. Sometimes it would be cloudy with nothing for me to look at except the outdoors and to imagine the cold of a February afternoon or the coming spring shower from the gray clouds.

The office itself was much larger and there were new leather chairs, a new couch, end tables, and lamps. A large collection of medicine bottles, medical books, and a series of old prints telling the alcoholic's demise added to the decor. It very soon became home, a place where I would feel secure enough to talk. My own chair in the same place at each session made it more home for me. My seat, with his seat in front of me, made it feel more like a conversation than an interview. He never sat behind his desk which would have created a barrier both physically and mentally between us.

I looked at Dr. Thomas and said, "I have to tell you something."

I don't remember why I decided to talk about my affair that afternoon. Maybe something had happened at home or maybe I just thought it was time. This was one of those embarrassing regretful things I didn't want to talk to him about. I knew it would have to come up sooner or later. I didn't want to talk about what I perceived to be my fault. It was hard to look at myself and see what was there. There was no way to soften what I saw as a flaw in myself and I didn't know but one way to handle it. I could either lie to Dr. Thomas and to myself or I could shoot from the hip. I decided shooting from the hip was the best way.

"I had an affair too."

"Oh, when?"

"It happened before Linc's, in fact."

"I see. How long ago was this?"

"I don't remember exactly, but it was after the dope case."

"That dope case always pops up, doesn't it?"

I smiled. "It always seems to be around... at least in my mind."

"So how did this affair happen? Was it serious?"

"Yes, at the time, I thought it was. Neither one of us meant for it to happen, I know that. It was just a case of being around each other, having a lot in common, and being attracted. And, I was so angry at Linc. I don't know how attraction works, but it doesn't happen to everyone obviously and some people have the stamina or sense to avert it."

"That's true. They call it charisma, don't they?"

"I've heard it called that. I just have to say I wish it hadn't happened because it didn't make me happy. In the long run, it made me miserable, but there didn't seem to be anything I could do about it at the time. I had fallen in love. It was that simple."

"Sometimes those things happen when we least expect it, but there is usually a reason behind it."

"I don't know about that. I just know I was profoundly miserable after the dope case, and before I knew it I was in this relationship over my head."

"This sounds very typical so far."

I smiled again. God, I hate this, I thought. I wish I could get up and run and go out and shoot myself. Do something constructive. I can't see how this is going to help. Here I am, a middle-aged woman with almost grown children, talking about an affair. It's not like I haven't done enough bad things in my life. My whole life has been a failure and a disaster from start to finish. Even my mother didn't like me.

Dr. Thomas was obviously waiting. I knew if I kept these thoughts up one more second, I was going to cry again, and I was so tired of that. It seemed all I had done in his office was cry, cry, cry. Half the time I didn't seem to know what I was crying about.

I cleared my throat and tried again.

"He was much younger than I was and ruggedly good looking. At least that's what I thought. He was very tall, with black wavy hair, those beautiful blue eyes, fair skin, and long slender hands. He was one of the black Irish, as opposed to those with red hair. He had a wonderful voice and a gentle way about him.

"But I think the thing that really triggered my interest was how I identified him with my father, not in the way he looked or acted or anything like that. He was in the wood business–pulpwood–and I had grown up in the lumber business. In fact, I spent a lot of time with Daddy in the woods when I was growing up. He had sawmills and later a planer. To me, it was all the same. I knew something about the lumber business, and I had missed being around it.

"You see I was so hurt, mad, and disgusted with Linc after the dope case that I retreated into myself and wanted to have nothing to do with anything I had known during my marriage to Linc. I felt let down and worse, there was no one I could talk to in the County. I felt Linc had betrayed me, his best friend. Everyone in the County thought I was just as guilty by association. I was his wife, and therefore everyone thought I had gotten part of the dope money just like all the rest of the lawyers. The truth is neither one of us got any, although there was plenty of opportunity.

"Of course, I talked to this man about this which was another mistake. In fact, that money was the joke or the subject of every dinner table conversation in the county for months. Did we take it and how much? But I have to say there was absolutely no one else to talk to. My father had died in 1973 and even though my mother supported Linc, she had no time for me. It didn't matter to her what I was thinking. She didn't want to hear it. She was too busy with her own life. I had married Linc. He had made a mistake and that was all there was to it. I should forget it and go on. She had other things to do rather than waste time talking to me about something that was water over the dam.

"I hated her for this, but I wasn't surprised. She had never supported me in anything. Why should she be willing to listen to me now? My sisters were little help. They had their own lives and what did it matter to them what had happened to my life. As they saw it, nothing had happened except I was disappointed. I guess, most importantly, I had learned as a child not to trust anyone with my private thoughts or what was happening at home. Growing up with an alcoholic taught me that."

Dr. Thomas interrupted. "Let's go back to why you think this man was like your father."

"You mean what reminded me?"

"Yes."

"Well, the way he thought about things. He was conservative and had the same ideas about business and government interference. It had been so long since I had heard this kind of thinking. Linc was not a businessman. In my mind, I was starving for what I had grown up with, the aura of the lumber business, the hard work, excitement, the gamble. Buying a raw material and turning it into a product to sell is not easy. It is essentially a corporate effort run by a hard-driving CEO."

"I see. So initially, this man reminded you of your father and this made you happy with the relationship."

"Yes, when I first met him, I wasn't immediately attracted to him. I was just so happy to again hear the things I used to hear about the woods, business, and a world I thought was gone for me.

I came to realize he wasn't at all like my father, but it took a long time. I was living a fantasy."

"So, how did you meet him?"

"His company bought some tracts of timber from my family. At the time, I was managing the timberland because no one else in the family was interested. It was a gradual thing. We did business deals and as time went on, I decided to go into business with him, which was the real mistake. It allowed us to be together almost constantly and that is when the affair really started. I felt so guilty for having broken Linc's trust and my commitment. I knew I was still in love with Linc even though things were going so badly. It was a terrible time. There was really a triangle for me and that is very hard to deal with. I had no idea what was really going on with me. I was being pulled in two different directions. I didn't want to abandon my children even though they were almost grown. I had no answers and no one to turn to."

"So, you were trying to please two people. Was there ever a real break between you and Linc?"

"Yes and no. Initially, I wanted to make a break and get away from Linc. I tried. I told Linc about the affair and asked him to move out. In fact, I told my whole family. My mother immediately asked Linc to move into her house and started an assault on me: a barrage of battering against me. She said I had no reason to leave Linc; he didn't drink, run with other women, or beat me. I was sinful, ungrateful, and she would do everything in her power to keep me from leaving Linc. She started a campaign in the family to get us back together. She called everyone in the family she could think of, including my cousin in Charlotte, to ask them 'to talk some sense' in my head, as she put it. I finally gave up, but I confronted her first."

"How do you mean?"

"I was so angry with her for not supporting me or even talking to me. But this silent aggression was the pattern she had always used. I didn't realize it at the time, but she had always taken the other person's side against me no matter what the issue. Anyway, it was late in the evening and I found her washing dishes.

"'Mama, I want to talk to you.'

"She turned her head but didn't take her hands out of the dishwater. She was a small woman, hardly a hundred pounds, but every inch and pound were perfectly placed and proportioned. She was very proud of her figure but never used it to be seductive. She stood with her back perfectly straight, feet together, hair was combed, her dress neat and pressed.

"'What do you want to talk to me about?'

"'I want to talk about Linc and me.'

"'There is nothing to talk about.' She turned her head back and continued to wash dishes, totally composed.

"My voice cracked as I spoke. 'Mama,' It was the urgency in my voice that got her attention. I knew by the look in her eyes she was disgusted and couldn't wait for me to finish whatever I had to say and leave. She had no idea I was about to give in to her. I leaned against the kitchen counter clutching the edge, fighting back the tears. 'I came to tell you,' I raised one hand and yelled, 'I am not going to leave Linc. As a matter of fact, I promise no matter what happens to me, I will not leave Linc as long as I live. And I hope you are satisfied. No matter what it costs me emotionally or any other way, I will stay with him because I have promised you. Do you hear me? I want you to remember this and think about it the rest of your life.'

"She looked at me, satisfaction slowly crossing her face. 'Good. I'm glad.' She picked up the dishcloth and went back to the job at hand.

"Her reaction was no more than I expected. But the hurt and humiliation were not over. I screamed at her one last time, 'I hope you will never know how much I hate you!' and left, crying uncontrollably.

"She did not call after me or call me later that night at home."

Dr. Thomas looked at the little clock on the end table. "That must have been pretty hard to take from your mother."

"Yes, it was."

"It's about time to end, but I think we made some inroads today."

"I hope so, I don't want to go through this too many times. I have been shooting from the hip this whole time and it is very hard."

"I know it is, but you hit a lot of hard targets today."

I felt good leaving, tired, but I had let Dr. Thomas see my darkest side. I had never meant to hurt anyone, but I knew I had. But–that wasn't true. I had meant to hurt my mother; however, I wasn't sure I had. She was hard to get to and I wasn't at all sure she understood what I was saying, except that her goal had been reached. It didn't matter about me. It had never mattered.

I knew I had hurt my children even though it was the last thing I wanted to do. It is so funny that once you are a mother everything else seems secondary in your life. At least that seemed to be the case in mine until the affair. Then the affair took over and I lost control of my life. I tried to hide it from everyone, but that never works. The children began to pick up nuances here and there, unusual moods on my part, and most obvious of all my efforts to indulge them with my attention. They sensed my attention was outward but was lacking on the inside.

I knew Lindsay was much more affected by the affair than Camille or Jimmy. She was the youngest, still at home and a teenager. She and I were very close, but she loved her Daddy too, and even though she knew about his shortcomings she didn't want to see him hurt. I understood this about her because of my love for my father.

I remembered one Sunday afternoon when the whole family had gone in different directions for the weekend. Lindsay and Linc went to the Commonwealth's Attorney's Convention. Camille and I went to a horse show and Jimmy and his wife had gone to the beach. Camille and I got home first, and she was taking care of the horses when Lindsay and Linc drove up. Lindsay went to the barn. I was on the porch so I could hear them talking.

"How was the show?"

Camille answered. Her animated voice was lower than usual. "It was good. Big Sal was clean in a couple of classes, but the competition was tight, and the times were fast."

"That's good. Did you have a good time?"

"Sort of."

"What do you mean? That doesn't sound good."

"Well, I think by next year Mom and Dad will be divorced and Mom will be married again, and I don't know what will happen to us."

"Oh! What makes you think that?"

"Just by the way Mom talks, and she called you-know-who last night and I heard her talking."

"I see. Well, I hope not. We will just have to wait it out I guess."

"Did you have a good time?"

Lindsay was sitting on the mounting block then drawing figures in the sand with a whip. "No, I didn't. Daddy didn't have a good time. He missed Mom because he talked about her the whole time and I didn't have a good time because I missed everyone being together. It's just a damned mess, but I'm not going to let it get me down and you shouldn't either."

She got up and went into the barn. I knew she was trying to soothe Camille by putting her arm around her or just standing close and looking at her. "Try not to worry, because I just don't think they are going to leave each other. Daddy wants to stay, and Mom is just mad. She'll figure this out and don't forget Grandma Jacobs. She's on our side. She'll turn the world upside down to make Mom stay."

"I hope you're right."

They came out of the barn together. Camille said, "Let's go in the house and see if we can find something for supper. I'm hungry."

I sat on the porch until dusk. I was stunned by the girl's insights, and mad at myself and Linc for getting us in such a mess. Linc hadn't made this mess. I had. But, at that moment I didn't know what to do.

I kept thinking about the affair as I drove home. Things I hadn't told Dr. Thomas, like the first time my lover kissed me.

It was an October afternoon. Warm air filled the woods, and the sweet smells of blooming sumac and a twinge of acrid hickory leaves wafted through the trees. Bright leaves lost their sharpness in the haze of the late afternoon sun. The dry earth gave up a feeling of richness under our shoes as we trudged through the mixed stand of hardwoods. We weren't talking. We walked purposely without talking, each of us wrapped in our own thoughts. We could feel each other's presence, the warmth of a body close by but not touching. The sounds of each other's foot-steps crushing the long dry leaves drifted beyond us. A hand reached up to pull back a branch to keep it from striking the other in the face.

The sense of closeness followed us, up the hills, along the creek, and finally to the road where we had left the truck. I had walked through the woods so many times with Daddy as a child, then as a young adult. I knew a lot about timber, and I loved being in the woods. I was never afraid in the woods. What was there to be afraid of? I could tell direction by the sun. There were no animals to be afraid of, and I saw the woods as a big room, quiet, private, and secluded from the world that I wanted so much to get away from.

We reached the truck and stopped to rest a moment before leaving. He reached in his shirt pocket to get a cigarette and lighter. I watched the movements of his arms and hands as he cupped the flame and stuck the pack and lighter back in his pocket. Then he drew long and easy on the cigarette and looked into my face as the thin smoke drifted away on the breeze. We still hadn't spoken. I remember thinking how I ached to feel the touch of his skin, of his body and the hardness of his muscles. The feeling swept over me like a wave and receded back to the sea. But his eyes were still there taking in my face as if locked in a beam of light.

Finally, the words came out. At first, they were suppressed then fell freely. They were spoken softly, earnestly. It was my voice, my words, that couldn't be helped. "I dreamed about you last night." The words lifted through the air, and suddenly there was the unex-pected answer back.

"I have dreamed of you many nights." I knew his face was closer, but I was powerless to move away. Moments later I felt the fullness of his mouth around my lips and the strength of his arms circling my body. My pulse surged and a glow came over me with the realization that he wanted me.

There was no taking it back for either of us. It had happened and we were both glad and sorry. The moment had opened and sealed our relationship. We didn't talk about going home, there was no need. "I'll call you," he said as I got out of the truck.

I smiled to myself. That was truly a romantic beginning. Something I had never had before. Linc and I met in the first grade and grew up together. Our first kiss was at age fourteen, sitting on the couch in our living room. In fact, I kissed him. He was leaving and somehow, I knew he wanted to kiss me, so I kissed him. There were romantic moments in our long courtship, many breakups and makeups, but the romantic feelings of falling in love before you ever touched were never ours. Linc and I were destined to live our lives out together as if the gods had laid out the map of our paths at birth. And maybe the gods know best.

A car zoomed past me, bringing me back to reality. I realized I must have been driving very slowly or the driver wouldn't have gunned his car to get around me. My mind didn't remain in the present very long because there wasn't much traffic. My mind quickly wandered. Were all love affairs as bittersweet as mine? Was there a pattern that people fell into without realizing the consequences? Did voodoo or something worse have a hand in it? Was the feeling so physically soothing because its spiritual or moral counterpart was so devastating? The memory of our meetings drifted through my mind and I knew there was so much more to this affair than chance or gods.

I came to think my father was as much responsible for this affair as if he had planned it. Daddy had taught me to love the woods, to love this kind of man, one who lived on the edge. In fact, I didn't know it then, but I was 'acting out,' as Dr. Thomas put it later in my therapy. What I had experienced so long ago was buried in my memory and all it needed was a nudge in the present from a man, and the circumstances to remind me of a love lost through betrayal in the most obscene way. My psyche was praying to find real love this time, but the same things were wrong. Deceit and betrayal played on different characters at different times, but the results were the same. The perennial seeds were planted long before; they were simply living out their rotations. The rotten seeds had been planted and it was my misfortune to reap the harvest. It was my destiny to see it through. I had no way of knowing this, other than the craving to love and be loved. Daddy was still the love of my life and my guide.

Most people who have affairs don't go to the woods to meet, at least not in the twentieth century. But we did and it was the most natural thing in the world. We would meet at a different timber tract each week and wander through the woods until we found an inviting spot near a creek or under an oak Then we would spread a blanket and lie down. The sun would find its way over us, then a breeze would cool us. Those afternoons slipped away quickly.

One afternoon it rained. Heavy rain sloshed over the hood of the truck and the clouds hung so low you could almost touch them. The trees in the background were dim outlines that mirrored grotesque figures lurking, listening, and waiting. We sat talking, holding hands, watching the rain, content to be together. He turned to me as if apologizing and I answered, "Don't worry, I am going to make love to you on every tract of land I own." He squeezed my hand and smiled, "God, I love you."

A stop sign appeared in front of me and I stepped on the brake. I was almost home. I had begun my quest to understand the affair. This was another step in unraveling the twisted rope that held my past. There were many more steps to take.

11

THE NEXT WEEK Dr. Thomas surprised me. I had just sat down when he said, "We didn't talk about Linc's reaction to the affair last week. Don't you think that's important?"

I was startled and dismayed. I didn't want to talk about the affair anymore and especially about Linc. I felt bad about it and I didn't want to be reminded of all the bad things I had done. It was hard to face what I regarded as my fault, but I didn't think I could say no to Dr. Thomas.

"Yes, I guess it is."

"So, tell me? How did you handle this with Linc?"

"Not very well, I'm afraid."

"Oh, how do you mean?"

"At the beginning, I was just enjoying my friend's company so I would invite him and his wife over all the time. I am sure this was hurtful to Linc to see how much I talked to another man and seemed to enjoy it and I hardly had anything to say to my husband."

Dr. Thomas interrupted, "Can't we give this man a name? I am sure he had one."

I smiled weakly. "Yes, His name was Pete."

"Good, I think we will do better calling him by name."

"It's funny but Linc was the one who introduced Pete and me. And he was the one who asked me to try and sell Pete some timber. Pete and Linc got along well. They weren't friends but were congenial."

"Linc could not have been nicer to Pete. It was his nature and as time went on this became very difficult for Pete and me. And I have to say the opposite was true for Pete. He was jealous I suppose, but he tried to put Linc down at every turn."

"How did this affect you?"

"It wasn't easy. I was mad at Linc, but I didn't like to see him hurt.

"I was so confused about everything because of the outcome of the dope case and the reaction of the people in the county. They blamed Linc for all of it and said he was soft on crime and weak. I had isolated myself from everyone, Linc's family, the public, and I even stopped going to church.

"Linc and I started going to his church when we were married even though I didn't like it. His whole family went there, and they made my life hell. Something was said in Sunday school class every Sunday to make me come home and cry all afternoon. Linc would never say anything to anyone to defend me, and I guess that had a lot to do with my anger at the time.

"I remember one time soon after we were married Linc did some presentation at church that his grandmother asked him to do. She was extremely religious and very opinionated. After it was over, she went up to thank him and congratulate him on a wonderful job. She turned to me and smiled with her hand on Linc's arm and said, 'Lesley, if anything ever happens to your marriage it will be your fault because Linc is so sweet.'

"I was stunned, but I didn't say anything and neither did he. There had been too many things like that said and never resolved. It all came down at once.

"When I had decided there was no hope for us or the marriage I tried to leave and that is when Linc finally faced the fact that things were very bad. It was like he wouldn't or couldn't believe I was really leaving. He said he would do anything to get me back, but nothing changed when I stayed. I guess that's one reason I was so devastated at his affair. The one thing I was holding on to about him after the dope case was that he wouldn't lie, cheat or steal, or run with women, but it happened, and I felt I had nothing left. That is certainly one reason I'm here. Somehow you've got to get me beyond all of this."

"That's a tall order and you know it's you that has to do the work."

"I know and it's only determination that keeps me going."

"What was the relationship between your mother and Linc?"

"Oh, she loved him and thought I was the bad one. She called him at the office and asked him to stay with her when he moved out. Linc was good to everybody and especially to her. He was happy to go there and try to stay in the family and maybe get me back.

"One Sunday afternoon he called and asked me to come to my mother's and go for a walk. It was in the fall and the colors were brilliant in the woods. There was a slight cool breeze and the leaves on the ground crackled under our feet. The countryside was so quiet it felt like we were walking in our own private world, but the distance between us remained. He reached for my hand and started to speak.

"'I want you to be happy, but I am afraid Pete will hurt you.'

"'Why do you think that?'

"'Because he is younger, and he doesn't understand you like I do.'

"'He might hurt me, that's true.'

"'So, you have thought about it.'

"'Yes, I have, maybe more than you might think.'

"'Your mother is worried about you and so are the children.'

"'The children, yes, but my mother is not worried about me.'

"'Yes, she is. We were talking last night, and she said she prayed you would be all right. She is afraid you'll do something you will regret later. I guess she feels you're in a crisis.'

"Tears came to my eyes. I knew what was happening and there was nothing I could do about it. Linc was sincere, there was no denying that. He had always loved me, and he loved me now. He had always done crazy things and somehow gotten out of them, but this time there was no turning back. He had broken his faith with me over the dope case and I had seen into his soul. He had deceived me, betrayed me and acted without honor. He had crushed my esteem for him and the pride I had once found in my marriage.

"Now I was expected by everyone–that is, everyone in my family–to forgive and forget. My mother thought the only important thing was to stay married. She didn't want to face the public questions if I left, and she didn't want to be bothered with my troubles. I knew instinctively it was not my feelings she cared about.

"Of course, the children wanted me to stay with Linc. He was their father and it was natural for them to want the family together. I could easily understand their position.

"I picked up a stick and began drawing in the dirt. It was a natural thing to do.

"I didn't have anything in mind. It was like I was doodling with a pen. I never drew things. I drew lines that intersect, never circles. I began to think my mind doesn't go in circles, it thinks from here to there, reason and result. That was what all of this was about. Linc had betrayed me, therefore he must go. In my mind it was so simple and straightforward. But this was real life, not doodling."

Dr. Thomas broke in. "That is certainly your thought pattern, and, in many ways, it has served you well in the past. So how did you reach a decision?"

"You might say in this case I didn't reach a decision. It was made for me."

"How do you mean?"

"Well, I have a cousin that is very close to me. He's a man, not a woman, believe it or not."

"That does not surprise me. Your life has been dominated by men."

"He called me one night and asked if I would meet him the next weekend. He wanted to talk to me about something. I knew what he wanted, but I agreed to meet him."

"Tell me about the meeting."

"By then it was late October, but the weather was still bright and clear. I wondered, as I drove through the countryside, how things could be so perfect outside when I was in such turmoil on the inside. The whole ordeal was wearing thin on me and I was about ready to agree to anything. I felt beaten.

"My cousin greeted me with a hug and a smile. 'Hey, you look great. I was expecting a bedraggled-looking woman, from all I have been hearing from Virginia. My telephone has rung off the hook. You've really got the family in Derbyshire stirred up.'

"'I guess so, Cousin. They've really dragged me through the wringer.'

"'I bet they have. Let's go to my room and sit and talk about this for a while.'

"The room overlooked a lake, surrounded by tall pines and Crepe Myrtles loaded with blooms; weeping willows hung over the edges, and geese and ducks could be seen sitting on the water waiting for twilight and a bountiful dinner served up from the depths of the lake.

"My cousin fixed us a bourbon and water and we sat by the window gazing out on the peaceful scene.

"He began. 'I want to hear your side now. Nothing but your thoughts and feelings are important to me now.'

"This was music to my ears; nobody had been interested in listening to me for so long. My story flowed. I didn't realize we had been talking so long until I noticed the sun was setting and the room was growing dark.

"My cousin sighed. 'Okay, let's go get some dinner.' He stood up. 'You know what the tragedy of all this is in my mind?'

"'No! What?'

"'That through all of this turmoil you didn't have anyone in Derbyshire that you could talk to. No woman that could under-stand your position; or even if she didn't, there was no up there for you to talk to as a friend.'

"'I hadn't really thought about it, but you're right. It's very hard to have a close friendship when you live so far apart.'

"The next morning, we were getting ready to leave. My cousin put his arm around me and said, 'Alright honey, this is what I want you to do. You go home and tell Linc to come home and you try this for six months. Then at the end of six months if you still feel the way you do now, you pack up and leave and nobody will say anything. I will see that they don't.'

"'Why do you want me to do this?'

"Because I don't think you care for this guy. I just think you are hurt and mad, but you still care about Linc.'

"'Maybe so.'

"I was too tired, mentally and physically, to argue with anyone."

Dr. Thomas looked at me for a long moment. "So, what you're saying is that there was no real reconciliation. You and Linc just sort of moved back together without any counseling or help."

"That's right and it was hard for me, but everybody else in the family was happy."

"You still have a lot of problems. I am sure you know that."

I knew that, but I didn't want to hear it. I wanted to be well and feel good. Why couldn't I?

12

Dr. Thomas and I did not pursue the affair as such anymore. At the next visit he said "I think it's time for us to look closely at your early childhood. Maybe there are some answers there for both of us."

I looked at him. What was he talking about? I had told him the most important thing I could remember. What did he want to know that could help now?

"Why don't you start at the beginning? On second thought, tell me a little about Derbyshire, about your grandparents, anything that left an impression on you. I want to know a little of the oral history of your family."

This was great for me. I had heard lots of stories, and all of them were based on fact. "Do you want to hear bad stories or good stories?"

"Both. I want to know what's made an impression on you. What were your ancestors like? Where did they come from? Who were they?"

"Okay, I can do that. The first thing you mentioned was Derbyshire and I have one word for that: poor!"

"It's that bad?"

"Yes. The word 'poor' comes to mind because in all my life, that's the one word used by everyone to describe life in the county.

Except in the fifties and later when they referred to my father. He was known as 'the county's first millionaire', 'a legend in his own time', and 'the richest man in Derbyshire County'. But that came later."

Dr. Thomas raised an eyebrow.

"When I was born, even he was poor. At that time there were two ways to make a living in Derbyshire. You could farm or cut timber. Some did both–my grandfather Jacobs did, in fact, do both. He had a farm, a sawmill, and a store until the crash of 1929 and the Great Depression that followed. But my grandfather died leaving a widow with four children: the oldest, a girl, my father who was thirteen, and two more boys. My father was the man of the house, but the house was collapsing. His father's alcoholism, and his subsequent death and the oncoming Depression, were causing its collapse. In his own mind though, Judd, as he was called, was already a grown man. At his father's death he directed the men to move the sawmill back home from a tract twenty miles away. Then he settled in to take over the farm. At that time the farm included more than a thousand acres.

"At thirteen, my father was like lots of other boys living in the country. He went to school when he had to, not to learn history or math, but to play baseball in the spring and fall, and basketball in the winter. Football was not played then at his high school. At night he hunted raccoons with a friend. They caught the raccoons live and fed them for a few weeks on milk, to give their coats a luster and make the meat tender. When they had enough to make the trip worthwhile, they delivered the dressed meat to butcher shops and cafes in Richmond and the hides to the tanner. These were Fulton Bottom and Shockoe Slip shops, where the poor whites and blacks ate. A lot different from now, don't you think?"

"Yes, it's amazing how things turn around in time."

"Anyway, this enterprise was my father's spending money throughout his high school days, which lasted until he was sixteen. By then the Depression was in full force. All the mills in the county had shut down. Tobacco was almost worthless as a crop, a chicken cost two dollars in the store, wheat was two dollars a bushel off the farm, and a veal calf was the only source of money if you were selling livestock. The women canned the vegetables and the men smoked the hog meat. If you were so unlucky as to not have either, you went to the poor house, or as many did, you literally starved to death."

"Really!"

"Yes. I have this on good authority–my mother, grandmothers, and our family doctor when I was a child. But Franklin Delano Roosevelt was elected president. This brought about a tremendous change in the county that affected everyone's life including my father's. In the three years since the crash and her husband's death, my grandmother had not been able to pay the taxes on the farm. Everyone and everything were broke. The Federal Government, the State of Virginia, and the County of Derbyshire were all broke. There was no money to be had. The New Deal was so simple. If there was no money, print it. If there were no jobs, create them. Get people to work; build schools, build roads, parks. If you don't have roads or parks to build, buy land with the printed money and create a state forest.

"Derbyshire got a new school. The new high school was built of brick and named Derbyshire High. Linc and I went to high school there.

"Anyway, some young men got jobs building the new school. Money began to trickle in, but not nearly enough. The politicians began to look around for more ways to spend money in Derbyshire. So, they created a state forest. The Federal Government would print more money, and lend it to the state to buy land at a fixed price of fifty cents an acre. The poor people with forty to fifty acres who were behind on their taxes, sold the land, but the county and state took it out of the taxes, which usually amounted to the price of the land. The Federal Government would not only help pay local and state taxes, but give the land back to the state in the form of a forest.

"In this way 23,000 acres were bought in Derbyshire from people not able to pay their taxes. After the deeds were signed and taxes paid, whatever was left was given to the owner. You only have to look in the deed books of those years and look at a map of the counties and you will see it's true.

"My Grandmother Jacobs sold five hundred acres of the home place, and paid the taxes on the remaining five hundred. All the land that was sold became known in the County as the government land, and to my knowledge, neither my father nor any of the family ever referred to their lost land as part of the State Forest. It was known to us, and called by us, 'the government land'. Everyone who has owned that farm from my grandmother to me has put every dead animal, horse, cow, pig, or goat across the fence on the government land. The buzzards still have their roosts on this fence line, waiting."

I looked at Dr. Thomas and smiled. "This is one good reason I think we are all Republicans and have been for generations.

"A CCC camp was built on the edge of the village of Derbyshire and the forest. My father's brother got a job there. But Judd was too old at sixteen. He remembered too much of what had been. Some of the people who had been bought out were friends, school mates, neighbors. He couldn't see himself burning their houses and filling up wells. And, the government had taken five hundred acres of his mother's farm because she wasn't able to make enough money, and he wasn't old enough at thirteen to really make a difference.

"At sixteen he went to New Jersey and got a job on a road force. I have one letter at home that he wrote during this time."

Dr. Thomas interrupted. "Would you bring the letter next time? I think we should keep on with this. And you said your grandfather was an alcoholic. Do you know if your father was ever sexually abused?"

"No, I don't. But I know my grandfather beat my grandmother when he was drunk, and I know he beat the boys as well. There must have been a lot of alcoholics in the family."

Dr. Thomas frowned and turned toward his desk.

I remembered to bring the letter the next week.

"I have the letter."

"Great, let's hear it."

"This one is to his aunt."

Little Falls, New Jersey

Dear Aunt Hannah,

I received your letter and was real glad to hear from you. I am alright and I am working every day. It has been real cold since I have been up here, and it has snowed four times since I have been up here. The work I am doing is not real hard and I don't have to work but nine hours a day. I have mead [sic] $47.25 since I have been up here. I will make more in a little while.

Tell everybody I say hello. I am really sorry, but I can't get Everett anything to do right now. It is just as many people up here out of a job as it is down there. But the people up here that have got a job get paid good. Maybe I can get Everett a job after a while. I will try cause I would like to have somebody to stay with from down home. Well it is time for me to go to bed. Write soon.

Love, Judd

"So, what do you think?" Dr. Thomas asked.

"I am surprised at how well he could write, because I know now he was very dyslectic. He was sixteen and in the ninth grade when he quit school and got this job."

"I wonder how he got the job in New Jersey."

"I wish I knew for certain, but I was told by a cousin that my grandparents knew a lot of people from everywhere because they had people come to hunt and they would stay a week or two. She thought one of those men may have had a business and gave him a job. It was a road construction job, but at sixteen it was a manly thing to do."

"It is indeed."

"But Daddy always knew he wanted to be more than just a

farmer in Derbyshire. When I was in college there was a professor who had a number of student teachers in Derbyshire when Daddy was in school. The professor told his class one day this story about Daddy, and one of his students told me.

"The professor was trying to tell his student teachers that they must be mindful of what they thought of their students, because they never knew what was ahead for the student, and often things were not as they seemed. Then he said, 'Some years ago one of my student teachers told this young man in her class that he should study more, pay attention and learn what she was trying to teach him. He replied, 'I don't have to learn this because I am going to have a bookkeeper to do it for me.'

"The professor went on, 'Sure enough, this boy Judd Jacobs has become a very wealthy man and his daughter is here at this school now.'"

Dr. Thomas smiled, "That's quite a story. Your father was a determined man."

"Yes, he was."

"Please go on."

"The winter in New Jersey was cold and the summer was hot, but Daddy had a job. That's what he always said when he was asked about it. He lived in a boarding house, went to work at dawn and worked until night. He never went to the fire to warm his hands, he never laid down the tool that he was using, he never took a pit stop except at lunch time; he would have been fired on the spot for any of these and many more reasons, but his reward was a paycheck. Daddy carried a bag lunch from the boarding house that always consisted of two hard boiled eggs and a sandwich.

"The summer of 1933 was hot and dry. Dust burned his throat and the sun turned his fair skin to scarlet, but he held on to that job.

"Christmas, he came home with all the money he had left after the barest living expenses. But he said the money was small compared to the education he learned from the road foreman. He always acknowledged this foreman taught him how to run his own business. But there was one other thing that my father understood so well and used to his advantage, and that was the class system and how it applied to his workers."

"Explain this."

"He understood it like the foreman from up North. You never asked someone to do something you weren't willing to do yourself, and you never made your workers feel there was any social difference between you and them, except for the money in your pocket.

"In Derbyshire in later years Judd was recognized as the man who could get more work out of his men than any other man around. For this he was hated by some but respected by those who worked for him. They got a paycheck."

"What do you think happened in your father's childhood that affected you as a child?"

I shifted in my seat. Dr. Thomas was always asking questions that made me analyze my thoughts and situations. "I think there were three things that really affected me as a child. The first, his father was a terrible alcoholic which means my father was most likely abused. Second, the Depression had a profound effect; and third, his father's death at such an early age. The Depression was as real to him the day he died as it was when he was thirteen. He was always tight with money and talked about it all the time. Even when he was rich, he acted as if he had no money. All of these things caused him problems that must have affected me."

"I think you are right."

"My father's mother's family was, at best, yeoman, in the socioeconomic sense, but in the old Southern sense, they were far less. Because back in the dark recesses of everyone's secret mind was the knowledge that my grandmother's Grandfather Pyle was an overseer on the Brooke Plantation. In the South, if you were white, there couldn't be a worse social curse than to be from an overseer's family. Praise God, I didn't learn this until I was a teenager. I'd have been heartbroken as a young child to realize that the greatest source of comfort to me, my Grandmother Jacobs, was not regarded by all as the angel of goodness I thought she was."

There was a slight pause and Dr. Thomas broke in, "You loved your grandmother."

"Yes, she and my father were the only people who ever held me and hugged me. I guess you'd say she nurtured me. She used to tell me about when she was a little girl and about her mother and father. I can remember her saying with great pride that her mother would run to meet General Lee at the big stone gates of Oakland to get a ride on Traveler. To me, as a child, this story was far grander than saying her mother was married in the parlor at Oakland. Then she would say how kind General Lee was to them, and how much everyone loved and admired him. Not a word was ever said about General Lee leaving the little girls on Traveler as a slave led him to the stables. The little girls wouldn't have expected to go to the big house.

"This was the only thing my grandmother ever told me about her mother. But she talked about her grandfather a lot. In fact, she seemed proud of the fact that he was the overseer at Oakland, the Brooke Plantation— just down the road from us now. He had stayed on the plantation throughout the war to take care of the property, look after the Brooke women, and save what he could from the Yankees.

"When Lee surrendered, my grandfather stayed on at Oakland with one mule, to try to raise enough food for his family and the Brooke family for the coming winter. It's always seemed curious to me as an adult that the lowest of the white social classes, thought to be the meanest and most hateful of human beings, could produce a granddaughter as kind, forgiving and loving as my grandmother. Where my great grandfather Pyle came from has been long forgotten.

"I guess what all this means to me is that somewhere in all the genes which allowed someone to be an overseer were a lot of genes of goodness which produced my grandmother.

"I only have good memories of her. I remember the way she rocked me, cuddled me and read to me. She would tell me stories like the ones I've told you. She told me others about my grandfather and how he loved horses and how he would be so proud of me. It just seemed to me that she was interested in me and my own mother wasn't."

"That's a bold statement. I'm sure we will hear more about that later. Please go on."

"After the job in New Jersey, Judd took a job on a road gang in Derbyshire working for the state. Three months later, he handed the foreman his shovel on Friday, took his paycheck and told the foreman. 'You are the last man I will ever work for as long as I live', and he was."

"Esther and Judd had decided to forge their relationship into a lasting commitment dedicated to bettering their economic situation. They were married in Washington D.C., then returned home on Monday to live with his family and work the farm."

"Tell me about your mother's family."

"Let me finish my father's first."

"You're right. Please, go on."

"The Jacobs side of my father's family was always a mystery to his family and the community. The first Jacobs arrived in Derbyshire County on a packet boat during the War Between the States. He had been injured in a battle around Richmond, and the Hutchins family from Derbyshire offered to give him a place to recuperate. This was the custom for helping Southern soldiers at the time. I always thought it was funny that he was shot in the hand. Doesn't that sound fishy to you?"

"Maybe he was just smart and thought shooting himself was the best thing to do."

"Nobody ever said that, but you may be right."

Dr. Thomas gave a mischievous smile. "You always doubt, don't you?"

"Yes, I don't trust any of them. His name was William Dolphin Jacobs. He fell in love with a Hutchins daughter, Mary Jane, and after a brief return to the war, they were married on Christmas Eve, 1863.

"After the war he told Mary Jane that they had to have an income, and the best way he knew to get any money then was for him to go to Washington, sign his allegiance to the United States, and apply for a post office in their community, Ashby. He did this and the family had a steady income until the post office was closed in the early 1900s.

"One of William Dolphin and Mary Jane's five sons and two daughters bought the thousand acres of land and built the house that my father called the home place, and I called home during my childhood. This son was my grandfather.

"It was the custom in those days for the man to have a means to take care of a family, and a house for his bride, before he married. Unless the man was independently wealthy, it usually meant a man was much older than his bride when he married. Such was the case with my grandmother. She told me this. Apparently, my grandfather had come to visit a neighbor as a young man, and during the visit he was introduced to a little girl no older than a toddler. She climbed in his lap and snuggled against his chest. He was so taken with her childish charms that he declared to her and the family present that he would make her his bride. Sure enough, sixteen years later he carried her across the threshold of a new home complete with all new furniture, including a new bedroom suite and dresser set.

"I can remember thinking about this as a child. How romantic it was and how proud I was to be living in a house my grandfather built. It's strange how things change. Now, no one lives there. The house is dark, and slowly all the appendages of a working farm are being pushed down and buried with bulldozers. Everything can leave, but the memories will remain as long as there's anyone who carries a thought of it from their past."

"You miss the place, don't you?"

"Yes, I miss the good memories, but I never want to live there or be there again. There's too much bad karma, too much I can't forget, too much I don't want to remember."

"I'm sure that's true, but once it's all out and we've put the whole puzzle together, it will be better. You'll see."

"I hope so."

He opened the door and another session was over. Why did these old memories make me feel so bad?

I didn't have another session until two weeks later. Dr. Thomas had canceled the week before. He sometimes had to cancel for court appointments and speaking engagements. My folder lay on his lap as he made notations. The folder looked thicker and a little frayed. I wondered how many pages of notes he had taken about me.

"All right young lady, where are we today?"

I knew the young lady part had to be a joke, but a nice joke. "I don't know. We talked about Daddy's family and Derbyshire the last time."

"Oh, yes. The place that is so poor." He looked at me and smiled.

"Yes, that's the one."

"Well, why don't you start today and tell me about your mother's family. How did they find this poor place called Derbyshire?"

"To put it in a nutshell, my mother's family, the Trimballs, were shunned when they came South. All her family on both sides was Yankee and there could be nothing worse in the South unless it was poor white trash. The South of *Gone with The Wind* was indeed gone by then, but the seeds sown so many years before were still sprouting in the new class structure of the rural south at the turn of the century. Writers like Faulkner, Caldwell, and Welty wrote their stories from memories of old tales. Legends told on moonlit porches or at family gatherings on bleak Sunday afternoons. Funny stories recited with bright fires warming the soles of cold feet on bony old skeletons who refused to die and who never tired of the same stories told over and over.

"These old stories were told to me by my mother's father and mother when I was a child and they filled my head and heart with the belief that class was an invisible, unbreakable structure that held us all within its perimeters. It was drawn at birth and held us through death. It could not be destroyed. Money was the only thing that built new generations of aristocracy. As my Southern History professor, Dr. Simkins, pointed out to me in college, 'Miss Jacobs, there is only one way for the South to rebuild its aristocracy: The rich must marry the rich. Then a new aristocracy will flourish, but you will never break the old'. I was sure at the time that he was talking directly to me."

"What made you think he was talking to you?"

"Because he knew my father was rich, and he knew Linc's mother was a Virginia aristocrat. The Virginia aristocrats could not be equaled anywhere in the South. He could see things I couldn't at the time. It was never a good idea for a poor boy from an aristocratic family to marry a nouveau riche girl with no pedigree."

"I see. And you had no hint of a problem from your family at the time?"

"No, I think Daddy thought that Owens was an old family, and I was moving up."

"So, they didn't object to the marriage."

"No, not really. They did see that Linc had no ambition. They objected to that, but they never talked to me about it. Someone close to Daddy in the community told me Daddy was worried about Linc not taking care of me."

Dr. Thomas made no comment, so I continued. "It was about 1900 that the runaway Yankee boy named Trimball met the orphaned daughter of another Yankee family, the Bells. I never knew much about this part of the family until much later. They had migrated from Canada.

"However, the Bells very much fitted the mold of the Trimballs because they were very religious, industrious, reliable people. They lived in the outskirts of Richmond. Ada Bell was orphaned as a baby and reared by her mother's sister and her family. The stepmother must have been good to her because there was never a whisper or a raised eyebrow to the contrary that I know about."

Dr. Thomas's beeper went off and I stopped talking.

"Please, go back to your thoughts. I interrupted you."

"Well, there were stories I used to hear that were all strange, but they left impressions as lasting as the images of a painter's brush. For instance, my mother hated Catholics and Indians. Why did she hate them so? I knew it was hate because of her expression and the tone of her voice. As a child it didn't make sense, but later I understood.

"The Trimballs came to America by way of Plymouth, Massachusetts. Not on the Mayflower, but soon after, in 1629. And, I think the word that carried the theme of her family was certainly 'Puritan'. My grandfather was Puritan, my mother was Puritan, and all my aunts and uncles. The Puritans had many good qualities—energy, fortitude, reliability, honesty, but they had other qualities as well: religious fanaticism, and intolerance. This thread of Puritanism bound my mother's life as tight as a steel cable.

"After Plymouth, the family settled in Rhode Island, then moved on to Vermont. Over a short span of time there were several Indian massacres that not only killed some Trimballs, but burned the events into family memory and legends as if they were prayers recited every Sunday. As for the Catholics, my mother always maintained that her family was Scotch Irish, which really wasn't true. They were English and descendants of an Archbishop of Canterbury dating back to James I, a fact which explains her hatred of the Catholics. All the Protestant Trimballs left England about 1629, the Catholic Trimballs stayed and welcomed Charles II back to power in 1663, when my ancestor was appointed Archbishop of Canterbury.

"Descendants of the Vermont Trimballs pushed westward until the late 1800s; they were homesteaders in the Dakota Territory. They were still Puritans, still religious, and now Methodists on a desolate prairie in the middle of a Depression in the 1880s. The depression of 1880 was not as tumultuous as the Great Depression of the 1930s, but most people thought it was worse. During this depression the lilting soprano voice of a female Trimball saved the family and the community. A widow named Sally, my great grandmother, was left with children and a farmstead, but she possessed what was regarded as an angel's voice. Knowing what was ahead of her and other families, she hooked up the family buggy in the summer of 1884 and set out alone to literally sing for her supper, not in a saloon, but on the revival circuit.

"Sally Trimball returned home in the fall with enough provisions to feed and clothe her family and most of her church family for the winter. The Trimballs survived, and a few years later my grandfather, at the age of thirteen, left home to make his way east. He and his older brother felt it necessary for them to leave and be on their own in order for the rest of the family to survive. The older brother went farther west, and though my grandfather never let a day go by that he didn't in some way look for his brother, the oldest Trimball son was never heard from again.

"At sixteen, my grandfather found a job as a milk delivery boy in Richmond. By eighteen, being a hard worker and a good teamster, he had a job driving a delivery wagon for the Miller Manufacturing Company. Granddaddy Trimball told me many stories of his delivery days, about how wonderful his mules were, and how sleek and fat they were kept. In softer tones, he told me how bad the roads and streets were in the winter. In a four-mule hitch sometimes a lead mule would fall down in a mud hole and drown before he could cut the harness off him.

"Ada Bell and Sidney Gaylord Trimball married and moved to a farm in the Winterpock neighborhood of Chesterfield county. But, as in my father's experience later, farming did not bring in enough money and a few years later, Granddaddy Trimball went back to lumber and became a foreman for the Ferguson Lumber Company. This job required Sidney to follow the saw mills, which meant living in the camps during the week and coming home on weekends.

"My mother, as the eldest child, had to assume more responsibility. She was six years old in the terrible flu epidemic of 1918. The family lived on Hull Street. During the epidemic, all the family became ill. Neighbors would not come in for fear of catching the dreaded disease. This left each household to care for itself. Both her mother and father were too ill to get out of bed, leaving my mother to care for the family even though she herself was suffering with fever and chills. She literally crawled up and down the stairs to bring them water and porridge and medicine. The doctor left the medicine on the doorstep.

"Somehow, they all survived, but that winter of sickness and death left its scars on my mother. She later treated her children as if every sickness were a major illness. This paranoia about sickness caused us as children many days of isolation at home. Fear followed my mother all her life, but I must add, in many instances, she overcame it with courage and tenacity.

"The First World War created a demand for lumber which made it harder and harder for my grandfather to come home on weekends. This forced the family to begin an endless succession of moves following the timber. In a few years they had moved through four counties, and finally to Derbyshire by the late twenties. The Depression was just around the corner, and true to its usual course, the lumber market was one of the first to fall. The Ferguson Lumber Company went bankrupt and my grandfather was out of a job.

"My grandfather had been through many hard times which prepared him for this day. He had enough money to buy the mill from Mr. Ferguson and he already had a tract of land.

"I am sure he surprised the neighborhood but didn't shock them when this happened. After all he did come from up north. Curiously, when he came to the Staunton community, the family moved into the upstairs of a house. The house later became a chicken house, so it is easy to assume that as a rental property it had not been too valuable. My mother and father met in the nearby school. My mother used to lean out of an upstairs window and wave as my father went by to the little school, a two-room grammar school. She was in high school then, two years ahead of him.

"Granddaddy made a go of the mill. He built a house on his land and had every intention of settling in the Stanton community for life. My grandmother, Ada, was tired of moving–twenty-three times in seventeen years. Granddaddy became a pillar of the community and an active Methodist.

"Granddaddy had bought a bankrupt company owned by an old Southern family, and it galled the community to have a Yankee, even if his heart and his pocket book were in the right place, telling everyone what ought to be done. I have to say here that one of his severest critics was an outspoken, intelligent, righteous widow–

later my grandmother-in-law–who said much too much money had been spent on my grandfather's Methodist parsonage, the church building, school house, and community buildings. The money should have gone, she said, to missions. Granddaddy, whose sister was a missionary to India, said charity begins at home.

"As a child, Granddaddy Trimball was, next to my father, my biggest hero. I listened to him as if he were a saint from heaven."

Dr. Thomas listened to my story with only a few breaks. I wondered what he thought, or what difference these stories would all make. I could tell there were many places he had made mental notes.

"Childhood impressions like these have a big bearing on a child's life. I'll see you next week. Okay?"

"Can I tell you one more thing?"

"Yes, of course."

"I've often wondered how my parents' lives and mine might have been different if we had not lived in a place as poor in spirit and resources as Derbyshire. I'm not a Presbyterian by faith, and I despise the idea of being in a predestined fate, but it often seems our destinies are set for us, and no matter how much we wrestle or attack them the end result is the same. What is meant to be, is. As a child, I felt nothing could be changed in my circumstances. As an adult, I know that they could have been changed. But it seems my destiny was to find my own way."

"That's a thoughtful observation. See what else you can come up with over this next week. There are lots of things in your parents' and grandparents' past that have a great bearing on your thoughts and actions."

I didn't understand what he was talking about then, but as my therapy progressed, I began to see that the values I treasured were deeply embedded in my past. I was not deeply religious, but I treasured my word, my honesty, my work ethic, my sense of loyalty, and my sense of fair play. I also began to see the effects of alcoholism, intolerance and abuse. I was cradled in all of them from birth.

13

AT THIS TIME, we had been six or seven years into therapy. I was more stable emotionally, and generally feeling much better. I kept thinking I was getting close to the end now. Soon Dr. Thomas would tell me I was all better and I wouldn't have to come back anymore. But that day didn't come and hasn't come yet. Camille says I will see Dr. Thomas for the rest of my life because I'll always need the medication, and maybe she's right. Dr. Thomas had switched my medication then to Paxil which worked well. He took me off Prozac because I had been on it so long.

Even though I was doing well, there were times when I lost control completely and had no idea what had provoked it. I had no idea then that the most difficult part of the hard-core treatment had not even begun. I would endure torturous hours of crying, not understanding what had happened to me, and the denial by my whole family that anything terrible had really happened to me. The day we began with my childhood was the beginning of this deeper therapy. Dr. Thomas was sitting in his high-backed red leather chair as usual, listening.

"I was born on Saturday, April 25, 1936 at ten-oh-six in the morning, at the home of my grandmother and grandfather Trimball in Staunton, Virginia. The family doctor delivered me. My mother went back home to her mother for the birth of her first-born. Where else could she find the security, sympathy, and knowledge her mother could offer? Childbirth was a scary proposition in 1936 especially when it was a home delivery. My grandmother had delivered her own five boys and two girls at home– all healthy and strong. She had also helped bring many of the neighbor's babies, black and white, into the world. Going to the hospital was out of the question for reasons of money and distance. It was fifty miles to Richmond and the nearest hospital.

"I was never told how long my mother was in labor, just that it was a terrifying experience and, in the end, it only produced me, a baby girl. I was told it was my father who was so disappointed. They said as soon as he heard it was a girl, he left the house without seeing me. If this is true, I'm sure it was very hurtful to my mother. However, I suspect everyone, including my mother, was disappointed in a female child. The only females of any species that were regarded as a premium in 1936 were dairy heifers. Females were then, as now, looked upon as disappointments.

"As I grew older, I began to realize what a mistake nature had made in my gender, and what a difference it would have made to me, and everyone else, had I been born a boy. I can remember going from fits of anger to depression, to guilt over being a girl and not a boy."

Dr. Thomas interrupted. "How did this bother you as a child?"

"Oh! Many ways. I used to like to go with Daddy wherever he was going. And sometimes I couldn't go, and I always knew it was because I was a girl. And sometimes he would be talking to a group of men and they would turn and talk softly so I couldn't hear, and that was because I was a girl. And my mother was always after me about being outdoors, and not brushing my hair, and getting dirty. I knew if I had been a boy, it wouldn't have mattered."

"I see."

"I was born a beautiful, healthy, eight-pound, twenty-four-inch girl baby. My head was covered with jet black ringlets. I had fat rosy cheeks, a perfectly formed mouth, and clear blue eyes. A picture of beauty they said, so why wasn't everyone happy? Besides being a girl, it may have been different for me if I had been a better baby. A bad baby, a difficult baby, cries, and evidently, I cried constantly for two weeks."

"I didn't mean to be bad. I was told I made everyone's life miserable by crying for two weeks. Doctor Landers said my mother's milk did not agree with me, or at least that's what they told me later. Somehow this was my fault, that I cried, that I was a girl, and, I guess, that I was even born."

"Do you believe this?"

"I guess I don't really believe it, but I sure felt it as a child. Dr. Landers tried every formula he could find. Finally, I stopped crying. They said a suitable formula had been found.

"The trauma of my birth followed me throughout my life. It was told and retold in my presence and for my benefit many times, when my mother felt I needed to be reminded of how much trouble I caused–even at birth. As a child it always made me feel bad. How could I have been so bad to cry, cry, cry? I was even more shocked on the day my mother died to be reminded of the old story of my birth."

"How did this come about?"

"Most of the family was in the lobby of Henrico Doctors' Hospital. Her oldest brother walked up to me and looked me straight in the eye as if it was something I needed to know.

"'You know your mother really suffered for you.'

"'I'm sure she did, but what are you talking about?'

"He leaned closer to me. 'I remember the day you were born. Oh, how your mother suffered! She screamed and screamed until I couldn't stand it anymore. I left and went over to Mrs Carter's and stayed until you were born. She really suffered for you.'

"I looked at him and nearly choked. My mind was racing. You son of a bitch, I thought; you sorry son of a bitch. You're a pious, sanctimonious, old bastard. How could you do this to me now? Can't you see how much I'm hurting from Mama's death already? You stand here telling me how much grief I've caused from the day I was born. You don't give a damn about anybody, or that God you talk about all the time. All you care about is your own damn skin and buying your way into heaven if you can. But I said quietly. 'Yes, I know, I caused her unbelievable pain throughout my childhood. I didn't know you had to leave when I was born. But thank you for telling me.' The pain, the hurt, the disbelief in his insensitivity overwhelmed me. I turned and walked away."

"That was a very hurtful thing to hear when your mother was dying."

"Yes, it was. I'll never forget the accusing look on his face while he was telling me."

After a few moments I went on with my story. "My mother stayed with her mother for six weeks before bringing me home. Of course, I don't remember any of this. I do wish I knew why I cried so much those first two weeks. They say babies pick up sounds, feelings, thoughts in the womb. I wonder if my crying was because I already knew what was ahead of me.

"So, I went home to the big farmhouse that my grandfather Jacobs had built for his bride before they were married. It was a two-story frame house with lots of gingerbread on the front and back porches, two chimneys, four large rooms and a big hallway upstairs and downstairs. It was an imposing house, larger than most in the community. My grandfather had quite a flair for planning. The house was surrounded by large yards and cement walkways. He carved his name in the fresh cement when it was built, *Ernest Burton Jacobs 1909*, four years before my father was born.

"He built a splendid white picket fence around a square acre of the front yard and made a half-moon driveway in front of the picket fence. The house was shaded by bright maples and sturdy white oaks, with all the dependencies a farm could need in the back. These included a smokehouse, chicken house, buggy house, tack house, cook's house, garage, sheds, barns, vegetable garden, orchard, and a lily pond his sister had put in the backyard."

"Sounds like an impressive place."

"It was in its day. They placed my crib beside my parents' bed in their downstairs bedroom. I'm sure this arrangement was the custom of the day, and I'm sure my mother thought she was doing the absolute right thing by putting my crib next to their bed. I just wish there had been another place for me."

"Why do you say that?"

"Because of what happened later. The room had one window on the side and double windows looking out to the front porch. A big wood stove provided heat, beside a dressing table with a skirt and matching covered bench. A round mirror hung above the yellow skirt with the big red roses. A bedspread of the same fabric and design covered the iron bed. A wardrobe stood on the opposite wall from the dressing table. My crib was made of iron with arches on the sides and one large arch at the head and foot. It seemed so small and high beside the bigger bed. Both beds were painted brown. An upholstered dark red platform rocker looked out from the foot of their bed, and another small rocking chair with the same yellow covering sat near the stove. An iron daybed, with a green cover, fitted under the double windows perfectly. The bed could be extended to make a double bed. It predated the modern sleep sofa but was used as the same idea. A thin brown wool rug with dark flowers covered the floor. There were pull-down shades and white fluffy curtains at the windows.

"As the days and months passed, I began to find myself waking up at night and pulling myself up on the thin rods to stand up in my crib and peer over the side. What woke me up? I don't know. Maybe it was voices or lights, or maybe at times, it was realizing I was alone in the room. Whatever woke me gave me a sense of dread. It was never a happy time and I can't tell you how old I was, only that when I look down in that crib, I can see chubby little feet, soft white skin on short full legs, and my hands are small on the railing. I feel very, very anxious and worried about what is happening around me.

"Maybe most people my age, who like me, slept in their parents' room, have as their first memories something of a sexual nature. I don't know, but with me, the sexual act between my parents is my earliest memory. I say it's my earliest memory because I am so tiny in my crib. And when I stand up in my crib, I have to stand on my tiptoes to see over the railing. I'm so scared about what's happening to my mother. I cry and cry for Daddy to stop because she is crying, and I can't get out of the crib. I shake the railing as hard as I can. I can see him on top of her, so big and she is so small, and I hear him say, 'I'm going to make you feel better', but it doesn't happen. Mama keeps crying and I'm crying, and Daddy's still on top of her. Then Mama realizes I am awake, and she says I shouldn't be watching and begs him to stop. And he says it doesn't matter.

"Finally, it's over.

"I sit in my crib crying and crying for Mama. Then she moves toward me and I get up and reach my arms over the crib rails to her. When she pulls me over in bed with her, I crawl over to Daddy and start beating him with my fists and crying and yelling 'Why did you hurt her?' Daddy laughs at me and holds my arms and says, 'Stop hitting me'. I don't understand, but I try to keep them apart by lying down between them. It seems strange to me that this could be such a vivid memory when I couldn't have been more than three years old. I stayed in their room until I was five when my sister was born. I'm sure there were many more times of equal anxiety on my part, and many more times when I witnessed situations that were far beyond my comprehension. Times that children should escape, but I was forced to be part. I didn't realize it then but trying to keep them from hurting or killing each other would become a big part of my life for as long as they lived.

"My first memories like this one were so scary because I couldn't get out of my crib. I knew Mama was hurting and I knew Daddy was the cause, but I couldn't do anything. I was trapped in my crib and I had to watch. Later, when I could get out of my crib, it wasn't any better because I still couldn't stop it and I would get in their bed and beat on Daddy with my fists. Then Daddy would catch me by the arm and carry me out of the room like I was a chicken flapping my legs and arms and screaming. He would drop me outside the door and lock it. Then I could hear and not see. But I couldn't bang on the door and scream because he would spank me, and it would hurt so bad. I just cried and waited outside the door until they let me in.

"I was so scared and worried because Mama was always crying.

One night, Daddy came home late and woke us up. He turned the light on and was fumbling around on the mantle above the stove. He was in his shorts. 'Where's that cocoa butter?' Just as he said that Mama started crying. 'Oh! Judd, no! I'm so sore, please don't, please don't. Oh, please don't.'

"He put the cocoa butter on the stove in a little top, then took a little pack and tore it open. He sat on the edge of the bed and put the rubber on. I had never seen this. And they didn't put me outside that night. I guess I observed my first rape before I was three. I know I hated him that night. Parents will do all kinds of these in front of children when they think they don't understand or maybe the parents don't care. I really think that night taught me to be afraid of men and sex."

"Are you sure it was rape and not passion?"

"If it was passion, it was different from any passion I have ever seen or felt since then. But I learned to love this man, adore him, some have said to worship him. He was my father, is my father. That will never change. And, for so many years he was my hero. As it turned out, he was my hero, but I came to see him differently."

"What happened to change him as your hero?'

"He became an alcoholic. It became a game for the whole family. Who was the best at denial? Who was the best at pretending nothing had happened? I was the best at trying to keep Daddy from drinking. I did everything. I tried to keep Mama from fussing with him. I tried to be as good as possible so no one would get mad. Then I tried to barter, which led to coercion on Daddy's part. Eventually I sold my soul without realizing it.

"And, I learned to hate this woman, my mother, whom I tried so hard to help as a toddler. This woman who was my birth mother, who brought me into the world, who cradled me in her arms as an infant, but she could never be a help to me as a girl or a woman. She taught me to hate her at an early age. The hatred grew as I got older; I learned the meaning of betrayal and protection. Both of my parents betrayed me in the most brutal way, but my love for and worship and devotion to my father grew in the same proportions as my hatred grew of my mother. The difference is I knew my father had a temper and could hurt me if he wanted to. I have learned to accept the fact that this woman was my birth mother, but throughout my childhood, I questioned it over and over in my mind. How could this woman be my birth mother? How could this woman I called Mama, be my real mother? Where was the mother who was supposed to cuddle me, kiss me, heal my boo-boos, talk to me, understand me, love me? I didn't understand what had happened to her."

"How long did you think that your mother was not your real mother?

"All my life. The thoughts were like waves. I would just know she wasn't my real mother. Then I would think. How could that be? I would convince myself for a while that she was my real mother, but it would never stick."

"This must have been hard for you."

"It was. Believe me."

"Are you sure this is the way you felt as a child?"

"Yes, I am sure."

My face flushed. How dare he challenge me on this?

"The first thing I remember as a child outside of the bedroom terrors was the great snowstorm of 1940, the year I was four years old. The snow began to fall early in the evening on New Year's Eve. The weather forecasts were very unreliable. The technology was not available to send the latest meteorologists reports flashing out every few hours. People relied on their own skills for the weather—their aches, their noses, the look of the sky, the sounds of wildlife, the abundance of berries and nuts. Whatever they used, my family was ready for what they believed would be a big one.

"Daddy had three sawmills by then. The farm grew the food for the men and mules. There were lots of mouths to feed on the farm and in the woods. Plus, four or five young white men lived in the house with the family. Cooper did not come to live with us until after the war began. This was a custom in the country. If you hired young white boys to work, you gave them free board. They could all sleep in one room and food was no problem for the cook. It simply meant adding more ingredients, not changing the menu. There was

156

plenty of room because my grandmother remarried, and Daddy bought the farm from her and the other children.

"My mother was the mistress of the house, and by then she had a yardman, a gardener, a cook, and various black children to do the errands for everyone. This sounds pretentious, but it was far from rich. There were always as many people around to work as you could possibly use. Food and shelter were the main things everyone wanted, and a farm could provide both. Every household had inside help and outside help, as well as men to work the fields.

"All these young boys had come in that Sunday night to be ready for work on Monday morning. There was a superstition among working people that if you didn't work on New Year's Day you wouldn't work the rest of the year. I have vague memories of the hustle to get ready for the big storm. The men were anxious all evening.

"Expectation and excitement were in the air. Were all the animals fed? Were the barns closed up? Was there enough wood on the porch for the night and maybe the next day? Was there enough antifreeze in the trucks?

"I have very clear memories of Daddy and all the boys sitting around the stove in the dining room that night. And I am sure the topic of conversation was the coming snow storm.

"On the morning of January 1, 1940, everyone in the house was convinced the snow had set in for a while. It was falling like a blizzard, fine, and fast with powerful wind gusts. The snow fell for days leaving the countryside blanketed and the snow three feet deep. The men by then were in a frenzy to get out of the house and back to work. But there was no work to be done. They fed the animals and helped move snow. The countryside was snowed in.

"I remember standing by the window in Mama's bedroom and looking straight out on the snow. If my hand could have gone through the glass, I could have drawn pictures on the flat surface or made a snowball. The reason I know this is because my mother raised the window one afternoon and took a pan and carefully dipped clean white snow in a bowl. She took the bowl back to the kitchen and added a little milk, vanilla, and sugar and returned to the bedroom with snow ice cream. We sat by the window and ate the snow cream. I thought it was the best ice cream I had ever tasted. We sat and ate, and I know I felt good, at peace. This is the one instance in my childhood that I can remember any kind feelings for my mother. She had made the snow cream, and we sat down together to eat it, just the two of us. We had a little tea party. For once, my mother had done something with me and for me.

"I have held on to this memory because I can feel the warmth of that afternoon and I can see her eating the snow cream and smiling. There were no harsh words, no frowns, no screams, no raised hands. Just Mama and me eating snow cream."

"I'm glad you have one good memory of your mother."

"I have never thought about it that way before, but I am too."

I waited a moment then continued.

"I remember one other thing that happened during the big snow. I wanted to go outdoors as much as anyone, but Mama thought it was too cold, too wet, and the snow was too deep. So, Daddy put my snowsuit on and took me in his arms outside to see the snow and take pictures. He had just bought a new tractor-trailer rig. He put me on top of the trailer and stood beside me for Mama to take our picture. The snow was even with the top of the trailer. I felt so important because I was just as tall as Daddy.

"That snow lasted most of the winter. The sawmills were shut down and the teams were already home because of the Christmas holidays. Daddy signed his teams on with the state highway department to help clear the roads. It was a hard and gruelling task for men and teams. There were very few motor graders at the time and those were assigned to the cities. There may have been one in Derbyshire to clear Route 60. Daddy started out each morning with three teams hooked to the snowplow: a very rough, home-made structure. Daddy and the men took heavy boards and nailed them together in the shape of a V. A log chain was bolted into the end of the V. On this chain, they first hooked three mules or horses to a doubletree with a whiffletree extension. In front of the three, they hooked another team on the chain, then one in front of the two, in effect forming another V. Because the snow was so deep, the lead horse had to break the track all the time which was exhausting work. They stopped every hour and changed the lead horse with another in the team. This changing of the teams continued throughout the day.

"I don't remember all of this, but Mama took pictures of the teams, and the snow of 1940 was talked about for decades. I do remember that I was fascinated with horses by this time, because of my father. Horses were such a part of everyone's life then because they were so necessary, but Daddy had a special interest in them. He liked to ride horses and drive a good buggy horse, in addition to having the workhorses. It seemed natural for me to love them too."

"So, you think your interest in horses came from your father?"

"Yes, but actually my whole family, on both sides, was interested. My mother's father loved horses too. I couldn't wait for him to come to see us on weekends so I could show him my horses. I remember so many stories he told about the famous harness horse, Dan Patch.

"I had my first pony before I went to school. His name was Billy, a very common name at the time for a horse or pony. Billy was very special, and I loved him so. He was large, black and white spotted, very gentle and just as lazy. I could climb all over him. He never objected to anything, even giving my dog a ride.

"I don't remember when I became Daddy's girl. The natural progression for firstborn daughters is for a tight bond to develop between father and daughter. This is probably true for all daughters, but certainly for the oldest daughter. I have read that the oldest daughter, if she is the firstborn, will develop her father's personality for the most part. I have seen this in other girls, and it was certainly true in my case. And sometimes little girls fall in love with their fathers and may become very jealous of their mothers.

"I don't remember feeling jealous of my mother. It seemed there was no reason to be jealous of Mama because there was so little open affection between my father and mother. And it certainly seemed to me and everyone else, that he preferred me to anyone. Usually, Daddy would make the first gesture to her, but it was rarely reciprocated by my mother. I can remember him coming home in the evening and trying to hug her and seeing my mother shrug it off as if it were unwanted or sinful or shouldn't be seen. I don't know which, or if all of these were true. I just know she wasn't affectionate with anyone. But I always ran to meet Daddy when he came home. He would pick me up and I would hug his neck. He called me Sugar Pie, Pumpkin, and Daddy's girl. He only called me by my name when he was mad or in a hurry. On the contrary, he always called my mother, Esther. It seemed Daddy did things for me and with me, and Mama did things to me. Except for the snow cream time.

"For instance, Daddy would take me on the horse with him. I would ride for hours behind him, along the sawmill trails during the week, and on the farm on Sunday afternoons. I would lean my head against his back and watch the trees, or the sky and feel the rhythm of the horse's gait. It didn't matter where I was going, how hot it was, or long it took. I was with Daddy and with the horses. These were the only two things I cared anything about.

"I don't know why I can't remember my mother holding me, singing to me, rocking me to sleep, any of the things that make children feel safe and loved. I think she felt she just didn't have time, or that she would be spoiling me to do this. It was during this time, sometime after the snow and before I started school, that I began to feel conflict between my mother and father more clearly. Daddy always wanted to take me somewhere and Mama always wanted to keep me at home. I had a dog and dolls and little tea sets, but my heart was always in the outdoors. This made my father happy and my mother very sad. I am sure she thought she was doing a very poor job raising me to be a young lady, because of all the time I spent with my father. And, to her, I was becoming a willful, loud, disobedient, awkward tomboy.

"At the time I had no idea what I was doing wrong because it seemed to me it was far more fun and exciting to be with Daddy than with Mama. In my mind Mama was bad. It was more and more evident to me.

"To make matters worse, my mother always knew exactly what was right for me in every situation. And she liked perfection. She never got over whatever disrupted her idea of perfection, and never forgave or forgot the cause of the imperfection."

Dr. Thomas listened intently but didn't interrupt.

"The heavy jet-black ringlets that I was born with were suddenly taken away. I don't remember anything about this happening, not even staying away from home a week or more. It happened soon after my first year. My mother left me with Aunt Hazel who was a kind wonderful soul. Aunt Hazel was a teacher and had raised a stepdaughter. For some reason, she rinsed my hair in baking soda, and it bleached it a beautiful, bright blonde. My mother was speechless when she returned to get me and vowed never to leave me anywhere ever again.

"After that, my hair became an obsession. Brushing it, curling it, and keeping it out of the sun became daily rituals. Rituals accompanied with admonishments to me and my father. She would fuss the whole time about the sun, dirt, play, sweat, hay, sand, water, anything that could disturb, mess up, or damage my curls in any way. She said I would never have that beautiful jet-black hair again, and it would never hold its curl like before. My hair grew longer and longer and became a thing to be hated by me.

"Aunts and cousins and friends told her my hair would be curly if she cut it short because it was naturally curly. But my mother wanted it long. As the years passed and I went to school, that fine thick hair became dry, broken, and bleached on top making it a bush completely out of her control. I was teased and tortured at school. My hair was so different from everyone else's, and the tight curls underneath couldn't be seen.

"My feet, as I have already said, were another embarrassment for me and trouble for her. I was born with fallen arches. The doctor suggested corrective shoes. They came in three colors–black, brown, or white–and one style: lace-up high tops. I had to wear these shoes all the time. I could never go barefoot. At first, I am sure I took them off whenever I could, but I soon learned that action produced a hail of screams and cries. 'Lesley, where are those shoes? You are the hard-headiest little piece I have ever seen. And wilful. You're determined to have your way, aren't you? You get those shoes right now and come in this house. All you want to do is run outdoors after the men. Just look at you. You're filthy! Your hair is a mess and your face is always dirty.'

"She would grab my arm and drag me to the house, half running, stumbling and crying. 'You worry me to death. You know that. Why can't you be a little girl like you're supposed to be? Get in that house. You've got to have a bath–with all I have to do. I haven't got time to be giving you a bath in the morning. You are not going outdoors the rest of the day. You hear me? I could just shake the stuffings out of you.' My mother was always worried, in a hurry, and angry about something.

"Then came the nightmarish bath. She would not run enough water in the bathtub, and she scrubbed me until my skin was red, but washing my hair was the worst. There was no baby shampoo and the long hair would get in my eyes and burn so badly when I was already crying. So, the bath was a torture chamber of cries and screams. 'Stop that crying, you hateful little piece.' She used that phrase so much, I knew it must be the worst thing anyone could be called. 'You'll have all the help in here thinking I'm killing you. Nothing could kill you. This water looks like a hog took a bath. And there are even cockleburs in your hair! Where in the name of heaven have you been? Hold still while I pull these things out. Don't you yell, I'll get your Daddy's belt. I ought to let him wash you anyway. He's the reason for all this and where are your underpants? Where did you leave them, this time?'

"She would catch the cocklebur or whatever it was and yank it out. 'This is ruining your hair. I could just take you and wear you out. Stop that crying! I mean it!' The pile of hair got bigger and bigger on the floor. I held my head to stop the pain, but my hands wouldn't cover my whole head and I didn't know where it was going to hurt next. After every piece of trash was yanked from my hair, she turned the water on full force and held my head under the spigot to rinse it. The water ran in my nose and mouth and I felt like I was going to drown. I would scream and choke, but it was only over when my mother thought my hair was clean.

"Then she pulled me out of the tub and put a towel over my

head and scrubbed it dry. It had to be dry even in the summertime before I went out of the bathroom because I would catch a cold. 'You'll catch a cold and be sick and I'll have to take care of you. Hold still. I'm not hurting you. I'm just drying your hair.' I had a headache, and my scalp was so sore I knew it was going to bleed and she would start all over. I learned to pray to get away.

"After the bath, I had to stay in the house the rest of the day and tried to be quiet. I didn't want to make her angry anymore.

"I began to stay outside more and more with my dog Lassie and my pony Billy. Billy was so kind and gentle. Totally lazy, but very willing for me to sit on his back while he dozed in the shade of a tree or grazed in the yard. He would follow me if I led him and he would play endless make-believe games as long as he didn't have to move too much.

"Lassie loved to play and when we were all worn out, I would go into the house and ask Aunt Pearl, as she cooked dinner, to fix me a bottle. My mother thought a bottle was fine. A child needed milk no matter how old she was. After I went to school, I would come home in the afternoon and fix my own bottle. So, at six and seven, I was still drinking from a bottle.

"Aunt Pearl was good to me, but she was the cook and had plenty of work to do, and she was not paid to look after me. I was never supposed to be in the kitchen keeping her from her work. Aunt Pearl was large and wore glasses and my mother said she could iron better than anyone she had ever seen. Aunt Pearl kept the irons on the stove all the time. Sometimes they were shoved to the back of the stovetop where they were just warm, sometimes they were on the front where the stovetop was a sunset red. She had an iron for every need. Big, little, pointed tips, blunt, thin, thick, narrow, wide. My mother said Aunt Pearl could iron a linen table-cloth into a perfect, wrinkle-free square, or the tucks in my dresses each tuck perfectly matched. We had electricity but the old irons were still used.

"Aunt Pearl would rinse my bottle, fill it with milk, and wipe it dry, and she always tested it on her arm to see if the milk came through the nipple. With my bottle secure under my arm, I went outside and lay down near Billy and put my head on Lassie for a pillow. This was about as perfect as I could imagine things to be. When I was tired, what could be better than to have my bottle, my dog, and my pony all with me. I would look up in the trees and watch the birds play, and swat the flies with my hands. They tickled my legs and arms and face. If nothing happened, soon we were all asleep. I would often awake to find kittens licking my bottle, or chickens pecking in the grass nearby. These were good times. All I had to do was stay away from Mama."

"Did Aunt Pearl become your confidant?"

"I'm sure she did, but I don't remember anything particular that I told her. Except I always wanted her to hold me, I wanted her to tell me it was going to be all right. I don't know why, but I needed assurance more than anything and I never remember getting that from her. Isn't that strange?"

"Yes, it is. But we will get into that later." He put my folder down. "Our time is up for now."

"Okay. Thank you. I'll be back next week." I always thanked him. I was truly grateful for what he was doing for me, although at the time many things were not clear to me. But that is the nature of my therapy. Sometimes it would be months before I recognized the significance of something we had talked about. I gradually began to see there were many things different in my childhood relationships than in those of other children.

I will never forget the time he said, "Mrs. Owens, you don't have to love your mother. She is your mother, but you don't have to love her."

This was a statement I had never heard before. It hit like a sledgehammer. The blow vibrated in my mind for several years. Slowly, with each memory of a blow from childhood, the meaning of the statement came to light. You can't love your mother if she doesn't deserve it.

14

———

Dr. Thomas's office was always so quiet. More and more it became a place where I could feel safe, a place of refuge. I looked up as Dr. Thomas began.

"We've covered quite a bit of your early childhood, haven't we?"

"Yes, it seems so. You know, I remember some things so vividly and others I can't seem to remember at all."

"That happens. Sometimes we forget or bury great portions of our lives when it's too bad to remember. What is the next big thing that you remember in your childhood?"

His comment stunned me. I thought I remembered everything. What could I not remember? That didn't make any sense. If I had buried it, how could I know what I couldn't remember? I shifted in the chair, trying to remember. "I guess the war made a big impression on me. I remember when the war started."

"You mean the Second World War."

"Yes."

"Good. Let's begin there."

"It was a Sunday night, I remember. We'd been riding around with Daddy looking at the mills and feeding the mule teams and horses. That was a Sunday afternoon ritual because the mules and horses needed to be fed. Also, Daddy always wanted to check on the slab pile and make sure the fire wouldn't get out before morning. Fire was always a danger because the slabs had to be burned all the time. When we got home my mother turned on the radio and we heard about the attack on Pearl Harbor. I didn't really understand what was happening, but I remember distinctly all of us sitting around the big radio standing in the living room. It was brown wood with black trim and had gothic, style arches in the top where the speakers were hidden. The station marker was on a clocklike face. The light inside the arches showed yellow. The dial was black with a red line like a thermometer.

"My mother fiddled with the dial each time the static got louder, and Daddy was saying constantly, 'Can't you get it better?' or, 'Be quiet. What did he say?' The tension in the air and their voices was so serious and foreboding that I felt afraid. I didn't realize it then, but there was every reason for me to feel frightened and afraid. The war news was a death knell to my childhood. From that night on, my world seemed to pass quickly from a childhood fear of Mama and baths to a new state of constant fear and dread.

"I feel compelled to say that my fear is in no way compared to the horrors experienced by thousands of children the world over during the war years. Theirs was a trauma I can only imagine and have no way of relating to. I know that now from reading about the atrocities and suffering."

"That may be true but fear affects us all. I am sure yours was just as real to you."

"My fear of the war was suspicion, fear of the unknown. I didn't know the meaning of the words I was hearing - like attack, bombing, devastation - but the anxiety they produced generated a constant sense of fear every time they were mentioned. These new fears were added to the other fears produced by my parents.

"I don't remember in detail anything about the days following the announcement, other than that the war became the focus of everyone's life. But it was not until we entered the war against Germany that my family came face to face with it every day. I am sure this was because we lived on the East Coast as opposed to the West Coast.

"The naval base in Norfolk was only one hundred thirty miles away from us, and German U-Boats were spotted there almost weekly. There were daily airplane watches throughout the county. Everyone had black draperies to cover the windows for the regularly scheduled blackouts. The women in every woman's organization knitted socks, made bandages, and contributed in some way to the war effort. My contribution until the spring of 1946 was to ride fence lines over the farm searching for worn-out horseshoes or discarded pieces of iron for the scrap iron drive at school.

"Then in the summer of 1942, after Rommel's defeat in North Africa, the first of his crack troops arrived in Derbyshire County as prisoners of war."

"Are you kidding? There were German prisoners of war in Derbyshire County!" he said excitedly.

Dr. Thomas seemed both amused and astonished that I would say such a thing. He looked as if it couldn't be true.

"No, I'm not kidding at all. It's true."

Then he seemed to get control of himself.

"It's so hard to imagine prisoners of war here even in the Second World War." Dr. Thomas stated, still appearing to be amazed that there were prisoners of war in the United States. To me it seemed as natural as the sun rising; however my children didn't know this until I told them, and many of my friends who did not grow up in Derbyshire didn't know it either. It would seem that it was one of the many little-known facts about the war that has not had broad publication. I don't know if it made it into any history books. Maybe this too is one of the things that people do not remember; like my own memories, some things get passed over and others become so significant.

I looked at him. I was definitely amused by his reaction. I had finally told him something he didn't know. I went on. "The old CCC Camp from the Depression and Roosevelt's New Deal was turned into a prisoner of war camp."

Dr. Thomas looked up again in disbelief. "What does CCC stand for? I'm not familiar with that term either."

"The letters CCC stood for Civilian Conservation Corps which was a brainchild of the New Deal. Camps were built to house these men near projects such as building roads through newly acquired forest land. When the war came the camps were empty and perfect for housing the prisoners."

It was obvious he was shocked by this statement. I smiled to myself. I liked this feeling of knowing something that he did not and being able to impress him. Recognition of any kind is something that I have since learned is very important to me. He's shocked by this yet it's as natural to me as pallbearers at a funeral. I went on.

"There were lots of prisoner of war camps all over the country. By then, nearly all of the able-bodied young men, unless they were like my father and the mill hands, had gone off to fight. There was no one left to do the work but women, and there weren't enough of them to raise the crops.

"Farm work became the job for the German prisoners in Derbyshire. They were taken out daily to do the work on farms. People were afraid of them, especially my mother. She was so afraid of the prisoners."

"You remember the German prisoners.

"Yes. They worked our farm until the end of the war. I was mesmerized by them. I'm sure their strange way of talking had a lot to do with it. I'd never heard a foreign language before. I always tried to stay out of sight, but I would listen to them and watch them for hours."

"I am sure they made an impression on you as a child."

"Yes, they did. I can even remember what some of them looked like. I'm ashamed to tell you this, but I have two letters at home that one of them wrote asking for food and clothes after he went back to Germany. I remember my father asking my mother to fix a package for him and his family. I know she didn't do it because she didn't think they deserved any help. She didn't like the Germans or any foreigners, as she put it. The real reason was she didn't want to be bothered."

"So, you think it was your mother's fault that nothing was sent."

"Oh, Yes. My mother was very unforgiving. She was hard and brittle."

"That's the impression you've given me over the time I've known you. You didn't like your mother, did you?"

My ears burned. I couldn't believe he had asked me that. I squirmed in my seat again. This session was turning into an endurance test.

"You don't have to like your mother. You don't even have to love her."

This time he had gone too far. "You told me that before. What do you mean? I've never heard that in my life."

"I don't expect you have, but it's true. There's nothing that says you have to love your mother, or even like her."

I was silent for a long minute. I wasn't going to answer him now, but I wasn't going to forget that statement either. I looked down thinking then changed the subject.

"My parents were fighting more than ever at night. I would wake up and hear my mother running through the house screaming and hear things falling over. I would get up and go to see what was happening even though I was always afraid because I might find something I didn't want to find. I would tiptoe quietly, hiding behind the door facing and peeping round. After I listened long enough to know that both Mama and Daddy were all right, I would go in and grab Daddy's hand or leg. I always ran to Daddy because I was afraid of Mama. She screamed at me during the day and at night, I knew she was mad and would hit me, too, like she was trying to hit Daddy. I'd try to get Daddy to leave the room wherever they were, but Mama wouldn't let him, so I stayed and watched her hit him and waited.

"As time went on, I learned that the fights were always about drinking. Daddy was drunk or had been drinking. It didn't matter which, either one produced the same amount of hitting, screaming, shouting, and crying on my mother's part. I didn't know when he was drunk or drinking, but I began to worry when Daddy didn't come home to supper. These fights always happened at night. The days were better because Mama wouldn't scream at Daddy when other people were in the house."

"How often did your father drink? Just on weekends, during the week? What kind of drinker was he? Did he drink often, but not so much, or was he a binge drinker?"

"At that point in my life, I can't really say. I just knew that his drinking was the problem. As I grew older, I thought he was a binge drinker, and he was at first. He'd get drunk on the weekends, that sort of thing, but then the drinking became more of a daily thing until he became a full-fledged alcoholic."

Dr. Thomas nodded in his polite and encouraging way that made me feel comfortable with him. "Go on."

"I didn't know it then, but other things were changing for the three of us. One particular night, Daddy was late getting home. I was still sleeping in their bedroom at the time because the house was cold, and wood was the only source of heat. We were all, including my baby sister who was born in January 1941, sleeping in the same room with the big wood-burning stove. Daddy came into the room and Mama met him at the door. She was shaking her fists and hissing at him like a snake to keep from waking the baby. I got up and went over to him and said, 'What did you bring me, Daddy?'

'I didn't bring you anything, Sugar. I didn't go anywhere to get you anything.'

"He reached in his pocket and pulled out some nails and said, 'See this is all I have. You can have these', and he dropped the nails in my hand. I said, 'That's all right Daddy, I'm tickled with these.'

"Daddy looked at Mama and said, 'Why can't you be like her? She's always glad to see me and is happy with anything.'

"This started a frenzy of crying and cursing from Mama, and then the baby awoke and cried. I tried to calm her even though I couldn't pick her up out of the high bed. I knew she was afraid like me. I didn't understand that I was becoming a pawn between Mama and Daddy. I wanted Mama to love me, but she always seemed to make me choose Daddy by doing something to provoke my sympathy for him. I never knew how these fights ended. They just dragged on until everyone was too exhausted or hoarse to go any further. I learned to dread the nights before I started school."

"That's a heavy load for a little girl to carry. It's a great burden for a child to try to keep peace between her parents. You didn't have much childhood, did you?"

"I never thought of it this way. No, I guess, I didn't. But there was one beautiful moment during this time that occurred at least two or three times a week. Without this person and these quiet times, my childhood would have been so much the worse.

"There was a country store about a half-mile from our house. Most every evening after supper I would go out in the front yard and wait to hear a car slow up on the road and stop at our mailbox. When it did it would be my Grandmother Garrett coming for a visit while her husband went to the store. Grandma Garrett, as I knew her, was my father's mother.

"Henry was her second husband. My grandfather had died when she was very young. To me, Grandma was as soft as a cloud, sweeter than the angels, and more loving than any mother I could imagine. If it was light enough, I ran to meet her, grabbed her hand, and guided her to the house. I can still see the little red pickup pulling away from the mailbox and purring down the road in front of a puff of blue smoke. After a few minutes with my mother, Grandma would take me in her arms in a rocking chair. She rocked and read to me from *Grimm's Fairy Tales*, a book she gave me for Christmas one year. The front cover reminded me of myself. There was a little girl with long curls snuggled in her grandmother's lap in an armchair. I only had to imagine my grandmother in the chair to make it perfect. I still have the book, tired and tattered as it is.

"There was no place I felt more secure than in Grandma's lap. Her softness shut out the world around us. I am sure that more often than not, I went to sleep in her arms, and she put me to bed.

"Grandma Garrett and my mother were as different as two women could possibly be. I knew this even then as a child and it's even more evident now as an adult. My mother was like I told: cold, hard, frigid, and brittle. I don't know how my father could have been lured to her psychologically. I am sure it was her physical attractiveness and her petite figure that turned his head. My mother had a public and private face. The public face could be the most forgiving and accommodating, and I am sure that my father never saw the private face until they were married.

"I never remember my mother rocking me, holding me, kissing me, or giving me a hug. I have wondered what my grandmother or my mother thought when I was in Grandma's lap and they were talking. I wonder if my mother ever resented or yearned for the closeness I shared with Grandma Garrett. Neither one mentioned it, but there I was quiet and happy. It had to be noticeable. I would lie back against grandma's soft body and watch my mother while grandma talked and rocked or read to me. It didn't matter. Now, as a grandmother myself, I think of those times and fold my arms just a little closer around the grandchildren whenever I can. There is still a deep hunger in me to love and feel loved."

Dr. Thomas looked at me and spoke softly. "I am glad you had your grandmother. I am sure she was to you just the comfort you describe, and you needed that."

I didn't answer for a minute because I was thinking about what he had said. It was so like him to be kind and try to bolster my ego at every opportunity. Thank God he was like that. I had had one psychiatrist who had challenged me at every turn, and it wasn't fun. I know too I picked up on Dr. Thomas's easy manner the first day I met him. It was another reason that made me ask to keep seeing him. I guess I had been badgered by enough men.

I looked up at him, suddenly remembering something. "I skipped something very important, I think."

"Oh, go back to it if you think it is important."

"I started school in the fall of 1942. I was ready for school but very anxious about getting started. My first-grade teacher, Miss Parker, was a friend and neighbor. In fact, the family lived on the farm just behind ours. Miss Parker walked through the fields each day and caught the school bus with me.

"My mother thought that, war or not, I had to have a new dress to wear the first day of school. That seemed to be a priority with my mother. She loved clothes and was not going to let me be overlooked in the clothing department. She often said she only had two dresses when she went to school, and she got so tired of them she could scream. Mother loved to sew, but she loved to shop even more.

"She found a suitable dress. One that I thought was absolutely beautiful. It was my favorite color–blue. It was made of blue polished cotton and white dotted Swiss. The collar and puff sleeves were set on a white yoke, and the skirt was gathered on a waistband of white. There was a wide matching sash that tied in the biggest, fluffiest bow. I knew I would have the prettiest dress at school that day. I couldn't wait to go.

"I can imagine the three of us, Miss Parker, my mother and I, standing by the mailbox waiting for the bus. It wasn't bright and shiny like the buses today. This bus was old and faded and made a lot of noise. The ride was long and dusty as we had to go along several dirt roads on the way. Several other teachers rode the bus with us. Now, as an adult and former teacher, I can't imagine how bad this must have been for them. Working all day, then riding the bus home with the same children who have, at best, been attentive to you, and at their worst been disruptive and disobedient. It seemed natural enough to me. I didn't realize until later that the presence of the teachers helped keep the older kids quiet. This came to light when the teachers for some reason didn't ride the bus. Then the big kids yelled out the windows and tormented the smaller children. They didn't torment me. My guess is I was spared because they were afraid of Daddy. Lots of people were.

"My father was getting rich by everyone else's standards and that gave him a lot of power. He liked to make fun of people and tease them. He was good to some, but he was mean too, in a childish sort of way. He would say anything to anybody, and he got away with it."

"Would you say your father was a bully?"

I looked down thinking. "Sometimes, yes. It was strange. He could be absolutely charming, and, in another situation, he was a tyrant. Sometimes he attacked a poor person with no defenses and sometimes he attacked the biggest guy around. He liked an audience either way, and if he led the attack he won. Sometimes I was so ashamed and felt so sorry for the other person. But I couldn't let anyone know I didn't support what Daddy was doing."

Dr. Thomas seemed to be thinking hard. "I see" was his only comment.

I went on, "Everyone, it is said, remembers their first-grade teacher. I certainly remember mine, Miss Parker. She was an old maid, but for me she was a substitute mother who made me feel safe. I don't remember her being affectionate in the modern-day-teacher way, but she was a big, tall woman who would protect us if necessary and discipline us if we needed it. I loved and respected her and wanted so much to be the best in her class.

"I knew I wasn't, in fact, I wasn't even close. It would take six more years until I was in the seventh grade for me to receive the compliment from her that I would take with me the rest of my life. It was a silly kind of thing, but it meant everything to me. I was in a play and needed a little white apron over my dress. Miss Parker kept the school costumes in a chest in her room. I was sent there to find an apron, but the only white apron had a bib and long ties at the top. We stood there dismayed; then, I took the apron, let the bib drop below the waist band, put it around my waist, and tied both sets of ties in a big bow in the back. She looked at me and burst into a smile. 'Lesley, you've got a real head on your shoulders.'

"I felt as if she had told me I was the smartest child in the world. I barely touched the floor as I went back to report to my sixth-grade teacher. Of course, the secret that I was so smart was mine to keep forever. Later, when my own children were in school, they were diagnosed as dyslexic–one more severe than the others. Looking back at my school life, childhood, and at other members of the family, I can see that the condition ran through my father's family. I suffered the consequences in school as did my father and my children. However, it gave us the determination not to give up–ever.

"I was so frustrated in first grade when I couldn't remember the words Dick, Jane and Sally. They were beautiful children in the books, and they had playmates Spot and Puff, but it was so hard for me to read the words, so I tried to memorize them. The dyslexia was showing its power. And to make it worse, there was a child in my class, a boy, who could already read and write anything. He sat at Miss Parker's desk and read her magazines, *The Grade Teacher* and *Classroom Teacher*, while I sat in the reading circle struggling to remember Dick and Jane. I used to watch him and wonder how in the world did he learn to read? He became my husband.

"It is hard to say why two people are attracted and I must say that in my mind, I was in college before I had any idea I was attracted to him. We were friends throughout school and dated in high school, but nothing serious. He says he picked me out the first day of school and went home and told his family that he had a girlfriend."

Dr. Thomas smiled in his gentle way and seemed to acknowledge that was a cute gesture for a boy to make. "Did he really?"

He seemed amused, I thought to myself. "Yes.

"Even if he didn't say that, it's become a legend in the family now. He told several older girls who rode his bus that he was going to marry me. I knew none of this at the time, but as the school years passed, it became more and more apparent to me that he was crazy about me. I'm afraid I used this knowledge to my benefit without much regard for his feelings. We knew from the beginning we would go to college, so we kept everything light and fun, not involved the way teenagers apparently are today. For us in the fifties, growing up was always in the future. You didn't grow up until you went to college.

"Four years seemed like such a long time, but it was the time girls used to find a suitable husband. A career for women was out of the question. I felt that growing up in Derbyshire had short-changed my perspective on life, and I was more than anxious to leave home and see the rest of the world. I don't think my husband-to-be saw it that way. He had the idea that the rest of the world was more or less like the area he called home. I am giving you these two opposing ideas to show you the basic differences between us. It has been hard for both of us, and I can't say why he was so determined to marry me."

Dr. Thomas interrupted and said in his quiet way, "I expect the smartest thing you ever did was to choose Linc for your husband. Have you ever thought of this?"

I almost laughed aloud. "You can't be serious. How could it have been the best thing I ever did when we have had so much trouble? I can't put it together now, but Linc and I are such opposites. We don't really agree on anything except, well, I take that back. We like the same kind of entertainment. We both like to dance. We both like the same style and period of decorative arts, but real values—that is another question."

"Linc has a quality you haven't mentioned. I think it is central to your remaining together through thick and thin."

Really, now I was the one that was in shock and almost angry that he could find the thing that I found to be me one of my biggest struggles could be even remotely good for me.

"What is it?" I said this almost curtly, hoping that my sarcasm and anger might show enough for him to recognize, but not enough for it to be actually real. I really could not imagine what this could be.

"Linc has allowed you to live your own life. I doubt there are many men who would have let you run your own businesses as you have and put up with your outbursts."

I was speechless for a moment. There was a long pause and we both looked at each other. Finally, I answered. "I won't agree with you now entirely, but I will acknowledge that because of my childhood, my adult life in many ways was a nightmare. Certainly, an experience foreign to anything Linc had expected. For this pain to him, I am deeply sorry, but for myself, I am so thankful that such a passive soul was able and willing to put up with my emotional explosions, hurts, and constant quest for power control, as well as my desperate yearning for love and attention."

Dr. Thomas looked at me with a half-smile again, encouraging and asking me in the way that was characteristic of his style. "That's quite an insight, young lady."

"I guess it is, but somehow I feel I knew that all along."

"You did. That's why you married Linc. The subconscious guides us much more than we know."

I bent my head and began tracing the diamond designs on the couch, as I often did when I was trying to figure something out. "There were other things that I noticed about Linc. He was never taught anything in the first grade because he could already read, write, and do math. As I said, he sat at the teacher's desk and read her teacher magazines. There was nothing for him to learn. So, he was set apart as the smart boy and the teacher's helper. All of us were in awe of him. He was odd. I remember him trying to show me how to hold the pencil to write. At that time we were not taught to print but to write. We went straight into cursive writing. I could not make those wide circles that would let me have a pretty handwriting. I remember him looking at me like 'why can't you do this', but he didn't say anything. I am sure he was curious."

"We are all curious when someone is different." Dr. Thomas glanced at the little clock on the end table. "It's time for us to end, but we made progress today."

That was music to my ears. I always wanted to hear that I was making progress or doing better, or something to satisfy my yearning to please everyone.

15

THE NEXT WEEK I began easily.

"In 1943, I moved to the second grade. This was a big jump because this was a split class of second and third grade. This marked the beginning of more trouble in school. It was not the first time that I realized all was not right in my world, but this really bothered me, and I did all the wrong things to help myself.

"I craved companionship and felt rejected by both boys and girls. This craving for companionship has followed me throughout my life. I became an outsider and more and more lonely and abandoned at play. I began to try to buy friendship from boys and girls. I would put a nickel or penny in a note and say, 'Will you be my friend?' The answer was always 'no' written on the returned paper–without the coin. Each rejection went straight to my heart."

Dr. Thomas interjected. "That must have been very hard on you. It's difficult to be rejected over and over and not give up. I take it you didn't give up." His tone told me this was a rhetorical question and that he was sympathetic to my stories and my problems. I needed so much to feel recognition and sympathy. I was constantly searching for encouragement too. I was beginning to see some of this as I retold my life stories to him.

It always made me feel so much better, if just for a minute when Dr. Thomas offered me even the slightest sympathy. "Oh, no I didn't give up. I just kept blundering along, making it more and more obvious to everyone that I desperately wanted friends and for some reason didn't have any. No one told me that if I weren't so pushy and tomboyish, I would have friends. This pattern continued right on through the seventh grade. Once the teacher caught a note in transit and made a big to-do. The notes stopped for a while, but my starvation for love and affection of any kind won out. The notes continued for the next several years. In school games I always seemed to be the last one chosen, or just before a poor girl worse off than I called 'Bull' Jackson.

"One girl in particular, the most popular girl in our class, used her position to lead the rest of the girls. They jockeyed for position within the group. The most popular girl chose her friend, who was always the next most popular, who chose the next most-favored, and so on down the scale. No matter the number in the group, they were listed in order of popularity from first to last. Favors within the group were also given out in order. I was never the most favored, but that was okay; I just wanted to be part of the group. I tried so hard to get the attention of the leader, but more often than not I was ostracized and left to stand at the window with my teacher and my sorrowful companion, Bull Jackson. I pitied her then, and especially now talking to you. I hate to say the derogatory term my classmates used with ease, 'Bull.'"

Dr. Thomas spoke up again. "Tell me about this person. She seems to be very significant to you."

"It never occurred to me then that I could have been called some horrid name such as 'Bull,' but if people had known what I had been subjected to, words like that could have been used for me. The only difference was one of class and physical attractiveness, I guess."

Dr. Thomas looked at me with a painful expression. "Girls who are sexually molested can take on mannish attributes in looks and actions, and thus the term 'bull dike' is levied against them. It's a sad commentary on innocent victims."

I looked at him stunned. I never knew how the term came about. "That's horrible. I remember how the boys used to giggle and laugh at her. It makes me hurt now. I know now that Bull Jackson had been robbed of everything–her virginity, self-respect, and acceptance. She had endured incest, poverty, torment by the school children, and the ridicule, scorn, and indifference to her family by the community.

"Her name was Edith. She was big, tall, large-boned, and awkward. She had a peasant build and attitude. She accepted her position, never making any accusations or pushing her way to the front of the line. She knew she belonged in the back and she didn't have the money to send in notes to try to gain power. She never had any money for anything."

"She really impressed you, didn't she?" Dr. Thomas asked, empathy in his tone.

"Yes. I'm sure that I identified with her more closely than I had any idea at the time. I have wondered how she saw school. Was it a place of reprieve? Was it a nice place to spend the day, and dread the nights as I did, or did she accept her terrible life? I will never know. Her face haunts me–dull brown hair with a part down the middle, sallow skin, washed-out blue eyes and broad, bull features. The nineteen forties that I remember showed little charity or compassion for animals or misfit humans.

"I had heard my mother talk about incest in the Jackson family. How rampant it was, and how many idiot minds and crippled bodies it had caused over the generations. Of course, this knowledge was scattered over the county because it came from the rural doctor who was the family doctor for everyone. He was the family doctor for my family as well as Bull Jackson's, my window companion. I wonder what he knew about my family and me. And this makes me wonder what other people know? And on it goes with no answers for me then or now."

"Do you know what happened to her?"

"No, I lost contact sometime in the fifth grade. I guess she moved to Richmond or another community. I never heard from her since, but I've never forgotten her either."

"She seems to have played a major part in your childhood, either as someone you would hope to never be like or someone whom you saw as a survivor at the time. It is certainly the norm that you would remember this now in a setting where you're trying to identify happenings which molded your life. Please go on."

"The third grade provided me with a particular lesson I have never forgotten. I attribute my resistance to ever telling a lie to this lesson from my father. It happened for the same old reason, my craving for attention and acceptance. Nothing meant more to me than being recognized by anyone, my teacher, classmates, friends, family. A hug was unheard of in my house other than from my father and grandmother.

"It began in a student assembly. The teacher up front made an appeal for donations to the Red Cross. She was trying to impress on the students how important it was for them to collect money for this cause. She pointed out one boy. 'Teddy I am sure you can get ten dollars from Mr. Rose who owns the farm your Daddy works'; and then 'Darlene you can collect dollars from your aunt in Richmond.' Hearing all these numbers and watching all these students getting so much attention made me desperately want to be recognized. I raised my hand quickly and practically shouted. 'My Daddy said he would give me fifteen dollars.'

"The teacher recognized me and repeated my name and the sum. For a second all heads were turned toward me. I had plucked their attention from the palm of her hand. Then I realized that I had to go home and somehow get my Daddy to give me fifteen dollars for the Red Cross Drive. I had given my word, and everyone had heard me. I just wanted to win the contest so badly. All I had to do was bring in the most money and the recognition would be mine again.

"The teacher had promised a money prize to the students who brought in the most money. I didn't care about the money, I just wanted to walk down that aisle and show the students I could do something. She did not say how much the prize would be.

"The days dragged by as I worried about how and when to

approach my father. I tried to get other contributions, but I had little opportunity. I was too young to go around the community on my bike. Finally, time ran out. It was late at night when I went into his bedroom. Daddy was lying in bed reading the newspaper. The bedside lamp shone on his face. I walked over to the bed and put my arm around the foot post. He kept on reading, paying no attention to me. I studied his face for a moment. I realized how frightened I was of him, so afraid he would turn me down. I forced myself to say 'Daddy, I need to talk to you.'

"He didn't put the paper down. 'What do you want?' he asked.

"'We're having a contest at school to see who can bring in the most money for the Red Cross and the winner will get twenty-five dollars. I know if you give me fifteen dollars I will win.' I couldn't believe I had said the words. They had come from my mouth. I gripped the bedpost waiting.

"He lowered the paper, his eyes met mine. 'Hum They are going to give you twenty-five dollars prize money. And you think fifteen dollars will win?'

"'Yes.'

"'Why do you think that fifteen dollars will win?'

"'Because I know what the other kids have brought in. And I just think it will win.'

"'All right, look in my billfold and get fifteen dollars, if you are sure you will win twenty-five.'

"'That's what she said. She told us in assembly.' I fumbled in his pants pocket and pulled out the fat billfold. It was thick leather and felt big and heavy in my hand. I opened it and pried the money flap apart. It was stuffed with bills as always. Daddy was making lots of money in the lumber business by 1943 and had promised me a horse. I thought about that as I picked through the bills. I carefully took out a ten and a five and put the billfold back. Daddy was already reading the paper again.

"I was so relieved to have the fifteen dollars in my possession. I ran upstairs and put the money in my change purse and went to bed happy."

Dr. Thomas made no comment, but there was a definite beginning smile on his face like he was amused.

"The next day in assembly my name was called to come down front and receive my prize. The students clapped for my success, but the prize was only a dollar fifty. I can still see the one-dollar bill, folded up with the fifty cents on top. It was then I realized I had to go home and tell my father that I had gotten only a dollar fifty. My happiness from the clapping was short-lived. I spent the rest of the day worrying about how I was going to get around this one. That night at the supper table Daddy asked, 'Did you win the twenty-five dollars?'

"'The teacher gave me only a dollar fifty. It was supposed to be twenty-five, but the teacher gave me only a dollar fifty.'

"'Where is it?'

"'In my change purse.'

"'Well, go get it. If she said she was going to give you twenty-five dollars she should have done it.'

"I got the dollar fifty and gave it to him. He put the dollar bill in his billfold and the fifty-cent piece in his pocket and went on with his supper.

"I knew I had lied about the twenty-five-dollar prize, even if Daddy didn't say any more about it. I swore to myself I would never lie again no matter what. It is strange to me now that I never questioned why I knew I had to bribe my father to get him to give me the money, or why he didn't let me keep the dollar and a half. In my subconscious, I knew money was always the key. Daddy would use money to buy anything. I am glad I learned not to lie. I just wish I could have learned it another way."

"I think what you see here is another betrayal," said Dr. Thomas. "We know you don't deal well with betrayal and you shouldn't. Children should never learn firsthand about betrayal. It is an ugly adult concept that has no place in a child's development. It breeds paranoia, suspicion, distrust, and a multitude of other neuroses."

"I see," I said, not sure if I believed him or not at this moment. I was trying to digest how reliving my childhood could help me now, and at the same time feeling compelled to tell him something else. "Something else happened in the third grade that I don't want to tell you about, but I guess I should. In fact, I know I should, but it makes me feel ashamed and embarrassed." I was looking at the couch as I talked because I didn't want to face him with the ugly revelation. I traced the seam around the cushion. "This has bothered me since I was old enough to figure out what I was really doing. I just know I was so innocent when it happened."

Dr. Thomas changed positions in his chair. "You don't have to tell me now if it makes you uncomfortable. We can come back to it, later."

"No, I don't want to make it easy for myself. I'm just getting up my nerve."

"I see." He smiled but didn't say anymore. Once again, he managed to acknowledge my pain and allow me to continue at my own pace with just a single gesture. His non-threatening manner was such a comfort.

I took a deep breath and began. "You know how kids want to spend the night with each other. Now they call it a sleepover, I think."

"Yes."

"I was going to spend the night with this girlfriend. It was always a real adventure because we got to ride another bus as well, and it was visiting a new home. It was usually a weeknight because our parents didn't haul us up and down the road like they do now."

He nodded in understanding.

"Anyway, that night several children had to sleep in the same bed, because the family was poor, and they had a lot of children and not a lot of beds. It was wintertime and cold, so we were very close together. I don't remember why I thought about this, maybe it was the closeness, or maybe one of them touched me in a vulnerable spot. I don't remember why, but I turned to my girlfriend and said 'If you lie on top of me, I know how to make it feel good.' She was reluctant because she didn't understand, but she followed my advances. The whole thing is so vivid in my mind and it makes me so ashamed. I have felt so bad about this for so long."

Dr. Thomas waited a minute then answered. "You shouldn't feel bad about this because you were not trying to molest your friend. You just knew a lot about sex and something made you think about it. It wasn't your fault that someone older had taken advantage of you when you were too young to understand."

"I see, but I don't remember anything about me, I just remember this."

"You don't remember why you got the whipping, do you?"

"No." My face flushed at the mention of the whipping.

"It's all the same thing. There were probably many instances of abuse. They are just locked in your subconscious. You have not allowed them to come to the surface yet. They are much too painful to remember."

"I see."

There was a long pause as if Dr. Thomas was waiting for me to say something else, but I wanted to leave this and get on with something more pleasant.

"I have to say there were some happy times in my childhood. The snow cream I told you about for one. They didn't last very long–maybe a couple of hours at the time–but for a short while they were nice. The important thing is I can remember them, too."

"I would like to hear a happy memory for a change. Tell me."

"There is one memory that I call up when the evenings are long, and the smell and sounds of spring or summer are in the air. Or on summer nights when I can hear the laughter of neighbor children and their friends, even in the country where homes are far apart. Sometimes it'll be on a quiet still evening when the air's heavy, and the darkness surrounds me making images dance in the light of the fireflies. They flitter off and on like twinkle lights on a Christmas tree, except I know these lights are real and there is a life in each one, and I always hope it is happier than my own.

"It was nights like these that make me remember my father's uncle Charlie and his wife, Honor. They were childless and lived on a fifty-acre farm. In fact, the fifty acres was cut originally from the same farm I live on now. I can see almost the whole fifty acres from my window in my home office. My great grandmother, Iris Garrett, a granddaughter of the overseer on Oakland, the Brooke plantation, gave each of her two sons fifty acres. The land was not the best or worst to be found, but Charlie and Honor treated the land as if it were their children. The consequences of this watchful care yielded a lifetime together. The money crop was tobacco, with enough land left over to support a team of horses, cows for milk, pigs for meat, and chickens, ducks, geese and guineas for eggs and meat, a vegetable garden, and enough grain and hay for the animals.

"Maybe once a month we would go to see them on a Sunday afternoon. It was a grand time for us as children, because Aunt Honor always had sugar cookies with raisins that she kept for us, and unlike my mother she didn't care how many we ate. Uncle Charlie entertained all of us with strange stories about the neighbors and their troubles that I still remember. He regarded these stories as news in the community.

"We would go on Sunday afternoon just before dark. In the winter we sat by a glowing fire and ate the sugar-raisin cookies. In the summer they sat on the porch while we chased fireflies and put them in a jar.

"The wetlands nearby were a haven for the tree frogs, the bullfrogs, whippoorwills, and katydids. Their voices provided the music for all sorts of fantasies that found their way from the dark woods. When the hoot owl woke up, we stopped and listened and looked for a ghost to float across the evening sky. When we got tired of chasing fireflies, I pretended I was riding my horse across the fields, jumping the panels of fence with the wind whipping my hair in the moonlight. Finally, we sat down on the edge of the porch and listened to the grown-ups talk, and held the cats, and petted the dog. Our thoughts, if any, centered on the tranquility of the night and how much we liked coming to Uncle Charlie's and Aunt Honor's."

"You paint a very tranquil atmosphere."

"It was all because Aunt Honor and Uncle Charlie lived a quiet, useful life. They didn't hurt or bother anyone. Neither were they jealous and they loved company, especially ours. Times were different then.

"Things were never tense or quarrelsome when we were at Uncle Charlie's. And when we went home, we didn't have to worry. Everyone would go to bed, and the next day was a workday which was always better than weekends. Daddy had to go to work and we had to go to school. The structure of the weekdays kept things better than the weekends. As we grew older, the sisters and I realized this, and we would try to plan things to keep us occupied on the weekends. However, I was always so afraid something awful would happen if I wasn't there. As a result, I rarely left on weekends so I could watch over Mama and Daddy. I am sure I knew there was not much my being there accomplished, except it eased my fear of not knowing what was happening. The awful fear of their fighting was always with me.

"I remember another good thing too."

"Oh, you are on a roll of good things, aren't you?" Dr. Thomas commented happily.

"I don't know about that, but this is a good memory."

"Let's hear it," he stated enthusiastically. He seemed genuinely pleased and interested in my life.

"It was always a happy time for me when the log teams of horses and mules would come home. This happened always at Christmas, and when the mills were moved from one tract of timber to another. Sometimes they came home at other holidays, such as Easter and Thanksgiving. I was charmed by the huge animals and the drivers and the heavy harness they wore.

"When Daddy said the teams were coming home that day, I would wait by the picket fence in the front yard as long as possible; or if it was too cold, I waited by the window in the house. At the first glimpse or sound, I rushed out to meet them, running down the road as fast as I could. I can still hear the soft rhythmic clip-clop of their hooves, the creaking of the huge steel-rimmed wheels on the log carts, and the jingle of the bells each mule and horse wore on his breast chain. The bells were heavy sleigh bells so the tree cutters could always tell where the teams were in the woods.

"These sounds in the distance sent me running down the road

until I found Grant's team and I would shout up to him. 'Let me ride!'

"He would stop. 'Lord, Mize Lesley, what are you doing out here? Does your mother know you out here? Here, get up here before something happens to you.' He would reach down and catch my arm and pull me up beside him with one easy swoop. His seat was one narrow slab of wood, maybe eight inches wide and twenty-four inches long. The seat seemed to me to be way up in the air and we were looking down on the team. It was scary except I knew Grant would not let me fall. This trust was all I needed to ask Grant, 'Can I drive?'

"'Well, yes, I guess so,' he would say. His big calloused hand would lay the lines in mine and a sense of power and importance surged through me. The lines were big heavy straps of leather, each almost as wide as my hand, with the ends draped across the axle below.

"'Look, Grant, I'm driving.'

"'Yes, you are, but don't go messing with this team because they know this is home and they're going to sleep in a barn tonight and rest tomorrow.'

"I wasn't really driving, and I knew it. The team would follow the one in front, and besides, all Grant had to do was give a command and they would have obeyed him, not me. I knew all this, but it didn't matter. I was sitting on the seat, holding the lines, watching their broad backs sway under the harness. I could smell the leather, the mixture of sweat and mud on their hides, and I could see the soft puffs of steam rise off their bodies and above their nostrils. I could call them by name, 'Belle' and 'Roady' and most of all I could pretend I was a boy and one day the team would be mine.

"It was times like these that made me realize how different things would have been if I had been a boy."

I noticed Dr. Thomas's eyebrows go up, but he didn't say anything. I did not want to get him a chance to comment further so I continued quickly.

"When the teams stopped, Grant jumped down and reached for

me. 'Now, you stand over there, I don't want you getting stepped on. These mules are ready to be turned loose.'

"I watched as he unhooked the trace chains and hung them on the clip on their breaching harness. Then the breast chains and the long, heavy tongue of the cart would drop to the ground and the team would march off to the harness house. There was a peg for each harness with the name above. Then mules and horses walked to the stable as teams for food and rest.

"When I had watched it all, every mouth fed, every manger filled, and every nose rubbed, I would sit on the steps to the loft and watch them eat for a while. By then, all the drivers were gone and there was no one but me and the teams and the barn animals who were all my friends. These were wonderful times. I relished them and tried to hold on to them and save them to think about when I had to go back to the house and face whatever the night might bring. These times could be recalled, days, weeks, months, and years later like now.

"These were the times of reprieve that would keep me intact and determined to survive, even when I did not know that survival was my goal. Living and dreaming horses was my escape from the hell I lived at home."

Dr. Thomas closed his folder. "Horses really did save your life, didn't they?"

"Yes, they did. No doubt about it in my mind."

"You're lucky to have been able to develop that interest."

"Yes, I know." He wasn't admonishing me, but I didn't like to be reminded that everything was not all bad. To me it was, and I didn't like him believing otherwise. I wanted to be the only one who could recognize any good in my childhood. But I couldn't say this. He had always been very kind to me even if I didn't always like what he said. I let it pass.

"Be careful driving home. I'll see you next time." He turned toward his desk.

I got up and left. I was grateful for the time to unload the inner conflicts and waves of anger that seemed to surface for no reason. Even today, there were so many ups and downs in my feelings as the session progressed. The usual pattern was to feel very agitated during the drive into town, and exhausted but relieved on the way home. Today I couldn't leave the session alone. I seemed so angry with both my parents, but especially my father. Nothing new had come out today. It was more the whole picture of my childhood that weighed on me, and most importantly what had happened to me so long ago that I could not let go.

16

IT WAS ALWAYS a mixture of dread and relief when I went to Dr. Thomas's office. I knew I had to go, I knew it would help me, but there was always that moment of hesitation when I thought about what it was going to entail. What I would have to tell that day? Rethinking during the week what had come out the week before. I couldn't see it then, but my real healing had begun with these sessions about my childhood.

Every time I went, I thought, now, what are we going to talk about today? I haven't the slightest idea, and what good is it going to do to rehash all these ugly things I remember? Why does bringing them up help anything? What is Dr. Thomas looking for anyway? Everything seemed to be a question. Where were the answers? I didn't know but I kept at the task.

This day I felt a little more relaxed and began more easily than usual. Dr. Thomas prodded me with a question.

"How would you describe yourself as a young girl?"

"I was ahead of my years–understanding the nature of animals, their habitat; and staying in the background for my own protection at home. In school life, I tried to buy friends. I was naïve and a tomboy. My companionship and identity with my father and the things which dominated his life, the sawmill business, the farms, and men's interests contributed to my tomboyishness. Daddy was my hero. I had come to worship him, and this adoration allowed me many things that perhaps would not have been mine had I not been so attentive and adoring of him. I had always disliked my mother, now I began to hate her. I thought her rage with Daddy all the time was the cause of his drinking."

Dr. Thomas spoke up. "I can see why you would think that. And often when both parents contribute to a child's misery, the child usually picks one and tries to make that one the hero. This is often a tough choice between two evils, but the child has to think at least one parent is better than the other or he would have no one."

I listened but I didn't like what he said. There was no doubt in my mind that my mother was much worse than my father. No real mother could make her husband whip a child and watch it happen. I wanted to yell this at him, but I didn't. I sat quietly for a moment. Then it came to me. I will tell him about Daddy's gifts. That will convince him I am right.

"Daddy used to give me nice things and do nice things for me. One of my gifts from him was a trip to the West."

"He gave you gifts, big gifts?"

"Yes, a lot of them. It seemed I was getting something all the time."

"That's interesting. Were your sisters jealous of you?"

"Yes, I am sure they were. But they were younger. Maybe I didn't pay any attention, or maybe I didn't want to think they were jealous."

"Tell me about this trip out West."

"Well, by 1948, the country had turned its attention inward and the war was becoming a brutal memory. Most of the men were home, including my uncles from the Air Force, the Army, and the Navy. And all of them on both sides of the family had come home without a scratch. I can't know how we were so lucky, because they were in the thickest of the fighting. One was a tank driver in Patton's army, one a fighter pilot who flew 98 missions over Germany, another a sailor on a submarine, another a foot soldier in the invasion of Sicily. There is no explanation for why some families suffered so much and others like ours suffered only the worry and heartache of loneliness for brothers, fathers, and sons. I am sure I am not the only one in the family who's felt a little embarrassed that we were so lucky. We couldn't believe we didn't have to pay our fair dues, even though we all supported the war efforts in every way. We were patriotic and never bought food on the black market or sold gas stamps for profit. The women prayed in church and cut bandages in the sewing circles."

"Your family was lucky during the war. Lots of families lost all their sons."

"That's true. I don't know why we didn't. My grandfather Trimball's roots were in South Dakota. He wanted to celebrate the good fortune of all his sons coming home by taking them to his homeland for pheasant season. His sister had a cattle ranch outside Wessington Springs. I was invited to go with my grandparents and one of the uncles and his new wife.

"At the time I had no idea what an opportunity was being given me. I knew I was the only one in my school going on such a trip, but I had no background for what the trip would mean. I was excited and eager to go to anyplace away from home. I kept a journal of roads, sights, rivers, cities, and events. Granddaddy had a new '48 Ford car and it seemed we flew across the country to South Dakota in no time at all and with no trouble.

"Aunt Ethelyn and her husband had seven children. They lived in a large farmhouse on lots of land, and had more cattle than I'd ever seen in one herd. In fact, everything about South Dakota seemed huge and different to me. Twelve people sat down to each meal at what seemed to be an endless table. If more hunters showed up, more leaves were put in the table. Loaves of bread were stored in the pantry with cakes, and pies in tins, and stacked on shelves to the ceiling. It was more baked goods than I could imagine anyone could eat. Aunt Ethelyn said you had to be prepared for whatever or whoever might come.

"I rode horses all day to the neighbors, whose house was so far away we couldn't see it from the road. The roads were not paved, but they were wide, and the ditches were very deep. They said the deep ditches would hold the snow. Windmills dotted the landscape in all directions. I had come to the windswept West and the dust swirled around the horses as we galloped down the straight corridor on the vast plain. Every once in a while, a tumbleweed would pass us as though it had somewhere to go and we were only ambling along, aimless and subdued by the swift wind. Then I would slap my horse with the reins and gallop after the tumbleweed, as Don Quixote chased imaginary enemies and tilted with windmills."

Dr. Thomas looked puzzled. "Why would you think of Don Quixote?

"Oh, because he was such a funny knight. He protected his damsels, but the ladies were all he thought about. He wasn't really a knight. He was make-believe, but so many people are taken in by that."

"You think he was a scallywag in all respects." Dr. Thomas stated with some edge to his voice that was unusual.

"Yes, all he was really interested in was sex. Everything else was a joke."

"So, you think Don Quixote was all about sex."

"Yes. Totally."

"That is very interesting that you would tie in sex with this trip. There is a deeper meaning here. We'll put it together later."

There always seemed to be a later time in Dr. Thomas's world. He was always saying we will understand that later. I was getting a little tired of later. I wanted to know now. But I went on with my story.

"Aunt Ethelyn's children were quizzical about why I had come. They were more quizzical about the fifty dollars my Daddy had given Granddaddy for the trip. To them, it seemed an unbelievable amount to give someone to come to South Dakota. It didn't really register with me, because I hadn't even seen the money. I just knew I could ask Granddaddy for money to buy gifts to take home for my mother and sisters, but nothing else.

"Also, I had a pair of white rabbit fur mittens with green leather palms. My cousins thought these were the prettiest mittens in the whole world. One of the girls especially liked them. She was crippled with polio and couldn't ride horses with us and go exploring. So, I left them in South Dakota for her. I heard that she wore them to school and a boy pushed her against the wood heater and burned the fur. She was heartbroken for having ruined the fur mittens. I understood what had happened, but I couldn't identify with the loss. Fur mittens were not a great loss to me.

"We were to stay two weeks. As the days slipped by, we were busy investigating the dugout used for protection against tornadoes, trying to understand the importance of the windbreaks around the house in guarding against the huge snowdrifts, and running through the lines of cottonwoods planted so the cattle could find protection from ice storms. It was a new and exciting world to me, so different from the orchards, woods, hills, valleys, and creeks at home. It was a world for which I had little understanding, but great interest in learning about. I wanted to stay, but the day before we were to leave came too quickly and I had to go into town to buy presents.

"The town was very small. There was a gas station, a café, and a hardware store that sold everything including souvenirs. Grandma wanted to help me choose the gifts, but I was sure I knew what everyone would want. I felt so grown up buying the gifts. I chose a tray with a pheasant painted on it for my mother, and Indian ponies for my sisters. For my class, I bought a little bottle of colored layers of sand from the Badlands. I had never seen bottled dirt before, but it looked just like what I had seen in the Badlands, so I knew it was real.

"Granddaddy had driven us out to the Badlands the day before. We drove along the highway and looked down on the treacherous gullies and broken rocks that would grow nothing. I listened to Granddaddy's stories of how the Indians had escaped with their lives so many times by going into the Badlands. Somehow, they miraculously found their way out before they died of thirst or starved. No living thing could last long under those conditions. Vivid pictures ran through my imagination, but more importantly the seeds of respect and tolerance for the Native

Americans were firmly planted in my mind where their growth was assured.

"The next morning, we packed the car to leave. I had not been homesick in the least. In fact, I had hardly thought about home. Aunt Ethelyn's house seemed so warm and the children were fun to be around. I tried to think of a way to get invited to live there, to grow up in South Dakota. Why not stay? We gathered outside for a picture. I was going to miss them. But Granddaddy said everyone at home missed me and I should go back. Everyone hugged me as I said goodbye. Finally, we were all in the car. I sat in the back seat so I could look out the rear-view window and wave as we drove down the dusty road to the highway for the last time.

"Granddaddy took us to Pierre, the capital of South Dakota, that afternoon. He thought I should see the capital. What he really wanted me to see was the Corn Palace in Mitchell. I couldn't imagine a building made entirely of corn. There were farms, windmills, cattle, pheasants, all things depicting scenes in South Dakota. The building itself covered a whole block. Late that afternoon we crossed the border into Iowa, and I glimpsed the last of the flat plains of South Dakota. The sun settled deep in the west as we were heading south over the river. I remember the long dark shadows that the bridge and the cars cast on the river below, an omen of things to come, but to me, it only marked the end of a beautiful stay in a place and time I would never forget."

"That sounds like quite a trip for you."

"Yes, it was. It's really like I can still remember every minute of that trip. It made me so happy for a while."

"Do you know why you can remember everything about that trip and there is so much you can't remember about your childhood in general?"

"No, I don't know why."

"Because I think you learned to bury things very early before you went to school. The older you got, the easier it became to bury whatever was unpleasant, or to be more exact, the horrific things that were happening to you."

I waited a few seconds, trying to take this in, then went on.

"It seems strange to me that I remember so little of the fifth grade except that I had the same teacher and there were still two classes in the room. I guess it was to save money, but each teacher had one full grade and half of another. This year my teacher, Miss Anderson, had the fourth grade and half my fifth grade. I had no idea how they divided the class between the teachers, but I suspected that most of the fifth grade in my class was the lower half of the class. My reasoning seemed solid because Linc and I had been split. He was in the sixth-grade room and I was in the fourth-grade room. Everyone knew that he was really smart. I don't remember being disappointed about my circumstances because I knew Miss Anderson.

"I don't know why I felt sorry for her particularly. There were many reasons that I could use. The most likely to me now is just a general feeling and identity with a person I recognized as equally lonely and inwardly unhappy as I was. Neither of us ever spoke to the other about our circumstances. I just remember her being very kind to me when she was not necessarily kind to others in the class.

"It is not fair to say that she was a typical teacher of the times, but there were others like her. Teachers were paid starvation wages. Miss Anderson not only had no money; she had no husband either. She lived with her mother and she was not attractive. She wore her hair in a bun, had metal frame glasses, and her shoes were the lace-up old-lady design. She wore a dark blue coat every day and a scarf over her head tied in the peasant manner. She had several dark dresses of the same cut and design with nearly the same print, which made them appear to be the same dress every day. She wore no make-up over skin that was grayish in color and accented by an almost dark thin mustache and thick eyebrows. She frightened some of the students, but not me.

"I don't remember her discipline; just that she was not able to keep order in the classroom. The year before there were two boys in the fifth grade who lived close to one another and played together all the time. They were constantly throwing spitballs, talking, laughing at Miss Anderson and making faces at her. Nothing worked! And unfortunately for everyone Miss Anderson ended up screaming, 'Now! Todd Jr.! Now! Jack Jr.! If you don't behave, I am going to send you to Miss Brown's office.'

"Miss Brown was the principal. The boys would laugh and say 'Miss Anderson, how are you going to send us? Are you going to send us through the mail?' There was another round of laughter. 'I am going to send you on a broomstick, which you deserve.' More laughter. Then she would grab them both by the shirt collar and march them off to Miss Brown's office."

"Children can be cruel, Can't they?"

"Yes, especially when the teacher has no control. Miss Anderson had everything wrong. She didn't have a clue about how to handle us. She always left the classroom door open so she could hear us. We never made any noise because we wanted to hear what was happening to the two bad boys. Usually, the next morning the mothers showed up before school so they could ask Miss Anderson's forgiveness and listen to the boy's apology. By afternoon something else was usually about to happen.

"Needless to say, I didn't learn very much either of those years. There was just too much to distract me. I did try though. I remember getting a D once on my report card in geography. For the rest of the year I practically memorized the book in order to do better. School was never easy for me."

"Miss Anderson needed a class in behavior modification, don't you think?"

"Yes, definitely, I feel sorry for her now. Then I disliked her just like everyone else, but I wasn't bad in class."

"I doubt that you were ever bad in class."

I smiled a little to myself. Maybe not, but how does he know?

"I did have a friend that year, who was one of the most popular girls with the boys and girls in our class. She was pretty. She had a mother who would take her and her friends places, and her hair was always in place. All things I yearned for. Especially, I wanted a mother who was interested in me and my activities. The only thing Peggy and I really had in common was clothes.

"My mother would buy me almost anything because she loved

to shop. Peggy's mother made most of her clothes, but they were fashionable and pretty.

"That reminds me that Bull Jackson was still in my class. She sat on the back row and almost never said a word. She learned to make herself as invisible as possible. There were many reasons why she wanted to be invisible. She was taller than everyone, even the boys. She was older, not bright, not attractive, and worst of all she was the product of incest. Bull Jackson–even now I cringe when I hear the name. In the fifth grade, I wanted to stand up for her when the boys teased her, but I wasn't strong enough. I just smiled at her and tried to be nice without calling attention to myself.

"But there was a time when all three of us found ourselves bound together: Miss Anderson, Bull Jackson, and me. On days when things had been bad at home the night before, I would want to stay in at recess and watch out the window instead of risking something happening on the playground to make my day worse. The three of us would find ourselves standing in front of the radiator and watching the fun outdoors. Somehow it felt safe. Maybe the three of us drew strength from each other. Maybe the others knew about me as I knew about them. Maybe we simply sensed each other's thoughts and had no reason to question or comment to each other.

"When I entered the sixth grade, I moved across the hall. Again, there were two classes, but I had been moved up to what I thought was the top of the sixth grade. I thought this because Linc had been moved to my section, and I knew he was the smartest student in the class. We found ourselves put in with the seventh grade with the principal, Miss Brown, as our teacher.

"Miss Brown was a very different person from Miss Anderson. They had several things in common. They were both old maids, they both lived with their families, and they had grown up in the same community. They were probably about the same age and they certainly dressed alike. However, as teachers, they were miles apart. Miss Brown was a great disciplinarian. Her words always meant something. They were never to be ignored or taken lightly. The girls and boys respected Miss Brown.

"Our year would have certainly been different if teaching us had been Miss Brown's only job. As the principal, she sometimes had to leave the room during class. Even then, Miss Brown had a way of monitoring us. She left the door open. Our voices would blare up and down the hallway as if they came through the speakers of a powerful radio. If she heard these voices the whole class was punished severely."

"No recess?"

"You know, I don't remember anything about what she actually taught. I just remember how neat and clean we kept the room and the respect we showed her. Miss Anderson only achieved minimum respect. Neither of them sought or received any show of love or affection. I do remember exactly what both of them looked like and what it felt like to be in their class.

"I always did my homework and tried to study. Sometimes it was impossible if Daddy had been late coming home, or worse yet had been drinking. At school the worst day of the week was Friday for two reasons. One—we always had our weekly spelling test on Friday right after lunch. I dreaded the test because I never did well. Of course, as I have said, no one knew it then, but I was dyslexic, and no matter how hard I studied, the words just didn't sound like the letters I heard. Even worse, Miss Brown graded the papers right after the test with everyone looking on, then put the grades on the graph in the back of the room. Of course, my grades were always the lowest and I felt so ashamed. Many of the smart seventh-grade boys would laugh and poke fun at my chart.

"The second reason for dreading Fridays was it meant the weekend was coming. Weekends were always much worse at home. Daddy would come home half-drunk on Friday night; he'd leave on Saturday morning and be very drunk on Saturday night. That led to a fight which lasted most of the night and the next day, Sunday. Enough time was taken out to go to church, which my mother hoped would cause some miracle to happen—maybe Daddy would stop drinking. My mother was not the only one to hope for a miracle. I did until the summer of my sixth-grade year."

"Worry was a big part of your life, wasn't it?"

"Yes, it was. I'm sure there were few hours of any day during my childhood that I wasn't worrying about what was happening with my father and mother. It's like they consumed me and there was no way to get away from them."

"That's certainly the picture you paint for me, but why did you stop hoping for a miracle in the sixth grade?"

"My parents were both Baptists. My mother insisted on going to church every Sunday. We had Sunday School every Sunday and preaching twice a month. But the fourth Sunday in June, of every year, was homecoming followed by a week of revival every night. This was the highlight of the church year and much preparation went into the event. The women of the church would meet beforehand and decide who would have the minister, his family, and the visiting minister to dinner each night.

"Thursday night was always my mother's turn. She and the cook would spend the entire day preparing the food, setting the table with her finest china, and making everything in the house as tidy and neat as possible. The meat course was usually steak and sliced ham. They were considered the best. The vegetables were always straight from the garden, fresh and abundant. There were new boiled potatoes, juicy ripe tomatoes of a blood-red color, yellow squash cooked with onions and butter, lima beans with butter and a touch of sugar, fresh beets sliced and dotted with butter, string beans cooked with a ham hock, and hot rolls. Dessert included several different pies, lemon chess, chocolate, and coconut.

"The ministers always seemed appreciative of my mother's efforts and always had seconds. Their conversation didn't interest me. Thursday being next to the last night of revival interested me. Tomorrow night, Friday would be the end for another year. We rarely missed a night of revival because my mother always secretly hoped that Daddy would be born again, saved, and stop drinking. It was always my wish, too. If Daddy would stop drinking all our lives would be different. I could stop worrying. That was my greatest desire.

"On this particular night, the ministers were dressed in their white Palm Beach suits with red ties and red handkerchiefs in their lapels. They certainly stood out before the farmer congregation. There were several hymns to begin the evening followed by taking up the offering to pay the visiting minister. Then the serious message began. There were different stories told, different verses read, but the theme was always the same: saving your soul. This visiting minister seemed to me to be sincere in what he was saying. Like God really could and would answer prayers and make things better. I listened all through the sermon, sitting in the second row between Mama and Daddy. I looked at them several times and I could tell my mother was really listening, but I couldn't tell about Daddy. He looked at the preacher, but I guessed his thoughts were about whether he had enough timber bought up, and if he had enough money in his bank account. I didn't think his thoughts were on his soul. The sermon became more and more stirring. The preacher's voice rose and subsided, with his hand motions and steps toward the congregation and back. I felt the Lord's presence in the church, listening. I just couldn't see Him.

"Finally, the most important moment of the revival came. The ministers gave the invitation for us to come forth and confess our sins to the minister and promise to do better. There was always a hymn. This night it was 'Just as I Am.' The minister began his plea as the congregation sang, *'Just as I am, without one plea.'*

"The minister's voice rose above the singing. 'Won't you come?' He raised his arms as if to beckon us out of our seats. 'Only God knows what is in your heart. He is the only one who can help you. Come before it is too late.' Someone comes down the aisle. 'Bless you friend. You have made the right choice.' A man went up and took the preacher's hand. The preacher leaned over and whispered in the man's ear, then raised his arms again to plead with the congregation. 'Don't hold back because you are embarrassed, or afraid, you should only be afraid if you don't come.'

"The hymn continued, *'with many a conflict, many a doubt, fighting's and fears, within, without, O Lamb of God, I come, I come.'*

"My hands were gripping the back of the pew in front of me, but the urge to move overwhelmed me and I felt myself pushing past Daddy to get to the aisle. Once there I hurried to the preacher and asked him to tell God to help me. I didn't say what for, but my thoughts were only on Daddy as if I were praying as hard as I could for him to stop drinking. The preacher released my hand, and as I turned to go back to sit down, I saw my mother and father coming to the preacher, too. My heart leaped. Maybe it would work. Maybe Daddy wouldn't drink anymore. As the hymn ended, I felt so happy and relieved. Maybe I had done some good. Maybe Mama was right. All you needed was faith.

"After the service, the minister came over to me and took my hand. 'Young lady you did a good thing tonight and I appreciate the influence you had on your parents too. God Bless you.'

"That night as I lay in bed, I thanked the good Lord for saving Daddy. I knew it was the Lord's work and I was only the messenger. I just knew a new day would dawn for all of us.

"I don't want to say here how the story ended. I want to be able to say the preacher and I were right, that Daddy was reborn that night and it was all because of me. That's what I want to say, but that isn't what happened. Daddy had not had anything to drink all week while he was going to church, but he couldn't make it past the next Saturday night.

"That Saturday night I knew that indeed I was in this world by myself. If God couldn't help me, nobody could. I had to rely on myself for survival. A door closed on my heart that weekend. I had already learned that I couldn't count on my mother and father, and now I knew I couldn't count on God. He may be out there for some people, but he wasn't for me. I felt rejected once again, and very angry."

"That must have been a very hard time for you. To be disappointed in a strong belief is a very damaging thing to your ego and confidence. And I am sure you were very depressed."

I nodded my head, yes. "I don't remember anything about it or how long I felt bad."

"I doubt that you do, but I know you felt very low for a while."

"I knew I had been selfish in asking God to help Daddy because I was really asking for help for me. It was the fights that bothered me the most. Maybe that was what was wrong. God knew I was being selfish in my prayers. I still go to church, sing, play the organ, but it is the wounded child within me that keeps me from believing in a God who stops fathers from drinking or who makes mothers kind to their children.

"Later that summer the Army decided they no longer needed to be in the horse business. All the remount stations were to be closed. These stations had supplied the Army with horses and mules since the Civil War. The remount station raised horses and mules and, in most cases, improved the stock for the local people by offering superior stallions for public use. Belmead was a remount station in the next county. It was on a 3,500-acre antebellum plantation built by the Brooke family. The Catholic Church owned it during the war and rented it to the government as a remount station. The plantation was large enough for a Negro boys' school, as well, which was also run by the Catholic diocese.

"The stables were on a high hill overlooking the James River and its low grounds below. Behind the stables were endless paddocks, riding rings, dressage arenas, and cross country courses to train the cavalry horses. In addition to the training stables, there were broodmare barns, breeding sheds, and stallion barns. The remount stations resembled the European breeding farms. Belmead was as large and productive as any. When the orders came to close, an auction was held and everything sold–horses, equipment, tack, jumps, and wagons. Daddy went to the Belmead sale and bought World War I wagons, dump carts, breaking carts, harness, work harness, parade dress harness, saddles, and so on.

"Not long after the sale, Daddy came home one evening and said he had bought me a horse and we would go pick it up Saturday morning. I couldn't believe my ears. I had wanted a nice horse to show for so long and nothing had happened. Now, with no prompting, Daddy had bought me a horse. It was one of the longest weeks of my life and it was one weekend I didn't dread. Nothing could dampen my excitement for a horse. I was twelve years old then and my interest in horses was set. Horses had been in my dreams, my mainstay for so long now, the one thing that never let me down and the one thing that was always there.

"I was up early on Saturday morning waiting for Daddy to say it was time to go. I sat on the seat beside him in the truck and imagined the most wonderful things we would do together. When we pulled into the stable yard, everything looked the same, except it was quiet. There were no soldiers in tall boots, no horses with their heads over the Dutch doors trying to see what was happening outside, no wheelbarrows rolling along the walkways going to the manure dump, and no anxious knickers from the stallion barn. It was quiet, an eerie quiet that made me sad. Daddy got out of the truck and slammed the door. 'Stay there. I'll be back in a minute.'

"I didn't dare move or say anything, even though I wanted to go with him so badly. I wanted to see the horse, but I waited. The sun grew hot and I stuck to the leather seat in the truck. I tried to rest my chin on the window, but it was too hot. Finally, I saw Daddy and another man coming across a far paddock. I couldn't contain myself any longer. I jumped out of the truck and ran to them. I had a real horse at last."

"'How do you like her?'" the man asked as soon as I got there.

'Oh! She's beautiful.' I could hardly get my breath.

'Her name is Lady Merci,' he said. 'That means thank you in French. That's her registered name. She's a Thoroughbred. Her mother was one of our best mares.'

"Daddy looked at her intently. 'You say she's three years old and broke to ride.'

"'Yes, they started breaking them at two years and then put them to work at three. There's not a thing wrong with her except she throws that left foot out in front and she has that little bump on her hock.'

"Daddy said slowly. 'Yes, you told me, but that won't hurt her for what we want.'

'No, she'll be fine for your little girl to ride around the farm.'

"I didn't know what they were talking about, nor the consequences. I was so excited to at last have a real horse. A horse that I thought I could show, too.

"The men loaded her on the truck, and we left Belmead for the last time. I watched out of the window, somehow knowing the scene before me was about to slip into time forever. As we headed for home, I turned to look back at Lady. She was a bright chestnut with a big star and one hind white sock. Her eyes were large and expressive, but you could see a little white on the edges. To me there was nothing wrong and I was going to make her the best horse in the world. We would win blue ribbons at the shows and she would be my best friend always.

"Daddy turned to look at her and said, 'Well, there's one thing for sure, you'll have the prettiest horse at the shows.'

"It was years before I realized the significance of that statement. Daddy never admitted or acknowledged any understanding of why he had bought this particular mare. And even now I am not going to accuse him of knowing he bought me a flawed horse when I don't know for sure. But I think what happened was that Lady was not included in the sale because she had two bad flaws. She had a capped hock which meant probably as a foal she had been kicked on the hock and it swelled, and the bump never went down. The other was she paddled with her right front foot, which meant the ankle bone was crooked and she threw her right front foot out when she moved. If this is not corrected as a foal it can't be corrected.

"Lady did become my best friend and almost constant companion. As I grew in knowledge and technique in riding, I became aware of Lady's shortcomings. I tried corrective shoes for her in the front and various liniments on the hock. It never occurred to me to think that Daddy had consciously chosen a flawed horse for me because she was cheaper. It's only since I began to learn the truth about other things in my childhood that I realized that my father could do such a terrible thing to me. There is no doubt in my mind that a cheap price was his motive for buying Lady.

"Realizing this is made worse because I was so innocent and trusting in his judgment and caring for me. It is hard for me to believe he would buy such a horse and watch me get beat in the show ring many times over when it had nothing to do with me. But

I was riding a horse that had too many blemishes to start with, many more than we could overcome and get a good ribbon. I loved Lady and kept her until she died. It breaks my heart now to think of all the work I did in training, and in trying my best every time in the show ring, only to have the cards stacked against the horse and me from the beginning. It was not a question of money. Daddy was well on the way to creating his fortune by 1948. I could have had a child-broke, perfectly built, blue-ribbon winner."

"You have a lot of things to overcome in this story."

"I am sure I do."

"There's plenty of time. We'll start back on this next time, okay?"

I stood to go. "Thanks, I'll be here." There was a lot to think about on the way home. I never knew when I reached a conclusion in therapy or really what precipitated it. I do know the drives home were as good as the drives to the office for thinking through events. I kept analyzing Daddy's motive in buying Lady all the way home. He knew there were several things wrong with her when he bought her. Was I worth that little to him? Was it simply a matter of money? He knew she didn't sell in the sale. It was easy to buy her because he knew the managers so well. Nothing seemed to come to mind that would explain things differently. By the time I reached home I was deeply depressed.

17

THE WEEKS ROLLED by as we delved into my childhood. I didn't know what we were looking for. It seemed I had told Dr. Thomas everything. But there always seemed to be more. What were we looking for? Dr. Thomas said we were looking for things in my childhood that related to the person I was now. It was true. All the little happenings were giving him a picture of how I related to my father and the rest of the family and my friends.

"The next fall I entered high school. It was the only white high school in the county. But we were not really in high school. It was the newly added year before high school. We were thirteen and entering the eighth grade. When Linc and I began the eighth grade, there were two classes of about twenty-five each, each one evenly divided between girls and boys. When we finished in the twelfth grade there were only nineteen left, many more girls than boys.

"That year I found many things different from elementary school. The first being that much older girls and boys rode the bus, stood in the hallways and ate lunch with us. I was very shy, and it took a lot of nerve just to walk around them. The boys especially were so old and grown-up.

"I stumbled along until Christmas when the most wonderful, amazing thing happened to me. The last day of school before the holidays was set aside to celebrate the coming holiday season. There was a Christmas assembly in the morning followed by a very special Christmas dinner with turkey, gravy, cranberry sauce, mashed potatoes, green beans, and hot rolls that were as light as any feather that floated across a chicken yard. Dessert was home-made yellow cake with white icing. And just for Christmas, the head cook, Mrs. Brown, no kin to the principal, put a piece of peppermint on each square of cake. On this day every student in the school ate in the lunchroom even if they couldn't pay the twenty cents. The principal kept a small stash of money in his office for such emergencies.

"After lunch, we all assembled in the auditorium to give out the many presents stacked high on the stage. We had drawn names before, and certain students and a teacher checked the roll that morning to make sure every student had a present. We all sat with our friends and waved our hands when our name was called. I don't remember who drew my name, and I don't remember the presents from my girlfriends, but I have a vivid memory of two presents from boys. My friends had teased me about getting presents from boys, but I had no idea it was really going to happen. No one was dating then, except on special occasions, and then it was with a group at a basketball game, a community dance, or church social.

"When my name was called for a big box wrapped in green foil tied with the biggest gold bow I had ever seen, I gasped for breath. 'Oh! Look. Is that for me?' The student delivering it said, 'That's what it says on the tag. Lesley, that's your name isn't it?'

"I grinned. 'Yes! You know that's my name.'

"My friends couldn't contain themselves. 'I bet it's from Mike.'

'No, I think it's from Linc,' said another.

"'Oh! You all don't know. Let me see,' I said. I untied the bow carefully. The ribbon was so pretty I didn't want to break it. The paper came off in one piece. Then my curiosity took over and the paper dropped to the floor and my hands tore into the box. I took wads of paper out of the box, but no present. I was almost at the bottom.

"My friends began to make comments.

"'Lesley, there's nothing in the box.'

"'That's a dirty trick.'

"'Who sent you that?'

"They grabbed the tag and looked. 'There's no name.'

"I dug to the bottom of the box and my hand felt something. 'Here it is.' I pulled my hand from the box quickly. There was a beautiful brown and tan billfold. My friends were impressed. 'Isn't that pretty?', 'We told you it was from Mike', 'Where's the tag?'

"My best friend said, 'See if it says, 'Love, Mike'. I know it does.'

"My patience was running out. 'Just wait a minute. I don't know who it's from.'

"By this time the paper, ribbon, box, stuffing were all on the floor. I had to find the tag. I began looking through the pockets in the billfold for something that would tell me who gave it to me. All eyes were on the billfold as I flipped through the plastic inserts. There on the very last one was a picture of a boy.

"'It is Mike!' they all screamed at once. 'We told you so.'

"Another friend said, 'Bet it says 'Love, Mike' on the back.'

"My fingers were trembling as I pulled the picture out. Sure enough 'Love Mike' was scrawled on the back

"A few minutes later my name was called again. This time my friends were much more vocal and confident. 'This one is from Linc for sure', 'Open it', 'Let's see what he gave you', 'I bet it's a pen. He's so intellectual.'

"This box was much smaller and not as prettily wrapped. But that didn't hamper my excitement over getting another gift from a boy. I unwrapped it quickly and took off the top and tore away the top paper.

"We were all quiet at once. Each of us looked in the box. Each of us was startled at what seemed to be the contents.

"There was a serious 'ah' from all of us as I took the second box from the package.

"'Oh, it's a box of face powder.'

"It began to register on everyone's mind. 'Oh, Lesley, Linc gave you a box of face powder.'"

"'Isn't that funny?'

"'Evening in Paris! Oh là là!'

"'Now, what are you going to do?'

"'See what the powder looks like.'

"I couldn't think why in the world he would give me such a strange gift. It wasn't as though he was my boyfriend or anything like that. He was young, my age. He was overweight, and in my mind not in the least attractive. And I had never heard of a boy giving a girl face powder in my life. But my curiosity was too strong. I had to look in the box. I wiggled the top and twisted it around until it came off. I held both parts of the box, one in each hand. For a minute no one said anything.

"Then there were peals of laughter from my friends as they poked a finger in the powder and flicked it in the air. 'Lesley!!! That's not powder! That's sawdust!' The laughter grew louder and louder. Soon everyone around us was laughing, except me. My humiliation was complete. I couldn't look up. I could only look down. I wanted the floor to open up and swallow me, seat and all, in one great gulp. I never wanted to be seen again by anyone. My supreme moment was gone forever. No one would remember that I had received two gifts from boys. They would remember only that one of them was a box of sawdust.

"The chorus around me continued. 'Did you see what Linc gave Lesley?'

"'No, what did he give her?'

"'A box of sawdust. Hahaha!'

"'It was in an Evening in Paris box.'

"'She thought it was face powder.'"

"'We all thought it was.'

"'That's awful. I'd kill him with my bare hands.'

"'Don't worry I think she's going to as soon as she can find him.'

"I had to get up and leave. I couldn't bear it any longer. I managed to grab all of my, what was now trash, and the billfold, and run.

"My homeroom was on the second floor and the steps were crowded with students talking about their presents and making plans for the holidays. I met Linc just as I walked through the door. 'How could you do this?'

"He was grinning. 'You mean the present?'

"'Yes. What else would I mean?'

"He kept grinning. 'I thought it was funny.'

"'Well, it isn't funny. It embarrassed me to death.'

"'I didn't mean to embarrass you.' He had almost stopped laughing now that he realized I was so serious.

"I was almost in tears at this point. 'You did embarrass me, and I never want to speak to you again.'

"By then I was near the trash can and everything in my hands went in it except the billfold. I turned to face Linc and held the billfold up. 'Mike gave me this and you gave me a box of sawdust!'

"Linc wouldn't give up. 'I just found the empty box and I thought it was a good joke.'

"'I hate jokes and I hate you.'

"We were both saved by the bell. I couldn't believe he could do such a thing and think that I would take it as a joke. We were saved again by not riding the same bus home. Mike and I did ride the same bus and I found a seat near him. Mike was in the tenth grade and much more mature than Linc. It made me feel better to tell him thank you. I could tell he was pleased that I liked it."

"Maturity is a great thing sometimes. This sounds like one of those times too."

"It's so strange that I put up with Linc all those times when he did such awful things."

Dr. Thomas smiled but made no comment. I went on to get away from the subject.

"Mike and I dated all through high school, but as is so often the case when we are young, my head was turned by more athletic boys. I was never attractive to the ballplayers for many reasons. The fact is, I was too much 'one of the boys' to be attractive to them. And I felt I was not pretty. I suffered from acne throughout my teens. My hair was not stylish, and I wasn't voluptuous which is always an asset as a teen. I have to say, had I been more feminine I would have been more attractive."

Dr. Thomas interrupted, "We've discussed how this comes about with girls who are abused. It's a phenomenon that often happens when the young girl wants to be attractive to masculine-type boys probably like her father, but only having her father as a role model she adopts the wrong signals."

"Yes, I can see this goes back to my father. I would talk to the boys about all the wrong things, like trucks, hunting, other girls. I didn't know how to talk like the other girls. And besides, Daddy liked me, and I talked to him about the business, and so on. And when I was teased, I fought back which was even worse.

"I was powerless to do anything about him or my home life. All the fighting at home made it imperative I keep up with the horses. Of course, it's possible to ride and be ever so feminine. But it's harder when you're forced to be in charge. I was in charge of the horses and showing. I made the entries, decided on the classes we would show in, what shows to attend, and what tack we needed to take. Partly, because I was five years older than my next sister, and because I had grown up thinking I had to watch out for both of them, I was the caretaker at the shows. My mother rarely went with us, and if she didn't go Daddy was always drunk, so I had to take on the responsibility."

I stopped talking for a minute to think. "You say being sexually abused causes many girls to become tomboys and grow into lesbians. I was certainly a tomboy growing up. And I understand this because I was with my Daddy so much more than my mother. He started taking me with him as a toddler and it continued throughout my teens. I went with him to the mills, to see his friends, and on business. Wherever he went, you might find me. I learned to think like a man. I missed learning what most girls learn from their mothers. I can't say why I didn't learn much from my mother. She was certainly feminine, but something was very wrong between us. I'm sure the alcohol made things worse."

Dr. Thomas nodded. "Alcohol makes everything worse for everybody."

I answered, "It surely did for us. I knew I was a girl, but I wanted to be a boy. I thought if I were a boy, Daddy would be happier.

Maybe if I was a boy, he wouldn't have to lie to me and say he wouldn't drink anymore, and then hurt me so badly by making Mama fuss all the time. Maybe if I were a boy, I wouldn't have to buy his love and my mother's by trying to be so good. Whatever the reason, the alcohol ruined my childhood and my adult life. I was under my father's spell and remained there until my ongoing liberation by you with therapy when I was in my early fifties.

"The one thing I am thankful for remains the fact that somehow my female gene was strong enough to throw off the violence and deprivation of my childhood. I have much sympathy for lesbians for what they have suffered. My heart cries out to them because many of them were not born lesbians, but were made lesbians by a parent. They have to live in a man's world on two fronts, sexually and socially. We who escaped this fate have only to live in the social world and live with the love–hate for men in our hearts that our fathers created. I know that my experience is only my own, but I feel it is in some ways typical."

"That's very insightful, Mrs. Owens, and compassionate on your part. You were very lucky to have been born with such strong feminine genes. But, who's to say, you may have been happy as a lesbian."

"No, no," I said. "I'm sympathetic but I'm straight."

"Yes, I think you are." He laughed.

"There was something else that happened in high school that directly relates to the whole story of my relationship with my father and with Linc. It happened when Linc and I were juniors."

"Please, let's hear it."

"There was a boys' club called the Future Farmers of America, or FFA. Nearly all the boys belonged because there was something to interest all of them: agriculture, forestry, or mechanics. This year they decided to sponsor a sweetheart contest as a means of raising money for the club. Each boy was to pick a girl, and the boy who raised the most money for his girl won the contest and she was the FFA sweetheart.

"They signed up on Friday afternoon and set a time limit of three weeks to raise the money. Linc and I had been dating all through high school, not steady, but enough for me to think he should sponsor me. I certainly wanted to have a sponsor.

"By the end of school everyone knew who the girls and sponsors were. And Linc had not chosen me. He tried to explain it away as he had the box of sawdust, but it didn't work. His story was that there was a lot of jockeying for position during the sign-up. Mike did not belong to the club. He was interested in art and debating and drama.

"A friend of Linc's came to him with a proposition. Tom was one of the best-looking boys in school and certainly the most popular with the girls. He was handsome, had a new car, played ball, and had a family with lots of money. In most cases, he had his pick of the girls. But, he had too many girls at the moment and went to Linc for help. There was a buzz in the classroom with all the talk about the girls. Linc was leaning over a desk watching another boy draw airplanes. Tom spoke quietly trying not to draw attention. His light blonde hair fell across his forehead in a swoop and his blue eyes were always twinkling even when he was serious. Even white teeth and a deep masculine voice made every girl's heart skip a beat. I heard Tom say, 'Linc, will you talk to me a minute.'

"'Sure, what do you need?'

"'I need to ask you a favor.'

"'Okay. What is it?'

"'Have you signed up for a sponsor yet?'

"'No, I hadn't thought about it, really.'

"'Well, good. Look why don't you sponsor Peggy?'

"'Okay. I don't care. I guess I'll have to sponsor somebody, and one's as good as another, but why do you want me to do this?'

"'Well, if you sponsor Peggy, then I can sponsor Nell. You'll really do me a favor because Peggy's going to be mad if I don't sponsor her and nobody else does.'

"'Sure, I'll do that.'

"'Now, I'll tell her that you picked her first and I didn't have a chance. Then she won't be mad at me.'

"Linc grinned and shook his head, 'You sure do have a lot of trouble with your girls.'

"'Isn't that the truth? They worry me to death, but I can't do without them.'

"That afternoon on the bus, everyone knew who had been picked. It was the latest news. But there was one big surprise. Me. All the girls thought Linc should have picked me instead of Peggy. Peggy and I were still good friends. So I was angry with Linc, and Peggy was mad at Tom, and everyone else was having a great laugh at our betrayal.

"Linc got lots of phone calls over the weekend from girls on my behalf. By Monday morning Linc realized something else had to be done. And Tom wasn't too happy, either. Nell refused to go out with Tom that weekend because she thought he would do something equally as bad to her, and besides, he'd told her he had broken up with Peggy. Peggy refused to go out with him because he had chosen Nell over her.

"I had told Linc what I thought of their little plan on Saturday night. As usual, he laughed as one of my mother's figurines went flying past his head and shattered on the wall behind him. It did get his attention and he agreed to go home early. I think he was shocked by my explosion. To me, throwing a figurine was a small matter. I did it to show him how he had hurt and humiliated me again.

"Monday morning produced some immediate changes in the sponsor list. Linc and Tom rushed over to the agriculture building before school to see the teacher who was the club sponsor. They ran in and I don't know who spoke first, but my guess is it was Tom.

"'Mr. Gray, we've got to make some changes in that sponsor list.'

"'Good morning!'

"'Yes, good morning, we're sorry but we've had a bad weekend.'

"'What's the matter? Do you have some girls mad at you?'

"'Yes. Are you kidding? They want to lock us up and throw away the key.'

"'I thought you weren't going to get away with that when you signed up.'

"'You didn't?'

"'No, you boys don't know much about girls. Girls stick together.'

"'Well, all we know is it didn't work, and we want to change it.'

"'All right, let's see what we need to do. Okay. Linc wants to sponsor Lesley and Tom wants to sponsor Peggy. Nell will be left out.'

"'Yes, but how did you know that?'

"Mr. Gray laughed. 'I think everyone knew but you.'

"Linc and Tom looked pretty sheepish when they came to class. Especially when one girl looked at them and said point blank, 'Did you change sweethearts?'

"The weeks passed quietly until the last day. There had been a lot of excitement about who had raised the most money and who was going to be queen. Everyone made bets privately. Linc had not raised much. I just didn't want to be left out. By lunchtime Peggy was leading and everyone thought she was going to be the Sweetheart. But Linc had left school and gone to see my father. No one knew this except the principal. Linc was totally confident and felt comfortable going to my father and asking for money to help me win the contest.

"Daddy's office was one big room with desks for the bookkeepers and himself. His desk was the closest to the door so you could talk to him without disturbing the bookkeepers at work. Linc has told me what happened.

"He knocked and went in slowly. 'Mr. Jacobs, could I talk to you a minute?'

"Daddy was sitting behind his desk looking at the mail. He had on his work clothes which were khaki pants and a shirt. His hair was rumpled, and he hadn't shaved. I'm sure he wanted to know why this boy who dated his daughter wanted to see him in the middle of the day.

"'Our FFA is having a sweetheart contest at school and I'm sponsoring Lesley. I've collected some money, but I thought you might help me make her the winner.'

"'I see. What are you going to do with the money?'

"'Different projects that we're doing for the year.'

"'Hmmm.' He turned a little and looked at the floor. 'How much do you need to win?'

"'I have about twenty dollars and I think Kevin has about thirty-five, as best I can tell, so twenty-five more should win.'

"Daddy turned to the bookkeeper. 'Write a check for twenty-five dollars and give it to Linc.'

"The bookkeeper got out the checkbook and laid it in front of him. 'Whom should I make this to?'

"'The FFA will be fine.' Linc was grinning. He had no idea it would be so easy to get another twenty-five dollars. And he thought this really should be enough. Those boys are going to be surprised and maybe Lesley will be happy.

"Linc put the check in his billfold and shook hands with Daddy. 'Thank you, Mr. Jacobs, and I sure hope Lesley wins. I really appreciate this, and the club will do something good with it.'

"'I hope you win, too.'

"Linc drove back to school in his father's '49 Ford. It was then the spring of 1954. He didn't have a car like many of the boys, but it didn't really bother him. He could use his Dad's car when he needed it, which was a better car than many of the boys had. The air was warm, and things seemed pretty good. He might even best them all and win this contest. 'It would be nice for Lesley,' he thought.

"He waited until two-thirty in the afternoon to turn in his money. Everyone else had turned in theirs and the whole school thought Kevin had won. Everyone was buzzing with the news when Linc walked into the agriculture building. 'Mr. Gray, I have some more money for the contest.'

"'Great! You just made it, didn't you?'

"'I guess so.' He fumbled in his pocket and grinned. He pulled his billfold out slowly and took a very long time to go through it.

"By this time everyone was standing around him waiting to see how much he had brought. Linc unfolded the check and handed it to Mr. Gray without a word.

"Mr. Gray looked at it and broke out laughing. 'Linc, I believe you won, boy. These twenty-five dollars will put you over the top.'

Everybody chimed in 'Greatttttt dayyyyyy Who gave him twenty-five dollars?'

"'Mr. Jacobs did. That's who. Linc, you were a smart boy. You waited till the last minute and went down there at lunchtime and got enough to win. That beats all I ever saw.'

"Kevin was the only person not laughing. He was shocked at first, then a slow scowl came across his face. 'Let me see that check.' He grabbed the check and looked at it carefully. 'It's twenty-five dollars sure enough. But, that ain't fair. You know it. I went out and asked a lot of people all weekend and Linc ain't done nothing but go down and ask Mr. Jacobs for some money so Lesley could win. That's what he done.'

"'Ah, Kevin don't be so jealous. Linc just out-smarted you.'

"'He did not. Everybody was supposed to turn the money in at the same time.'

"'There is nothing wrong with him waiting.'

"'That's not true. It wasn't fair, I tell you.'

"'You'll just have to work harder next time.'

"'That ain't gonna happen because there ain't gonna be a next time.'

"The boys were still laughing as Kevin left the building to get his car and go home. He was a poor loser, but to them, it was still funny. Linc had beat him and all the others fair and square. It was so surprising because it was out of character for Linc to do something like that."

"It sounds like Linc really came through, doesn't it? He seems to have put a lot of thought in this."

"Yes, I have to say I was really impressed."

"I know it helped your self-esteem for a little while anyway."

"Yes, except that it was Daddy's money that won. Later that weekend Linc told me he just wanted to do something nice for me. He thought I would like being the FFA Sweetheart. I was just as surprised as Kevin when they told me. Everyone seemed fine with my winning, but I felt strange because I had always been conscious that Daddy's money had been at work. I knew I would never have won if Daddy had not given the money.

"The night of the banquet Daddy and I both were invited. Linc made the announcement of the winner and presented me with the jacket. It was great to win and be pronounced the sweetheart, but I knew in my heart it wasn't true. There were lots of other girls that most of the boys would rather have had as sweetheart, but no one said anything.

"It was not until Daddy was introduced and he stood up that I really understood why he had given the money. It was for his own pride and prestige. It was written all over his face and manner. He was so proud of his ability to be able to buy this prize for his daughter. I'm sure he was glad I gave him the opportunity, but he had won the prize.

"I didn't wear that jacket much for several reasons. The first was, I had never won many things–some ribbons–and there was not going to be another opportunity to be a club sweetheart, so I wanted to keep the jacket clean and perfect. The other was, I was not really comfortable wearing it because it made me stand out and called attention to me. I knew somehow that I didn't reflect what most people thought a sweetheart should be. For what I lacked in not wearing the jacket, I made up in getting it out of my closet and looking at it. It was the source of many fantasies over the years.

"The jacket is still with me. It's stored in my attic with other objects that bring back memories from long ago. It's moth-eaten and yellow from age, but it will never lose its luster for providing one beautiful but shadowed moment for me."

18

AFTER EIGHT YEARS, Dr. Thomas and I had covered all the material of my family's background, and my childhood until adolescence, and nothing had emerged to indicate a greater problem to me. I thought we had solved all my problems. The doctor knew better. I was much more at ease with him, my depression was better, and I had learned a great deal about my emotional well-being and how to understand my need for attention and affection. But the real problems remained. I still had terrible nightmares, I still broke into rages, and there was a deep sense of a great loss in my life. What was the problem? What had caused this wide chasm in my life? There had to be an answer. I was much closer to knowing that day than I could guess.

"Good morning! What's new and different this morning?" Dr. Thomas sat down. Still, after eight years, he seemed a youngish, trim, handsome man with a confident, easy manner. He wore glasses and smiled a lot. I had always felt at ease with him, never intimidated as I had been with so many men. I knew his office by heart. I could picture it in my mind, and I could call it up whenever I wished. I knew every piece of furniture, every picture, the lamps, every accessory, the clock, the box of tissues, the funny little pasteboard statue of him and his wife on his desk. It must have been made on his honeymoon.

They were a yuppie-looking couple, happy, relaxed carefree. She was pretty, with dark hair and a slight build. The statue always gave me a feeling of hope. It was a promise that things could be better, no matter how bad I felt.

I said, "I have only one thing on my mind. I want to know what happened to me?"

He looked at me for a long moment. He held my file which was at least four inches thick, resembling a well-used book with tattered pages sticking out around the sides. It was going into its ninth full year of use. I thought, 'That's a long time to see a psychiatrist'. I had watched the folder get thicker and thicker over the years. I had made progress. I no longer screamed and yelled and beat up on people, especially my husband. The medicine and the therapy had helped me to keep my anger under control. But there were times when the old wounds would open, and the depression would pull me into the muck and mire of self-hatred. I would soon learn who was responsible for that condition.

"Well, let's see." He looked at me for a long while. My statement didn't seem to be a surprise. It was clear that he had already given this a lot of thought. He kept glancing through my file and looking up at me. Finally, he put the cover back on his pen and closed the file with the daily charge sheet on the outside. He began slowly turning the pen in his hand.

"For patients who have deep-seated subconscious secrets, we have a truth serum that will unlock these long-closed doors during what we call Amytal interviews. But I must warn you, they are very dangerous because you are going against nature."

"What do you mean?"

He fidgeted in his chair and looked very serious. "You know, when a child is molested, the pain is often so bad the event is locked in the subconscious and never allowed to come to the surface. This simply allows the conscious mind to exist, to be free of the terrible fear. The conscious mind pretends the event or events never happened. Then when you dig these memories out, you have to be very sure that the conscious mind is ready and willing to handle whatever the terrifying memories are. And they are horrible. Or you would be able to remember them."

"I see." I felt chilled as he talked. I ran my finger over the pattern in the couch cover. I had never heard of anything like this. But, above all, I wanted to know what had happened to me.

"And there are only three times that we ever use this method. Number one." He struck the pen against his finger as he talked. "When the patient is suicidal, and we have exhausted every means of medication and therapy to get to the bottom of the cause. Number two, when the patient is totally out of control as far as harming others is concerned. And number three, when there is something physically wrong like holding one's arm in the air constantly, an action that impairs the patient's well-being. And even then, we do very few of these treatments. I do maybe one a year. It's rare because I must stress again, it is so dangerous."

I looked down. "I guess that eliminates me because I'm certainly not suicidal. I don't yell and scream as much anymore, and there's nothing physically wrong with me except I can't remember and I can't stop crying." I reached for a tissue and struggled with the tears running down my cheeks and gasping for my voice. "I can't stand it when I cry, but I always do."

He looked at me and nodded quietly. "It doesn't matter if you cry."

I dabbed at my eyes, smoothed my hair, got another tissue as the tears continued to stream despite all my efforts.

He looked at me thoughtfully. "Your case is different because you've been struggling with this for so long, and particularly this time. What has it been? It's been several months now that you have been talking about what really happened to you as a child."

"Yes. It all started one night about a month ago with this movie on TV. I don't know why it set me off, but I've been thinking about what happened to me ever since. It was about this man who had sexually molested his daughter. He had lied and deceived his wife into thinking she was crazy by giving her drugs. And he was a doctor."

"I see."

"It had nothing to do with what I thought had happened to me, but now I don't know."

"You mean you think it could have been your father."

"I don't know. That's the point. I've never known what happened. That's not true. I've always known what happened, but not how or when or who. I just don't know." The tears now had turned to sobs and I could hardly get my breath enough to talk.

"I know you don't know, and we can do an Amytal interview. It's just that you have to realize how dangerous this is, and you have to be prepared for whatever you remember. Do you understand that? You should give it a lot of thought."

"I will. I just want to know the truth. It's as though I have been living a lie all my life. If I thought it was one person, and if it was really my father, I want to know it. Besides, it couldn't have been the crippled man. I would have awakened before he got halfway into the room."

"So, when do you want to do this? I will be away about a week for Labor Day and then I won't be away again until Christmas. I want to be here after we do this. It will probably take about three sessions and you will have to be in the hospital as a day patient to do this. It usually takes about six hours for the serum to work through your system. And your insurance will not pay for this. These interviews are never covered. It will probably cost three thousand dollars all told."

"I'm not making this up. I know something happened. I just can't remember. I remember the same thing now as I did that morning, nothing has changed in fifty-some years. I have been carrying this around. I want to be myself. I want to be rid of this dark secret."

"Yes, I understand. You just have to be absolutely sure you can handle whatever it is."

"I want to tell you something about my father that I remembered. It is crude and awful."

"Let's hear it."

"I don't remember how old I was, but I was little. Daddy had to go see a black man about working. When we got there the man was not there. A woman with a baby in her arms came out to the truck. Daddy looked at the baby and asked if it was a boy. She said yes and Daddy said what a fine big baby boy he was. Then he called the woman by name and said, 'Let me see that baby nurse', and she did. I don't know why I remembered that now, but I remember how I felt. I was embarrassed and ashamed."

"From what you've told me before, I think your father was a functioning alcoholic long before anyone knew it. That is a very strong statement even for the forties."

"Maybe he was drunk then, and I didn't know it. I remember how he leaned over to the woman to watch the baby pull at her nipple and push her breast with his hands. He wasn't a young baby. He was big and seemed so strong. I remember how Daddy was so intent on watching him and the grunting sounds the baby made. Daddy was making sounds too, sounds I can't really remember, but it was like he wanted to grab the baby and pull him away from his mother. And the baby would give him some great surge of happiness. It was hard to tell which one was gaining the most pleasure, the baby from nursing or my father from watching.

"I couldn't tell if the mother was embarrassed; she was just watching the baby and smiling. No one paid any attention to me. I wanted to cry, but I rubbed my toes in the dirt instead and listened and waited. It was a horrible scene to me. I was so anxious. I remember the woman was barefooted like me and she had on a brown dress that opened in the front with nothing underneath.

"Finally, Daddy said we had to go, and he told her to take care of that baby and to tell her husband something about work. Then he reached down and grabbed my hand and walked toward the truck with me in tow. I stood on the seat next to him. I always wanted to ride standing up. He started the truck and I turned and watched the woman walk back toward the house with the baby. I remember I wanted to go with her, she looked so calm carrying the baby and I thought she would be good to me. The truck went down the dirt road slowly and we all, the truck, Daddy and I faded out of sight. I can't remember anymore."

Despite all my efforts, the tears were still coming, and as soon as I walked out to the reception area, I was crying uncontrollably with heaves and sobs as though my heart would break. The receptionist could see I was out of control and took me back to the kitchen area for a cup of coffee and a time to get myself together. I cried for ten minutes by the clock, but I had no idea why I was crying. I just felt as though everything had been taken away from me. My old life, my father, everything I remembered as good had suddenly turned bad and there was nothing I could do to stop it. It was as though I knew what had happened to me, but I couldn't stand to admit it. I hated myself for feeling that way. It felt like I was betraying someone rather than the other way around, being betrayed.

To cry until I was exhausted and never know really why I was crying had been the pattern of my life. There was always something that started the tears, but there was always a deep, deep sorrow that I couldn't name. It was a terrible time.

But this time there was a deep realization that raked every fiber of my body. I knew in my heart that the father I loved, adored, respected, admired was the one responsible for my years of suffering. I wanted to die right there and never have to look another person in the eye. My thoughts kept saying there must be a mistake. It could not be true. My Daddy wouldn't do these awful things. The clock was right in front of me. The minutes ticked away. There was also a mirror. It showed me, through the clouds of despair, that my eyes were swollen, my cheeks were almost raw, and my expression was that of a mourner who had just confronted a terrible loss. I forced myself out of the chair and walked out the door. It was my first effort towards facing my past and my future. I managed a weak thank you to the receptionist as I walked past her.

I drove straight home, fifty miles, in silence. The countryside whizzed by the car as I sped down the road. There were times I had to think about where I was on the road. The time passed with the miles until I pulled into our drive. The dogs met me, wagging their tails, and I heard the guinea hens chirping as I went in the house and fell exhausted on the bed. I was one more session closer to the truth and the end of years of carrying the burden.

A few days later I awoke during the night from a dream that I can't remember, but my immediate thought was to get away, get away, but from what? I cringed in terror, a terror I couldn't recognize. The realization of lying in my own bed and feeling these emotions and 'not knowing' sends the mind to depression. The body experiences a weakness so debilitating I thought I would never want to get up again.

This was the first of my dreams that I would later find were directly connected with my problem, but they would start in earnest after the Amytal sessions. In this dream I did not remember any of the characters or faces in the dream, but rather the body language. My body was telling me how horrible the dreams were to become. My body was preparing me for what my mind would accept later. It is so strange the way your subconscious mind protects the conscious in a way that we will only allow the conscious mind to remember what it is ready to accept. The path through the dreams was to be long and torturous. But I learned quickly to say to my family that they were only movies about bad things that make me cry and shudder and cringe in fear.

19

IN THE NEXT SESSIONS, Dr. Thomas and I talked about the Amytal interviews. What they would be like and how they would be done. I was very nervous and apprehensive at first.

"Tell me how these interviews work."

"Usually they are done in three sessions. Two days, like Monday and Tuesday, then skip Wednesday and do the third one on Thursday."

"Do I go to the hospital?"

"Yes, but only for the day. You would check in about eight o'clock and we would schedule the session for say ten o'clock. It will probably last about an hour."

"Will I be awake?"

"Yes and no. What we do is put an IV in your arm, then feed the drug slowly into your bloodstream. You will be aware of my voice, but you will be in a kind of euphoric state floating between the conscious and unconscious mind. A nurse will be with you checking your blood pressure to make sure you don't go under too deep. This serum slows your heart down. We want to make sure we keep you in this world."

"I hope so. I'm not ready to check out just yet, no matter how bad I feel or what I want to know."

"So, after we finish, you will go right to sleep and rest for a couple of hours. This is very draining, and you will be tired. When you wake up, you can have lunch. We will be monitoring your blood pressure every fifteen minutes throughout the afternoon."

"When can I leave?"

"That depends on what comes up in the interview. If we get into some very heavy material, which I hope happens, then it may be late afternoon. And you must have someone to drive you home. You'll be in no condition to drive."

"I can see that. I'll get Lindsay to bring me."

"She doesn't have to stay with you. She can have the day for her own, but she will need to check in with the nurse's station a couple of times to determine when to pick you up."

"I understand. I don't know what I would do without Lindsay. I feel comfortable with her because she seems to understand what I'm going through and the others don't."

"I am sure that's true. She's a very sensitive person and her training is a big help. The main thing you have to remember about this is that it is going to be extremely debilitating and it will take up your whole week. And you must be prepared for whatever comes up. I can't stress this enough. You must be ready to see and feel whatever comes to your mind. I think you are, or we wouldn't be talking about this."

"I think I am ready too. I don't know why I say that, because I've no idea what I'm going to remember, or I'd remember it now. And I know it isn't going to be pretty."

"That's true. Are there any more questions?"

"No, I guess we've covered all the bases."

"How do you feel about it?"

"Well, I'm anxious, but I want to do this. There's no question about that. I've lived with this hanging over my head for so long. I want to get to the bottom of it. I want to be me. I'm tired of living the life someone else gave me. I'm tired of making decisions like a zombie, denying what's in front of me, loving people out of fear."

"We've talked about this before, but you know you fit the profile of a Stockholm Syndrome member."

"Yes, like Patty Hearst. She joined them to survive. Because she joined the gang everyone assumed she was really a member. She lived with them, fought with them, so she was one of them."

"Some people call this brainwashing, but it's really a deep desire to survive."

"I can see that."

"And, as in your case, the younger it begins, the harder it is to break. Your Daddy knew when he whipped you, you weren't ever going to tell. That was already deeply entrenched in your mind. And your mother wanted verification through the whipping that her husband could not do such a thing. That whipping, or beating is a better word, served as a double-edged sword. Your mother and father both felt secure after it was over. You proved you belonged to your father, and your mother could look the other way and not worry. It worked for everyone, except you."

"So, in order for me to live a so-called normal life, I locked these horrors in my subconscious and pretended to Mama, Daddy, and the rest of the world that I loved and adored him. I followed him and copied him. I defended him. All the time trying to win his love and the deep hope that if I was good enough those horrors wouldn't happen again. When my efforts were never good enough and the horrors happened again, I felt betrayed. Then the emotional outbursts came, and I became the crazy one in the family."

"Yes, that's it, and until we can unlock those horrors buried in your memory, external things will continue to happen that will remind the subconscious of the betrayal and another outburst will occur."

"So, let's find out what they are if we can. I know I'm ready."

It was a bright, beautiful November day, a day that belongs in October rather than November. The air was warm, the leaves a crisp golden, red, bronze, deepest purple, and forest green. It was not at all the kind of day that you might associate with the dark, swirling, depths of the subconscious, but that's where I was headed. Lindsay was not driving me as planned. Her truck had broken down in Lexington over the weekend. I rode in with Linc. He dropped me off in front of the hospital then went on to a legal seminar in Charlottesville.

I walked up to the front doors and a buzzer sounded. All mental hospitals are locked. Every door, every window, every drawer, everything that is not a piece of furniture is locked in its proper place. The only things left to be carried off or stolen are tissues. Boxes of tissues are everywhere, on every counter, every desk, toilet, bedside table. Everywhere a hand might be able to reach for one. They are there to cry in, buckets and buckets of tears.

The nurse took me to a little room equipped with a stretcher, and cabinets with drugs. Her keys jingled as she unlocked drawers. Keys are attached to belts so they won't be lost or laid down, and so patients can't take them. Can you imagine a patient with keys to all those drug cabinets?

The nurse tried to ease my tension by talking. Her name was Mary. She had a soft voice and an easy way about her, but no matter how many questions she asked or how hard she tried to distract me, my thoughts were on one thing. What was I going to remember? I wanted to know. I released the tension by crying and insisting to Mary that I wasn't scared.

Dr. Thomas came in and, as always, his presence gave me confidence.

"How are you?" It was always his first question.

"I'm okay." My sometimes answer. "But I know one thing."

"What's that?"

"I am mad at my Daddy this morning. I don't know why, but I am."

"Well, let's see if this Amytal can help us find out." He looked at the nurse. "I see you have everything ready. Excellent, we can get started then."

He moved around to the right side of the stretcher.

"Now, this will be just a little stick, nothing to worry about." He picked up the butterfly IV and the bottle of the drug. Such a little bottle for such a big job, I thought.

"You're good with a needle," I said.

236

"You shouldn't have said that because this vein isn't good. We'll have to try another."

Seconds passed. The second vein was no good. I could tell because he was frowning, but still, there was no pain.

"I should have used the first one," he said. "Let's try this again." The IV was in place. Mary began to squeeze the blood pressure pump. "Now count backwards for me from 99."

I began to count backwards, "99, 98, 97, 96, 95, 94, 93, 92, 91, 90..." I could hear my voice as if I were completely conscious, but my eyes were shut, and I felt a dream world around me.

"That's good. That's far enough." The doctor's voice and words were soothing. I felt safe even though I knew nothing of what was to come. His voice came through again.

"What were the holidays like at your house when you were a little girl?

"Awful."

There was no hesitancy in my reply, I felt compelled to say the words as soon as I heard the question, and I knew the answer immediately. It was as if the information was rolling from a tape.

"Why were they awful?"

"Daddy was always drunk."

"Every holiday. Christmas, Thanksgiving, all of them?"

"Yes"

"Did your mother fix dinner?"

"Yes"

"What happened then?"

"Mama fussed."

"Why?"

"Because Daddy was drunk."

Dr. Thomas's voice broke in: "What would you do then?"

"I would try to think of something to change the subject, to stop them from fussing. I'm trying to help her with the dishes, so she won't fuss."

"What is your Daddy doing?"

"He's finished eating and is getting up to leave."

"And your mother, too?"

"Yes."

"And your sisters, what are they doing?"

"They're leaving too, to go play."

"And leave you by yourself?"

"Yes."

"So, what are you doing now?

"I'm leaving too. I'm taking all the dishes into the kitchen and trying to make everything neat."

"Did your Daddy get drunk other times?"

"Yes, on weekends."

"Did your mother fuss at him?"

"Yes."

"What happened then?"

"Mama fussed and tried to beat on him."

"Why?"

"Because Daddy is drunk."

"What do you do then?"

"I am trying to help her, so she won't fuss.

"'Mama, I'll wash dishes today, so you can rest.'"

"What did your Daddy do then?"

"He got mad. He always got mad."

"Did he ever hit your mother?"

"Yes."

"Hard?"

"Yes."

"More than once?"

"Yes."

"Did your mother ever have to go to the hospital from it?"

"No."

"What did you do while he was beating your mother?"

"I followed them around to try and stop them. 'Mama, stop,' I screamed. She has a coat hanger to beat on him. Now, he has it. 'Daddy, Daddy, please stop, don't hit her anymore. Please stop. She didn't mean it.'"

"Where were your sisters?"

"They ran away. I told them to."

"So, they weren't there when the fights happened?"

"No. Sometimes they were there."

"What else did your Daddy do on weekends?"

"He went away."

"How did your mother feel about that?"

"She fussed. Because she wanted to go somewhere too, and she knew he would go with his buddies and get drunk."

"What else would he do?"

"He would lie. They both lied."

"Your Mama and Daddy lied?"

"Yes."

"What did your Daddy lie about?"

"What he was doing and where he was going."

"Did he lie about anything else?"

"He was sneaky."

"What kinds of things was he sneaky about?"

"He would do things people didn't know about."

"Did your Daddy take you places?"

"Yes, when I was good. I tried to be good all the time."

"Did your mother think you were good?"

"No. She always thought I was bad. They all thought I was bad."

"Did, your Daddy take your sisters places?"

"No."

"Did your mother want your Daddy to take you places?"

"Yes. She didn't want me around. She didn't care."

"Why?"

"Because she thought I was dirty. They all thought I was dirty."

"Why did they think you were dirty?"

"I don't know."

"Did you want to go with your Daddy?"

"No."

"Why didn't you want to go with him?"

"I don't know."

"Did your Daddy want you to do any other things?"

"Yes."

"What other things did he want you to do that you didn't want to do?"

"Sit on his lap."

"Didn't you want to sit on his lap?"

"No."

"Why?"

"I don't know."

Much harder crying.

"It seems like sitting on her father's lap would be a nice thing for a little girl to do, doesn't it?"

"Yes."

"We are going to stop now. Is there anything else you want to tell me before we end?"

"Yes, I want to tell you about the whipping."

"You mean the whipping we know about."

"Yes."

"Was the whipping bad?"

"Yes, it was awful."

"Why did you get a whipping?"

"Because Mama thought I had been with a man. She found stuff on my underpants."

"What did she do?"

"She was mad. She made Daddy whip me."

"All right, we'll have to stop now. You just relax."

More crying, wrenching sobs.

"He whipped me so hard and made the blood run and I had scars on my legs, and I couldn't let anybody see my legs for a long time."

"It's all right now. We have to stop. Just relax. Take deep breaths and rest."

There was more crying. Dr. Thomas opened the door and the stretcher started down the hall. He and the nurse walked steadily without talking until we got to my room. Then they helped me up and onto the bed. I felt so wobbly and groggy, but I knew what was happening.

Dr. Thomas spoke to me. "Just rest and take a nap. It's O.K. They'll bring you some lunch later."

I lay on the bed going in and out of sleep. A nurse kept coming in to take my blood pressure.

I began to think back to the interview and more pictures came to me. It made me cry again just as I had through all of the questions of the interview. The reality of the desperate feelings flooded over me! The desperation of wanting to make myself feel better, to make my world of holidays happy, not sad, engulfed me. I never in all my life as a child had a happy holiday.

I could see my mother in the kitchen fixing dinner. There were all the same things. Her homemade rolls put down in perfect rows on large flat bread pans sitting on the radiators in the kitchen to warm and rise. There were at least a dozen to a pan. The rolls were perfectly round, rising like the snowball cakes in the store without the color or the coconut. They were mounds covered with butter that made them glisten, and the aroma of the butter and dough made you swallow because you could taste the bread and it wasn't even in the oven. You could tell when the bread was done because the dough had stretched until there was a fine film on top that would be the brown crust when they were brought to the table.

The scene kept moving just as I remembered it happening when I was a little girl. Mama was watching the clock. I always knew it was more to see if Daddy would make it home rather than if the meal would be on time. We rarely had company, for holidays or otherwise, because Mama didn't want to be embarrassed by Daddy. If he was late, we would make trips back and forth to the kitchen to watch the clock. As the time passed, Mama's frown got deeper and deeper, and we all knew what was coming.

Mama sat at the table. Her face was drawn. Her best tablecloth, china, and silverware were placed around the table with crystal goblets and fine china cups. We, the sisters, always set the table and cleaned up the kitchen after dinner. No one talked. I sat to Daddy's left always, my sisters sat beside each other on the right. As I got older, I tried to fix a centerpiece of flowers, or cornucopia, or wreath, to make the table more festive. Mama and Daddy faced each other as if they were pairing off for a boxing match.

Daddy carved the turkey. His face was fiery red from the liquor. He tried to say something, but he only stuttered. Nothing came out. This only happened when he drank too much. He carefully placed the meat on the plates without saying anything. The plates went around the table and were piled high with all the favorites of the holiday. At least half of it would be left uneaten. My mother always spoke first, always the same words. "Why do you have to ruin every holiday?" And my father's voice came back defiant, "I ain't ruined anything. Why do you fuss all the time?"

"Because you're drunk as usual. You do this every time," she shouts.

"I ain't drunk. I'm sitting here as nice as I can be. I washed my hands and all."

She frowned and raised her voice. "Shut up. You've ruined our dinner as you always do."

"I ain't ruined nothing, I don't see how you can do this all the time."

Mama would point her fork at him. "What do you mean? It's not me, it's you. You don't love these children or think about them."

"I do so. I buy them anything they want, and you too, you know I do." He picked up a turkey bone and gnawed it.

"You think money will buy anything, even happiness."

"I know it won't buy happiness or you'd be happy," he snapped back.

I'd try to butt in by saying, "Daddy, I rode Lady this morning and she was really good. I hope we do good at the horse show next Saturday. Sarah rode Ace, too."

My mother would throw a glance at me. "That's right, take up for your Daddy. All you care about is those horses anyway. You're just like him."

"Esther, leave that child be."

Daddy sometimes reverted to the old usage when he was drunk or upset.

He looked at me. "She's not doing anything."

His head wobbled slightly and all I could see was the pain in his light blue eyes.

Nothing was ever different, even as an adult, when we all went home as mothers with families. Daddy was still drunk, and Mama was still carrying on. She was fixing dinner, fussing, and complaining. Nothing changed until Daddy died.

In my own home, the holidays were times of terrible stress, too. I tried to erase the terrible memories of the past by giving a big Christmas party every year, in an effort to fill the house with cheer and wipe out those old memories that lodged in my subconscious. The parties never really worked because somehow Christmas was always a time of deep depression.

Now the endless scenes from my childhood were so vivid. I could see my mother at one end of the table–tiny, sullen, hurt, trying to eat, but choking on her anxiety, and her need to reach out and scratch my father's eyes out for ruining another holiday dinner. My father sat at the other end of the table–his face purple-red, gobbling his food, but trying to put his best foot forward. My sisters and I ate quietly knowing that any minute it was all going to explode, and one or the other of our parents would get up and run from the room.

We would sit there with whichever parent was left and try to make some sort of conversation until we were finished eating. I was always the last one to leave because my sisters had thought of something to do and I was left to contemplate how it could have been better. Why did it always end this way? What could I have done?

More pictures were flashing through my mind. The awful fights, the awful nights, the awful sights that I didn't want to see or hear. But there they were, right in front of my eyes, zipping by like a ticker tape. Mama in her nightgown chasing Daddy through the house screaming, "You yellow bellied son-of-a bitch, I could kill you. Why do you keep drinking when you promised me with your hand on the Bible that you would never drink again?"

"I didn't mean to, Esther, and besides, I ain't had much to drink. I just had a few drinks at the fish fry."

"Yes, I know. There with all your buddies while I am at home with these children. You promised you would come home and take us somewhere this weekend. Damn your soul. I wish I could get my brothers up here and tie you to a tree and beat you within an inch of your life."

A figurine went sailing by his ear and shattered against the wall. He turned his head just in time to get the blow of a shoe in his face.

"Mama, stop," I screamed, knowing things were coming to a head fast.

"Get out of my way," she yelled. Her face was in contortions. She grabbed a coat hanger and started beating Daddy across his chest.

"Stop it, Esther, don't make me hit you."

He made no impression on her. My heart leapt to my throat as I watched him grab the coat hanger and swing it across her thighs. I knew how it hurt because I remembered the lashes I got. She was crying now, and the sobs ripped through my head. I raced to grab Daddy's arms and hold on.

"Daddy, Daddy, please stop, don't hit her anymore," I begged. "Please stop. She didn't mean it." I felt the rage in him subside as he lowered his arm and the coat hanger dropped to the floor. Mama dropped in a heap as Daddy ran back to the bedroom and slammed the door. It was over for the night, but another fight had taken its toll on our lives. There was no escape for any of us.

After an hour or so I began to see white pages unfold before my eyes. It is a steady roll until one of them is a building. It looks like a high rise maybe, but the next page shows more buildings like the first. They look like short high rises, with an open space like a parking lot underneath some of them. They seem to be on a hillside and on both sides of the street. Somehow, I know I've seen these buildings. There is something so familiar about them. They are stucco and the windows are like square boxes.

Then it comes to me. I know exactly where these buildings are, but I don't want to go in. They are part of St. Emma's School at Belmead in Powhatan County. Daddy had mills on Belmead Plantation during the war. He was there every day for four years and I was with him a lot.

There is no one else there now but me. I wait because I dread this, and my feet are glued to the street. Somehow, I have to go inside through the open space underneath. It's dark and I don't want to go, but I make myself move step by slow step.

Somewhere in that dark cavity, I see something, and as I get closer I realize it's a man sitting down with a little girl on his lap. She is facing him, and she is naked, and her legs look so small and thin hanging down over his thighs. The man has one hand on her buttocks and one hand on her head. He pulls her body to him then pulls it away and I see his penis, long and hard sticking straight out. Then he pushes her head down on his penis and her curls fall around it. The force of his hand causes the huge red penis to disappear in her mouth and the man throws his head back in a wild jerk.

After a few seconds, I know the little girl is me and the man is my father. My eyes fill with tears. Tears replace the pictures and the horrible realization and rejection sets in. I couldn't believe what I had seen was possible. The sexual acts played out. I couldn't believe those people were me and my father. Neither one was possible, but I now knew the deep, deep hurt that released the sobs. At long last, after more than fifty years, I was seeing the truth. Crying, I have learned, has different tempos, rhythms, depths, amd voices that seek to let out the pain. The release of tears is like a river that ebbs and flows on pain. Humans are the only animals who can shed tears, cry, scream, shout, and moan all at the same time. We have all these means of release. I hope we are the only animal who can relive the same pain over and over again as I was doing at that moment. I hope animals can forget pain, but I know they can't. I know the reason that we don't remember is a form of protection. I just wish there was a less painful way for children and animals.

I began to play every memory of that horrible scene over and over like a video camera in my mind of that horrible scene. It rolled on and on until I felt sick to my stomach and my head throbbed like a hammer was pounding inside. A nurse tried to calm me, but after a few minutes of explanation, she realized I needed to cry. My lunch went untouched and the sun began to fade in the afternoon sky. The nurse called Dr. Thomas at his office and he prescribed something for me. She came in again with a little white pill and a glass of water.

"Here, honey, take this and you'll feel better soon. It will quiet you down."

Between sobs I took the pill and fell back on my pillow.

"That's good. You'll feel better in a few minutes."

She checked my blood pressure and left the room.

I lay on the bed numb, waiting for anything. Finally, I dozed off.

Camille picked me up from the hospital. I didn't feel like talking to her. I just sat and watched the countryside go by. Finally, I knew why my life had been so tormented and why no amount of pills could kill the pain I couldn't name. We rode in silence. I wasn't physically or emotionally able to talk. I rested that night in fits and starts and waited for what was to come in the second interview.

20

I WAS EXHAUSTED the next morning but determined to see the day through. Lindsay took me into Richmond, but we didn't talk. I was still too wrapped up in the memories of the day before and too focused on my own thoughts. Lindsay went with me into the hospital and a nurse took me to the same room. I recognized the tape, gauze, needles, tubing, strips already cut, ready for the IV.

The same nurse came into the room. She was to be with me throughout the interview that morning. She was young, attractive, bright, and she recognized my tears already. It took only the recognition of sympathy to send me into a stream of tears again, and the statement that what I had seen couldn't be true.

"Yes, it can be true. It is true. Everything you remember is true. You have to believe it's true or you can't shed the awful guilt that you've carried with you for so many years."

"But it can't be true. It just isn't possible," I wailed.

"Yes, it is true. Your Daddy was a sick, sick man, and your mother was probably worse. They did a horrible thing to you and you didn't deserve it. You were just a little girl. How could a little girl help herself? She couldn't help herself nowadays and certainly not in the forties." She turned and picked up a pillow and put it in front of me.

"Here, hug this pillow tight and pretend the pillow is you when you were little, and the pillow is just a little girl. She's hurt and scared and has no one to help her. Everyone has hurt her. The people she loves most in the world, the people who were supposed to take care of her. Hug the pillow and say, 'You're going to be okay. No one's going to hurt you again.' Can you do that?"

I nod my head.

"Say it, please."

I hug the pillow tight and look down at it. "No one is going to hurt you again. I won't let them. I will take care of you."

"That's good. Can you tell her again? She is so scared."

I nod and murmur "Yes" through the tears.

"Good girl. Now tell her. She needs to hear it so badly."

"'No one is going to hurt you again. They're both dead. They can't hurt you anymore. I love you too much to let anyone hurt you again. I'm going to be strong for you.'"

"Good."

The door opens and then Dr. Thomas comes in. The tears rush again.

"I remembered something else, but it can't be true."

"That's good that you've remembered something else, but let's get started then you can tell me. Maybe more will come through, then."

He put the needle in place and asked me to count backward slowly from 100.

"99-98-97-96-------"

"Good, now tell me what you remembered."

"I remembered going to this place in Powhatan where Daddy used to go all the time when I was little."

"What was this place like?"

"There were lots of buildings on both sides of the street."

"What did they look like?"

"They looked like old-fashioned institutional buildings. They were made of stucco and they had square windows."

"What else did you notice?"

"Some of them had open spaces underneath like a parking lot."

"Where were you when you remembered this?"

"I was standing in the middle of the street and I knew I had to go into one of these buildings and I didn't want to."

"Why didn't you want to go in?"

"I was afraid of what I would see."

"Did you go in?"

"Yes."

"What did you see?"

"It was dark, and I didn't want to go in, but somewhere deep inside in a corner I could see two people."

"Who were these people? And what were they doing?"

"I was sitting on Daddy's lap facing him and I was naked, and I could see my legs hanging down over his."

"And what else did you see?"

"I could see his hand on my backside, and I could see his penis, and he pushed me on it, and then he pulled me back and pushed my face down on him, and I choked, and I saw him jerk his head back and make a face."

All this time I knew I was crying, and I wanted to get away from telling the doctor, but I couldn't, and I wanted to die from the hurt.

"Do you think this is true?"

"Yes."

"Did your Daddy take you to this place many times?"

"Yes."

"Did your Mother know where you were going?"

"Yes."

"What did she say?"

"Nothing. She didn't care if I went."

"Did your father ever take your sisters to this place?"

"No."

"Why didn't he take them to this place?"

"My mother wouldn't let them go with Daddy. I was the only one that she wanted to go with him."

The doctor began to take the needle out of my arm. He talked softly and slowly. "Just rest now. Take some deep breaths. We are going back to your room now. You can rest and take a nap."

There was more crying.

"I tried to be good. I always tried to be good, but they didn't like me. None of them did. I just wanted them to love me and I couldn't understand why they didn't. I would do anything for them if they would just love me."

"It's all right now, you just try to relax. You are going to be okay. Take some deep breaths."

The stretcher began to move, bumping across the threshold, turning down the hall. I could hear people in the hallway. Patients began to follow the stretcher.

"What's wrong with her?"

"Where has she been?"

The nurse said, "She's going to be okay. We're just taking her to her room."

This didn't seem unnatural to me. In a mental hospital there are few barriers between patients and staff. Patients feel free to ask or say whatever comes into their minds. Also, there is a bonding among the patients. We must look out for each other, no matter how sick we are. It's the doctors and nurses against us. They have all the control. The one most important question among patients is who is your doctor? Then they know a lot about you, and they tell you whatever you need to know.

It felt so good to stretch out on the bed and pull the blanket up around my chin. I was covering myself from the horrible exposure that left me feeling naked and alone. In two days, my whole life had changed. Everything that I had ever thought about myself or my family was stripped away like peeling paper off a wall leaving the ugly glue and shabby sheetrock exposed. I had nothing left to think about but the abuse. Over and over again the pictures went through my mind and there were no answers for "why."

I had tried so hard to be a good girl when I was little. I had tried for my mother and my father. I had told the doctor so. What I remembered was what was in my mind. The Amytal won't let you lie. When the doctor asks a question, you have to answer. There is no other answer. It's there before you and you have to say it. You have no resistance.

The nurse came in every fifteen minutes to check my blood pressure. Sometime after lunch a woman came in and stood over me.

"Hello, I'm Vernell, your roommate."

"Hi." My voice was weak, and I didn't bother to move. What difference did it make if I could hardly see through my puffy eyes, but I could see enough to know she was big and African-American. She was looking at me under the covers with my clothes on. In a mental hospital nothing is odd. You feel safe to be yourself.

She looked down at me searching. "What did they do to you, honey?"

"Nothing, I've just been crying."

She continued searching. "Can I get you anything?"

"No, I'm okay."

She stood another few minutes still searching. "Well, I got to get out of here. I'll be back."

She left in a hurry. Not running from me or getting away from me. One of the unwritten, but clearly understood rules in a mental hospital, is that if you are not restrained in some way, you do not stay in your room. You have to get out and mix with people. You can sit on the hall floor, you can sprawl out on the couch in the reception room and sleep, you can talk on the telephone all day, you can eat, smoke cigarettes in special places, but you cannot stay in your room. Wanting to be by yourself, away from other people, is a very bad thing for your mental health.

I learned this quickly during my first stay on the psychiatric ward, at Saint Mary's in 1989. It was the safest, most wonderful place. The outside world was totally shut off; I didn't have anything to worry about. It was a feeling I have never forgotten. I guarded against remembering this feeling of security because it would be so easy to succumb to the depression and go back to this beautiful feeling of safety which I had never experienced before.

It would have been so easy to succumb to that feeling now. It would have been so easy to say I wanted to stay and let my life slip away as an invalid watches the world from a wheelchair. Or, I thought of the patient at St. Mary's who never spoke a word and spent her entire waking time looking out the window. That would be the easy way. I would never have to go on with these treatments and face the awful truth about my childhood. I lay on the bed all afternoon. I could not get up. I was too physically drained.

Vernell kept coming in to check on me. But she would stay only a minute. She couldn't understand what they had done to me or why. Usually, if someone stays in bed, she is in the ICU section and restrained in some way. A nurse kept checking my blood pressure and talking to me. There were no more hidden pictures appearing.

Finally, the sky was getting red with the sunset when Lindsay appeared in my doorway. She helped me up and we walked out. We must have made a curious pair, a young beautiful blonde woman with an older woman on her arm who looked as if she had just lost her best friend. Some of the patients followed us to the door. We had to wait until a nurse could unlock the doors and escort us out.

The nurse looked at the patients gathered around and said, "You can't go out now. You'll have to wait your turn. Alice will take you out to smoke in fifteen minutes." Maybe some of the patients just wanted to slip out of the door and be out in the real world. But nothing seemed real to me. My world had been shattered by glimpses into the past, a past kept under lock and key for so long.

21

_____

THE NEXT MORNING I was quieter. I had the same nurse who took me to the treatment room and set up for the procedure. She was comforting and quiet. We waited as she tried to reassure me that this was not my fault. It was not my fault that I had been abused. It was not my fault that I had been depressed all my life, and it wasn't my fault that I had to relive these awful memories. It was the filth of a sick mind that caused it. It was not just the sick mind of the abuser, my father, but the equally sick mind of the facilitator, my mother. She had allowed it.

The nurse said, "You can't have an alcoholic without a facilitator, and you can't abuse your own daughter without the help and knowledge of her mother." Maybe, better said, you can't continue to abuse the daughter without the mother's knowledge. My mother was both; she facilitated my father's drinking and she knew about the abuse. My father was a monstrous alcoholic as well as a child-molester. And my mother helped him be both. So, who was the sickest: my father the perpetrator, or my mother the facilitator?

My feelings jumped from vicious anger where I could have torn my mother and father apart, literally limb from limb, with my own strength and bare hands, to a feeling of complete defeat and apathy. I would become an enraged animal, pacing the bars of my cage, snarling and biting the bars of the fence that kept me from reaching my prey. When the frustration subsided and my anger turned inward, I would retreat to a corner and lie down to nurse the deepest depression and thoughts of my self-destruction. Sometimes I even wanted to forgive them as a good Christian would try to do, and sometimes I wanted to turn my back forever. The truth is, I knew I had only scraped the surface of my understanding and there were miles and miles to go. And then, there was the endless process of grieving. Grieving for what happened and what could have been.

The doctor came in.

"Good morning. How are you this morning?"

"I'm fine, but up to my old tricks as you can see." By that, I meant that I was crying. "And I have something to tell you before we start. You know, horses saved my life when I was little. Well, Daddy had a shop where he fixed the harness for the logging horses and I used to go and help him fix the harness. And I don't know what happened there, but I know there is something about that shop that isn't right. I can just feel it."

"Let's explore that first after we get started. Lie down and relax. We'll get this needle in as quickly as possible. In the meantime, tell me about your new dogs."

"You mean the Salukis?"

"Yes."

"Let me ask you something first."

"Certainly."

"Why do you ask me to count backwards?"

"Because when you start slurring your words it means the drug has taken effect. That way I can gauge how much you need. It's a very delicate process. If I give you too much, you will go to sleep. Too little, the hypnotic effect is gone."

"I see. One more thing."

"Yes."

"These interviews last about an hour, so how much do I remember when it is over?"

"That all depends on the person, but usually you remember the lightest part of the interview. In other words, you remember when you have the least drug in your system. Administering the drug is a very imperfect science. The hospital will not allow any taped interviews so whatever information is left from this is what you remember. But you know the important thing is how much information comes out during the time, not what you remember."

"You mean letting the pressure off the subconscious is the important thing?"

"Exactly, getting it out of its confines, releasing it to the conscious mind is what counts."

"It's kind of like letting the steam out of a pressure cooker."

"Yes, that's simplifying it, but that's exactly what is needed. All of these awful memories act like steam and they have to go. Any more questions?

"No." Time ticked away as I described the Salukis. I talked about them until the crying subsided and my voice was almost normal.

"Now, count backwards from 100."

I counted slowly and distinctly.

"Are you feeling the effects of the drug?"

"Yes."

"Are you going off into limbo?"

"Yes, somewhat but not enough."

"Can you count again for me?"

My eyes were shut, and my body was euphoric, but I knew exactly what was happening in the room. Then it all seemed to slip away to the questions he asked.

"Tell me about your father's shop."

"He fixed the harness there. It was a big room with all the tools and harnesses and everything you needed for the horses."

"Did you go there?"

"Yes."

"When did you go there?"

"I went with Daddy to fix the harness."

"When did you go?"

"We would go at night after supper."

"Did you like to go?"

"I loved to go to fix the harness, but–" I could hear long sobs.

"But was there something there you didn't like?"

"Yes." I continued my crying

"What didn't you like about the shop?"

"I didn't like to go upstairs."

"Did your Daddy make you go upstairs? What was up there?"

"There were bags of feed."

"What did your Daddy make you do when you got up there?"

"Lie on the feed bags with him."

"Did you want to do this?"

"No."

"Did he ever tell you not to tell?"

"Yes. He told me not to tell Mama."

"Did you ever get a whipping other than the time we have talked about?"

"Yes."

"Who whipped you?"

"Both of them whipped me."

"Your Mama and your Daddy whipped you many times."

"Yes." Loud wails. "Yes, yes, many times. Mama always whipped me with a belt. I was so scared. I can see her coming at me with the belt raised. Her eyes hated me, and her face was all scrunched up."

"Why did she whip you?"

"I was bad," I could hear more sobs. "I was bad, but I tried to be good. I always tried to be good, I wanted to be good, but I was bad."

"Who said you were bad?"

"Mama and everybody thought I was bad. They thought I was dirty."

"How do you know?

"Mama said so. But I tried to be good. I tried not to be dirty, but I didn't know how."

"How could a little girl be dirty?"

"I don't know, but Mama said I was every time I went with Daddy. I just wanted to go to the shop because of the harness. I didn't want to go because of Daddy. I used to go out to the pastures and lie down and talk to the horses. They never hurt me, and they would listen, and I would lie in the grass and talk to them while they ate."

"How old were you?"

"Little. I was real little, but the horses wouldn't hurt me. I could hardly reach the top of the anvil on the bench when I went to the shop."

"How long did this go on? Until you were bigger, probably until you were a teenager?"

"I don't know, but a long time."

"Do you remember telling me about seeing your Daddy sitting on the stump with you? How old were you then? Were you bigger then?"

"Yes. I was lots taller."

"This is enough for today. You can relax now, and we will take you back to your room."

Still my crying filled the room. Sobs and sobs that wavered, rose and fell as the heartbeats.

The door opened. The last interview was over. I had lived through it again.

"You will probably have more memories for a few weeks. Don't worry. You will be alright. Just rest now and try to relax. I will see you next week in the office."

Back in my bed, I rested. I didn't try to think. I had thought enough. It was finally over. I knew what had eaten at the core of my soul all these years and it was nothing that I had done, but I felt angry and guilty. I couldn't sort them out.

My roommate came back. "I looked for you last night. What did they do with you? Are you alright?"

"Yes, I'm fine."

"You ain't fine, but if you stay in this place long enough, you'll be fine. Just remember that. I gotta go. I'll be back."

Vernell left for the last time. I had not gotten to know her, but we connected in the strange way people do when they recognize hurt in each other. I had no idea why Vernell was there, but it didn't matter. Maybe the courts had put her there, maybe for an overdose, maybe because of child abuse. It didn't matter. We were two women in the same place, from different backgrounds with different problems, but we were bound together by the same invisible bonds. We were both victims. I recognized Vernell as a fellow patient in a mental hospital and she was concerned about me. She tried to help by showing her concern. That was enough for me.

22

IT WAS the fourth day after my last interview. I was desperately tired, but otherwise able to function in day-to-day life. My biggest concern was how would I ever believe what has happened to me. I knew in my mind what happened, but my heart told me it couldn't be true. I remembered so many good things about Daddy even though they may have been or were indeed lies.

On the one hand, I knew I should hate him and my mother. I knew they are like figures in the horror stories from the depths of Dante's hell. I also remembered how Daddy called me Sugar and Pumpkin and how he sometimes defended me to my mother. Then I thought, maybe I made all this up. I remember the snow ice cream my mother made me. It just isn't true. No father could treat his daughter as I remembered it.

Even as I write, my mind is clouded with images of my father never having time for me, of my desperate attempts to reach him, even when I was little, to beg him to stop drinking so the house would not be always filled with anger, cursing, and screaming. I remember how embarrassed I was as a teenager to be told, by a neighbor girl who was also a classmate, that her family could hear my mother and father fighting. And how they would sit on the front porch and listen.

I think of all these things now, and I feel I am five or seven or three people or however many different people there are. They are all plastered on the walls of the room and there is no center of me. I am fragments of somebody I don't know, but I want very much to find me. This thought, to find myself, my real self, well and whole, makes me keep going. Back in the summer when these thoughts and memories started, I wanted more than anything else to know who the man was. I wanted the man who had caused the whipping —whoever he was—not to get away scot-free as if nothing had happened. My wish was to get well, be free of him and his legacy, to live the rest of my life in peace.

Somehow, I had to reconcile the two men I knew. The father I learned to love in order to survive, and the father who betrayed me in the cruelest way. This would be the only way I would find peace. Peace is a word I know nothing about except as a word in the dictionary with an imaginary definition. To experience rest without worry, life's daily routine without dread, and joy without guilt is what peace must be like in real life. I just wanted to find this peace within myself. I know the road is much longer than I can imagine but much shorter than the fifty-some years that I had been searching.

The telephone rang while I was in the barn. Lindsay was going to ride my new horse. He was really old, but he was new to me and I hoped he was going to be my hunting horse. I bought him at my last horse sale, from a woman horse trader whom I had grown to respect. I had the feeling that she had been badly abused in her life as well. She was so masculine on the surface, but there was a gentleness and sincerity about her that belied the fierceness she projected. I answered the phone reluctantly.

"Hello."

"Mrs. Owens, this is Susan in Dr. Thomas's office. How are you?"

"Oh, fine." I was so used to lying about my feelings. I learned very early, and very young to never say how I felt. It meant my lip would quiver and I would begin to cry because someone had shown some interest in me, or I would boil inside trying to fight off the intrusion into my private world that I wanted to remain private. The simple answer "fine" was always the right answer no matter who asked.

"How are you?" I returned the amenity.

"Good. Mrs. Owens, Dr. Thomas has an opening at twelve o'clock today. Could you possibly come in? I know it's short notice."

Hearing her voice made me want to race to Richmond. She was a nice person and always sweet and gentle to me. I almost screamed over the phone, "Yes, I can come. What time is it? I have ten forty-five."

"Can you make it?"

"Yes, no problem. I'll be there."

"Good. Dr. Thomas just wanted to get you in here as quickly as possible."

"Thank you, Susan, thank you so much."

I hung up the phone and yelled to Lindsay. "I'm going to see Dr. Thomas. I'm sorry, but I have to go."

"Don't worry, Mom, you need this. I'll ride your horse."

I raced to the house, my head spinning with what I had to do to get there on time. I would take Racine, my male Saluki, with me and go to the vet after I saw Dr. Thomas. After the vet, I'd go on to the stockyard and meet with the manager. Then back home by nine o'clock. It would work. There was no time to really change clothes, just comb my hair, get my bag, fix my face, get Racine in the truck with the crate, and I would be ready.

The hour to Richmond was my time to think about what I wanted to talk about. This had been my routine now for over eight years. The only thing was whatever I thought about was not usually what we talked about. Therapy is a tricky thing. It usually doesn't work the way you expect. And today there was nothing I wanted to talk about. But I wanted to feel better. My life's goal was to feel better. And I knew there was only one way to feel better. Face it. But it seemed in my life and my family I was the only one facing it, the only one who had ever faced the demons in the closet.

I sat in his office in the same place, on the couch. My usual seat, since I had relinquished control of the sessions at least four years before by giving up my seat in his red leather chair. I remember the day. I told him I felt that by him sitting on the couch and me sitting in the leather wing back chair, I had control and since he was the doctor, he should have the control. We switched that day and the couch has been my seat ever since.

"Well, we had three full sessions, didn't we?"

"Yes."

"Who have you shared this with?"

"No one."

"Really! Are you kidding? I would have thought you'd have told someone."

"You must be kidding. Tell my family? No way."

"You mean not even Linc? If my wife had been put in the hospital and this truth serum administered, you better believe I would have been at the door wanting to know what happened."

"But you aren't Linc. He doesn't want to know, and I don't want to repeat all these awful details to him."

"How about Camille and Lindsay, or your sisters? Are they interested?"

"My sisters would die before they asked me about this. I haven't spoken to Lynne since that Friday when she told me about Daddy and her. I talked to Sarah this morning, but nothing was mentioned. She can't stand to hear anything bad. Camille is so much like her and Lindsay knows everything anyway through her work. She doesn't know the details, but she knows what could and probably did happen. Lindsay has been a lifesaver to me these past few months."

"Well, just because they didn't ask doesn't mean they don't love you. They all knew what was going to come out anyway, don't you think?"

"Yes, certainly the sisters, and Lindsay and Camille too, I guess. Sarah just can't handle bad things."

"You are from a family who can't handle bad things."

"Yes, and I married into one, too."

"You mean Linc's family."

"Yes. Can I tell you something now? I don't know why I have been thinking about this, but I have. All of last week."

"Okay."

"I have been thinking about Linc's brother. I don't know why I have been thinking about this, but he's mean. You know how in World War Two movies, the German officer will be telling someone that he's going to a concentration camp, and in this calm, deadly voice he explains why and how and when it's going to happen. All the while he is turning something in his hands, or fiddling with something on a table, anything but looking at the person he is talking to."

"So, you think he is a Nazi?"

"Yes, that's exactly what I think. He was so mean to me when Linc and I were first married. I can never forgive him for all the hours of torment he subjected me to at his mother's dinner table. He is one of a few people I know who likes to put the knife in you and turn it. And that's what he does. He loves it. It gives him some sort of high to get one up on someone in an argument."

"I don't know if you're dealing with another force in this man's image or not."

"I don't either. Maybe I am just talking about him in order to not talk about my own family."

"It could be."

"I do know everything I have ever said about him and all of Linc's family is true."

"I'm sure it is."

The hour continued without much mention of the interviews. I just didn't want to talk about them. It was time to leave before I could bring myself to mention them.

Dr. Thomas stood up. "I think you're doing pretty well. We'll do more piecing this thing together next time. How about next week? Are you scheduled?"

"I'll be here."

I was there the next session and through the fall and winter. Thanksgiving Day was a beautiful day outside warm, sunny, bright, everything that nature could do to make us all feel good and be happy. I know I've been happier in the last eight years of my life than at any time before. The reason I'm happier is all because I had finally gotten help for the abscess which had been eating away at my soul all my life. I always knew something seemed to be wrong with me, but I didn't know what. I was different, no matter where I went or what I was doing. I reacted differently from other people. I was odd, somehow. I had a temper and didn't mind showing it. Sometimes I didn't want to be angry, but I couldn't help it.

One year when everything was ready for Christmas, all the ornaments glistened on the tree in the hallway beside the stairs. The sun shone in the front door panes making fire shadows and streaks of color dance across the tree and making the ornaments come alive. I knew it was going to be a glorious Christmas. But, as always, the sun went down, and the colors faded, and the ornaments were still, and the false glow of the strung lights went on, and the Christmas tree took on the air of dark magic, and I knew it wasn't real. The house took on the air of dreaded expectation with each ticking minute on the grandfather clock opposite the tree. When Daddy had not come home early in the evening, I knew that this Christmas would be no different from the rest.

We all sat in the den, before the TV, waiting, my mother, the sisters, and me. No one said anything, but we knew what had happened and what was going to happen. The atmosphere intensified until finally my mother went to bed in disgust and the sisters followed. When I was older, I sat up because I knew what was going to happen. It didn't matter whether I went to bed or not. When daddy came home, the house would explode with my mother's anger. All the lights would go on. The pounding of their bare feet on the floor sounded like a train running through the house upstairs and downstairs, interspersed with my mother's screams as she chased him cursing, throwing things, and sometimes he crashed against the furniture. I followed them, always hoping somehow to prevent one or the other from killing each other, and usually hoping they would kill us all and get it over with.

I think now how funny or extraordinary it was that I didn't call someone to help me or tell someone about my plight at home. But I know so well why I didn't. I was so afraid someone would find out the horror of our situation. I couldn't bear the embarrassment of admitting that my father was a drunk and that made my mother a raving maniac. There was an unspoken pact with all of us–not to tell–to keep the secret. This must be one of the strongest bonds in an alcoholic family.

I went fox hunting in January at Greenfield. The weather was miserable, and the footing was worse. The hunt met at the farm where I grew up, the home built by my grandfather. It's only two miles away from where I live now at Hunter's Hill, but I have only been back a few times since I left it for good in 1991. My sister owns it now.

El Niño had been dousing us with rain almost constantly since the New Year. The trails were ankle-deep and even the fields were miry. I tried to save my horse as much as possible, but I know it was a strain on him.

After the hunt, we had the hunt breakfast in the barn. The same barn my father built for us after I begged and pleaded, for years, for a horse barn. At that time horses were my lifeline. Now I know what I pleaded for was more than a lifeline; that lifeline was paid for with blood money. I didn't sell my body for money. It was just taken away from me. The barn was the result of several things. Probably some guilt and some ego–Daddy wanted the fine horses too, and a fine stable to keep them in, and I begged for the barn, and perhaps there was some love for me. As loathsome as I feel about what happened to me and all of us, there is a part of me that will never believe that Daddy didn't love me in his own way. He didn't love me as a result of the sex, but because of what I did for his life. In New Age thought we were soul mates.

Usually, the hunt breakfast is set up on tables near the vans, but the rain had chased us in, and the smoked turkey, ham biscuits, brie, wine, and cakes were served in the aisle. I watched and mingled as people joked, and laughed, and talked about the mud and the fox line we hit early on that morning, and how this day compared with other mornings before it. The smell of good wine and food and rain and horses mixed together with the faces of old and young and the music of human merriment. I was transfixed with the triumph of the moment when I recalled the days and months and years my sisters and I had spent in this barn, with only ourselves and our dreams for the horses to keep our minds from the dread of our parents in the big house at Greenfield.

Helen Atkinson Maplethorpe, the writer, and her hunt club were our club's guests, and I had to be there. She was totally accessible and could not have been nicer. I don't know why we are all surprised in a way when famous people are nice. It should be the other way around: that we expect people to be nice until they prove themselves otherwise. Anyway, I could immediately sense her sincerity and genuine interest in all the aspects of fox hunting. She was the master of her hunt and has the manners that should be there. I don't know why I was so taken by her ease at being with other people, but I sensed a depth in her concerning others that made me feel so at ease.

I did all the usual things, complimented her writing, asked for her autograph, and made small talk. I didn't mention that I had two books published or that I wanted to give her a copy of each because they are about horses.

The vans and trailers parked in the field which was always called the "big field," and where as a child I chased our horses for hours trying to catch my horse to ride. There was Big Billy, Little Billy, Bailey, Patches, Lady, and Daisy. They were all so smart about my catching them, and I was a little girl, but tenacious. I would try to drive them back to the barn, but they would always turn just before they got to the gate and run the other way back towards the creek. Each time I thought I couldn't go back after them again, but I always did. Sometimes when it was hot, I would fall exhausted in the grass and cry and cry and cry because they wouldn't go through the gate.

It wasn't until I was a teenager that Daddy built a barn just for the riding horses and fenced off several small lots just for the horses. By this time, we had the show horses, and I had advanced in my understanding of horse psychology enough to catch them without the small paddocks.

That day in January, I looked around the field and thought about how many tears had been spilled on that ground, and how many hours of frustration spent when no one would come to help. When the horses finally would give up and go through the gate, it was sometimes only minutes before Mama called me to supper and all my work had been for nothing, because the horses had to be turned back out to pasture. The 'big field' taught me a good lesson in never giving up.

Any child expects and wants her parents to love her and when they don't, then the child must find a way to survive. I was very lucky at this. I did find a way to survive–first by disassociating from the bad times, and second by seeking to make Daddy love me by trying to do what he wanted. I learned to ride like a warrior, sing like a nightingale, support him in wanting to be a giant in the lumber business, acknowledge his desire to be known as an honest businessman, and not condemn him for drinking.

When my mother did nothing but fight him at every turn, it was very easy for me to replace her screams with soothing words and knowing looks of support and praise. The one thing my mother and I always agreed on was trying to stop him from drinking. As a teenager, I found the best way to prevent his drinking was to make a deal. It worked for the short-term but cost me so much for the long term.

When we were children the hunt club was in the outskirts of Richmond and we, for the most part, were the only people in Derbyshire with show horses. The people who could afford them weren't interested, so except for the friends at horse shows, we shared a very lonely life with the horses.

We had no one but ourselves to talk to then about the horses, and we couldn't even confide in each other our fears about the situation at home. It was an unspoken truce that we maintained among the three of us, never to mention the unspeakable even when we thought about the unthinkable. We turned to the horses when we couldn't turn to each other.

Now my sister owned the barn, the hunt club had moved to Derbyshire, and this Saturday the barn was full of people and horses. Remember, in Derbyshire things have a way of turning around, the upper end is South and the lower end is North. The tables had turned again. The hunt club was here, not there. How different it would feel to me without the scars from my childhood.

El Niño hung around for months as the winter slipped into spring. It had dumped its worst on us for three days. The clouds hung heavy as I strained to see through the constant spatter on the windshield. Each time my Jaguar met an oncoming car or truck, a wave of water was thrown over the hood. Then one wiper struck it head-on, and for an instant the view was clear. It rained on me all the way to Richmond. At last, the warmth and dryness of the doctor's office were a welcome sanctuary.

We had been working with the outcome of the Amytal interviews over the winter. I knew what I had seen in the hypnotic state of the Amytal, but rationalizing that with the conscious mind after fifty years is asking a lot. My mind told me all my memories were true, but my father had totally deluded me with his dreams of his goodness. It was so hard for me to accept the ghastly pictures of reality, and even harder for me to reconcile the symptoms of a sexually abused childhood as an adult. I wanted so much not to believe the things I remembered. I wanted them to be a nightmare that would go away, and which I wanted to go away more than anything in the world. I didn't want to believe anything bad about either of my parents, even though I knew these things were true.

Dr. Thomas recognized all of this and another series of Amytal interviews was scheduled.

23

THE AMYTAL HAD CALMED me greatly for a period of about six months. There were fewer outbursts of rage and less depression. But, as the year passed and another spring edged closer to summer, the nightmares became more intense and more frequent. I had been subject to nightmares since childhood. There was one recurring nightmare that followed me through childhood, and even today I feel the terror it produced.

I would dream that I was in the big red barn at home, the one my grandfather built, and this huge brown bear would appear and snarl at me. He always seemed to come from behind the steps that led to the loft. I was in the aisle and he would chase me to the steps and up to the second floor. I would run frantically to scramble up the pile of hay, reaching for anything to grab a hold of. I could hear the bear breathing hard and running across the floor trying to get me. I would cry and scream for help, but nobody came. Then when I could hear his paw sweeping through the air to catch my leg, I would wake up dripping in sweat and completely out of breath. The terror of being chased and nearly caught gripped my body until I stretched my legs to make sure I could move.

It seems odd now that I never went downstairs and told my mother or father that I had a nightmare. Maybe subconsciously I knew all along who the bear was. But then I just lay awake for hours too afraid to move. This nightmare was always followed by several days of dreading the nights to come because I would have to close my eyes and pray the bear would not come.

Dr. Thomas and I recognized the bear as a symbol of my father, but a bear was much less traumatic than living through the abuse again in a dream. As a child, I'd felt the bear was just a brown bear breathing and blowing hot air after me. As an adult, I knew the bear had the movements and gestures of a man. He was simply hidden in the brown hair.

There were other dreams equally as horrifying, but none that happened over and over as the bear chase did. I have wondered if the nightmares corresponded in time with the abuse. If so, it was a double whammy for me to survive the abuse and later be confronted and have to survive the bear. My nightmares were the basic reason for this set of interviews.

The weather that spring was warm, and the flowers were brilliant. I remember the azaleas especially. They cascaded around the foundations and formed mounds of snow along the fences. The shades of melon and salmon were bordered with cranberry making it hard to distinguish whether they were bowls of sherbet or frothy summer drinks.

This series of interviews was to be done at Saint Mary's. I was glad to go back to Saint Mary's. I had no bad feelings about going back, only anxiety about what I would learn. It was good to think about going back to the place where I had first gotten help. Lindsay took me, as usual. There was a great deal of construction going on, and we had to walk around many new areas before we came to the elevators. Upstairs on the seventh floor, there was little change. There were more signs, but the doors leading to the psychiatric ward were the same. I looked in and felt my heart plunge. No matter how good my memories, the fact was the same; this was the unit where they treated people with mental illness. I swallowed hard, took a deep breath, and pushed the intercom button. The buzzer went off and I heard myself saying. "Lesley Owens for Dr. Thomas."

The locks clanked and the door was ready to open. Lindsay kissed me on the cheek and promised to be back in the afternoon. She often tested patients there for the doctor she worked for, so she knew the routine and most of the doctors.

I pulled the door open and walked into the hallway. The air was thick with hospital smells but there was little noise. I could hear talking behind the nurse's station and there were several patients on the floor. A nurse met me and directed me to the room where the voices were heard. I took a seat at a table and looked around. There were lots of patients, nurses, counselors, and several women who seemed to be like me. Then I remembered Dr. Thomas was to do four interviews that day which was highly unusual since he only did a few each year. But it just happened that he had four people who needed them, and he decided to do all of them the same day. We all looked very different from each other.

One of the women was very young, probably in her late teens. She sat in a chair to herself and seemed very disinterested in what was going on around her. She was blond with blue eyes and fair skin, slight build, and small features. She was pretty by anyone's standard. I wondered what had happened to her to cause her to need this treatment at such an early age. But that was good. At least hers would not drag on all her life as mine had.

Dr. Thomas came in a few minutes later and took her with a nurse into one of the little rooms that opened off our sitting room. The door closed behind them and I imagined the nurse putting on the blood pressure gauge and Dr. Thomas trying to get the IV started. I hoped her veins were large and cooperative.

There was another lady who appeared older than me and very sad. She was tall, thin, with gray eyes and short gray hair. She reminded me of a school teacher. She was probably very bright, worked hard, and had very high standards that over time had caused her a lot of pain in the classroom. I tried to make eye contact with her, but she hardly moved and my efforts to smile at her were useless.

The fourth woman in our little group was totally different. She came with an entourage: a woman who was obviously her friend, and another doctor. There was much going back and forth, much talk and fluster about this woman. I wondered what could be wrong with her. She certainly didn't seem to be sad or depressed. It was rather the opposite. From my viewpoint, she was demanding a great deal and never seemed to stop talking. Everyone seemed to want to please her. I was betting it would be hard to do.

I was so enthralled with my little group that I had overlooked what else was happening in the room. A little parade of patients was circling the tables in the center, including mine. They weren't saying anything to themselves or anyone else. They just walked around the room. I watched for a minute then realized that a very tall man in his late seventies was apparently leading the little group of women. He was unusually tall, maybe even six feet four inches. He had on brown corduroy pants and a brown shirt and he wore glasses. He must have been a professional of some sort. Now his work was forgotten, and his mind was totally absorbed in making the circle around the room.

I looked up at the clock and it said 10:30. Within almost the same second, a little voice from the corner of the room said, "I've got to go home to milk my cows."

I couldn't believe what I was hearing, but there it was again. "I've got to go home to milk my cows."

I looked hard and there in the corner was a tiny little woman telling the nurses again. "I've got to go home to milk my cows."

One of them answered her. "Minnie, it's not time to go yet. It's only 10:30 and you don't milk until twelve o'clock. You go back and sit down, and we'll call you when it's time."

"No, it's time now for me to go. You don't understand." She walked away from the nurse and began to follow the little parade. She caught up with the leader and walked with him, looking up at his face.

"I've got to go home to milk my cows."

He didn't answer her or stop walking.

She tried again. "I've got to go home to milk my cows."

He gave no indication of seeing or hearing her.

She was showing signs of frustration as she yelled at him, "You can't hear and you don't talk either, do you?"

I guess I was the only one paying any attention because I thought it was funny, but no one else seemed to notice. Minnie stopped walking with the man and went on to someone else. I began to think about a dairy family and how this life must have affected Minnie. Everything on a dairy farm revolves around milking time seven days a week. Obviously, that woman had both a large dairy and a good dairy, or she wouldn't have been worried about it. Somehow in the impaired reaches of Minnie's mind, she knew if she could just get home to milk the cows everything else would be all right.

I wanted to tell her it was all right. This frail, little woman in the gray cotton dress wore wire-rimmed glasses and a knot of gray hair at the nape of her neck. To look at her, I knew she could have been anything, a teacher, a librarian, doctor. Now, she was a little woman reduced to begging to be allowed to do the one thing that had given her a sense of accomplishment in her life, or maybe it had been her livelihood. I didn't know. I do know I identified with her and wished for her pain to leave.

I was the last of the four women that morning to start the interview. I wasn't afraid or worried. In fact, I looked forward to the euphoric state and the deep sleep which came afterward.

The nurse and Dr. Thomas began talking as they got the blood pressure and the IV in place. I wasn't interested in their conversation until the nurse said she had been to a wedding in Derbyshire over the weekend. My ears immediately tuned in because it was so unusual. Then she said the wedding was at seven o'clock in the morning and I thought–only in Derbyshire!

This series of interviews went well, but my focus was adolescence rather than childhood. It was so hard to believe what I was remembering, and yet I knew it was true because it connected so many things that had happened later.

It was Daddy's daily routine to come home at lunch from the mill because the main office was attached to the house. He would eat lunch, then open his mail and talk to the bookkeepers. After a short nap on the couch in the den, he would go back to the mill. It was about this time of day and about life at home that the interview concerned.

I don't remember the question that put me in this time frame or place. I just remember seeing Daddy pulling me by the hand on a hillside in what we called the big field at home. I was trying to get away and begging him to let me go. It was a summer day with the sun shining brightly. I could see myself trying to hit him to let me go, pulling at his hand and begging through tears all the while. He kept walking, not paying any attention to me. It was as if he were in a trance or really angry. I had seen him like this many times.

I soon realized we were on the path going to an old house where his aunt had lived. It was on our farm, but it had been abandoned for years. It was a small Williamsburg-type house with a little porch out front, a well, some scattered trees, and a few common rose bushes, yuccas, daffodils, spirea, and lilacs. There were many cottages around like it.

We had to cross a creek where I had played cowboys and Indians on horseback with my cousins. We had laid out towns and ranches and villages all along the creek bank, but I had never allowed them to cross the creek. We children never went near the old house. There was never any reason we should cross the creek or explore the house or grounds, it was just that my father owned the place and I said we couldn't go there. I never knew why I didn't want to go there, until this interview. Then I realized Daddy was the reason, and this interview was explaining it.

He continued across the creek and up the hill to the cottage. My terror grew as we got closer. I could hear our footsteps across the floor of the porch. The door scraped on the sill as we entered the dark cool little room. Another crime was about to be played out.

Here the interview ended, but I must include something that happened when I was in my early thirties involving this house, Daddy, and me. It happened the day I signed the papers to have Daddy admitted to Tuckers, the hospital for alcoholism. That was one of the worst days of my life and certainly the worst to that point.

The alcohol had become uncontrollable and depression made him suicidal. Linc, my mother, and I all agreed Daddy had to be committed after one of the bookkeepers called me to come get him at eight o'clock in the morning. He and my mother were wrestling over a knife in the front yard. He was attempting suicide. Linc had assembled a doctor, a guardian ad litem for Daddy, and a judge to hold a hearing. It fell to me to sign the papers for his commitment because my mother refused. I called one of my sisters for support and she said, "You take care of it. I can't stand it," and she hung up the phone. All of this took place in the den at home. To me, it was the most distressing and embarrassing two or three hours. I wanted to become invisible, but I had to sit there and answer the questions. My mother refused to come downstairs.

The sheriff came to take him to the hospital. I couldn't understand at the time why my mother would go with him in the sheriff's car to the hospital but would not come downstairs to have him committed. Again, I was acting as a true wife and my mother was the enabler for him. She had always been.

After they all left, I had been so emotionally exhausted I turned to the one thing which had saved my sanity all my life. I went upstairs and found an old shirt and jeans and went out to the horse barn. I put a bridle on my old mare, my first show horse, the chestnut mare Daddy had bought for me when I was twelve. I didn't even put a saddle on her but found a bag to use as a saddle. I jumped on her bare back, with only the bag to keep my clothes from getting too sweaty, and went tearing across the fields at a full gallop. I had no idea where I was going. I just wanted to get away. I found myself lashing her with the reins as the tears raced across my face. Once again, the tears and sobs were racking my body and I had no idea why.

The old mare flew across logs and ditches. I rode low and yelled in her ear to go faster. When we had both run our bodies out, I found myself at the creek across from the old house. Lady was in a lather and blowing hard. I slid from her back and drew the reins over her neck. She dipped her head onto my chest and leaned heavily against me. I was sorry for having abused her but glad for being able to ride off my anger and hurt. I led her over to a stump and sat down.

I don't know how long I stared across the creek before I realized where I was. The scene didn't look the same as it had when I was a child. The house, the trees, the bushes, and the well had been bull-dozed up. The knoll the house sat on was smooth grass, now in a pasture. The creek was at the bottom of the hill. That was about all that was left to recognize, except the foreboding feeling for me that lingered there. I sat for a long time letting Lady cool out and letting my thoughts wander. I had many memories of the house, riding by on horseback with Daddy, driving there with him. But still, I could not make myself cross the creek. The times I couldn't remember kept me from crossing the creek. Finally, Lady and I walked back home without realizing any of the connection, except for the sick feeling.

These were two instances in my life when my body and mind refused to go when I had no idea why. This interview explained my reluctance as a child and as an adult to go near this house. In both instances I had no idea why, nor did I spend any time worrying about why. It was simply a place I didn't want to be. Our subconscious protects us from so much.

24

IT WAS July and it was hot. The whole northeast was in a severe drought and it had not rained in Derbyshire for weeks. The past week of hundred-degree temperatures had baked the ground like biscuits baked too hot, too fast. They come out of the oven hard, flat, and cracked. The leaves on the trees were wilted and drooping, thirsting for water. Every day the hot wind wrenched more and more water from their fiber.

I watched the sun rise fiery red, lighting the countryside with an intense orange white hue that carried the waves with it. The heat penetrated the open windows and filled the room with suffocating layers of air, one on the other. I dressed slowly and drank coffee. Minutes later I realized the coffee had made me even hotter and sick to my stomach.

At 7:30, Lindsay arrived to take me to the hospital for another Amytal interview. She was the only one I trusted. Anyone could have driven me to Richmond, but who was willing to go to the psychiatric ward at St. Mary's to get me? There were some in the family who could have done that too. But no one else had my confidence as Lindsay did. I know this is because she arranged my first hospital stay, but mostly it's because she understood what I was going through and did not give me useless answers to comments.

She answered me directly and validated my pain. I finally realized after ten years of therapy what psychiatrists did in therapy. It's like my mother-in-law once said, 'Oh, it couldn't be that bad. Go out and enjoy the beautiful day instead of dwelling on your feelings.' Or worse still, when she once said, 'You know that person didn't mean to hurt your feelings. You have to forgive them.' On the other hand, the psychiatrist says, 'Why do you think you feel so bad? Why do you think this person is so mean to you?' Or, 'That is a very mean statement to make.' Friends sometimes try, but they have no understanding of how to help real pain.

Lindsay and I talked all the way to Richmond about my problem. How had Daddy been able to abuse me? Why didn't I just hate him as a child? Why didn't my mother protect me? Why didn't my sisters really believe me? Why didn't they want to talk about it? All questions I had been over and over. I had no answers, but she listened with compassion.

At the hospital, I registered, and we took the elevator to the seventh floor. It was all the same as last year. It was a short walk to the big double doors and the red button with a sign that said *Call to Enter*. Three simple words, but they meant no one entered unless his or her name was on a list of the names of all patients and staff. You were a patient if you had some type of mental trouble. The horror of this ward was that so many patients were there as a result of abuse by another person.

Lindsay punched the button and explained who we were. The doors opened and a pretty blond nurse smiled and said, "Hello, Mrs. Owens, we've been expecting you."

She gave Lindsay a phone number to call in the afternoon to see when I could go home. Then Lindsay was gone. I was left in the hallway with all sorts of people milling around, doctors, nurses, technicians, aides, counselors, patients. I quickly picked out the patients from the staff, particularly the men. One man stood by the nurse's station. Every minute or two he asked, "When can we go out for a smoke?" Nobody paid any attention. "Isn't it time to go out for a smoke?" A nurse looked at the clock. "You have ten minutes yet."

She didn't look any different from anyone else because

everyone dressed the same. However, the staff wore badges, and patients didn't. Doctors wore suits and ties.

A nurse came by with a clipboard. She looked at me. "Mrs. Owens?"

"Yes."

"How are you this morning? We're going to be in this little room for a while, just to get you ready."

"Yes."

She had a big ring of keys. She chose one and unlocked the door. We entered and I sat in front of a little table.

"Now just let me go get my tray and I will get this IV started."

She came back with a tray, put a tourniquet on my arm, and began patting the veins.

"I have small veins, so you're going to need at least a point twenty-three gauge butterfly needle."

She picked it up and looked. "I hate to use this because it's so big, but that's what he wants."

I didn't say anything. She continued to pat my arm, my hand. "All right dear, let's try this one." The needle started in, the pain made me tense up. "I'm sorry, honey, just a little further."

The second push felt stronger and my arm became rigid.

She put on one piece of tape and tried to draw back the blood, nothing.

"Look at that. It's gone. I knew that needle was too big. I'm going to use a smaller needle. I don't care what he asked for."

"He had the same trouble the last time. I bet he stuck me five or six times before he ever got it right."

"I'm going to use this 123-butterfly, and I am going to put it in the big vein in your arm."

"That's fine. Just tape it good so it won't roll off again."

When she finished, we went into another room with a bed, a blood pressure machine, and two chairs. I looked at the nurse. "I need some tissues."

"Why are you crying?" she asked.

"Don't worry, I cry all the time. I was just thinking how unnecessary all this is or could have been."

"Yes, why are you doing this?"

"Incest. Isn't that something? My own father. I don't understand. Why was sex so important? I was just a little girl. I am mad. Damned mad, at the world and especially my daddy and my mother."

"Your mother didn't protect you?"

"No. She knew about it, too."

"You have every reason to be angry."

"At some level they all knew, I mean the whole family. And I was always trying to protect my sisters."

"It doesn't seem right, does it? You know, you look familiar to me."

"Oh, yes, I've been here before. Last year. You were my nurse for one interview. I recognized you."

"Now, I remember. We don't do many of these. In fact, yours was the last one until today."

"That's right, it was last May and here I am again in July, and it was ten years ago yesterday that I began all this. I made it about fifty years before I landed in the hospital. I carried all that damn stuff around for fifty years. It's like I had both legs cut off and one hand tied behind my back all my life, but I still made it, to some extent. But I could kill my daddy first, then all of them who didn't help me, an innocent child."

The door opened and Dr. Thomas came in. "Good morning. How are you?"

"The same. I'm crying, but you're used to that."

"Yes, I've seen you cry a few times." He moved over to the bed and began looking at the syringe and needle. He looked at the nurse. "Is everything okay? I see the butterfly is in the main vein in her arm."

"She has such tiny veins."

He looked at me and smiled. "We know about that, don't we?"

I nodded but couldn't speak.

Dr. Thomas said, "I need a ten cc syringe."

The nurse leaned over the tray. "There isn't one there. I'll run down to the supply room and get one."

I had finally stopped crying enough to make a comment, hoping it would be a light joke. "I have plenty at home in the horse barn, if you want to get one of those."

Dr. Thomas was amused. "I should have told you to bring one."

Finally, everything was in place and the lights turned down. The nurse began the blood pressure pump. Dr. Thomas's hand was on the syringe.

"Take a reading every minute," he said quietly. Turning to me, he said in a soft voice, "Are you feeling any relaxation?"

"Yes, some." This was always the best part. A wonderfully relaxed feeling of safety and security would spread over my body and into my mind. It was all right. Whatever was going to happen next was all right.

"Can you count backwards from 100 for me?"

A few more minutes passed.

"Can you count backwards from 100 again?"

This time the drug had taken effect, and I closed my eyes and waited for the sinking away to wherever the drug allowed me to go.

I have forgotten the beginning of the interview because I remember thinking it was all trivial. That it was not important. Why were we talking about those unimportant things? I felt agitated and wanted to go on and get to something I didn't already know. I kept answering the questions though.

Suddenly I felt scared.

"Where are you?"

"I don't know."

"What do you see?"

"It's like I am looking down on this awful black yucky pool. It's slimy and I am afraid."

"Why are you afraid?"

"I am going to fall in it and it's a long way down and it's deep and it's so black."

"What else do you see?"

"It's like it's a silo and I am at the top looking down and I don't want to fall."

"Are you going to fall?"

"Yes, I know I am going to fall."

"Do you think you will be hurt?"

"No, I just don't want to go down there."

"What's in that pool?"

"It's full of demons."

"What kind of demons?"

"I don't know, but they are there."

"Okay, we're going to stop now, but I want you to listen to me, will you?"

"Yes."

"I want you to go home and think about those demons tonight, all right?"

"Yes, I will."

By this time, he had taken the needle out of my arm and put a Band-aid on it. The nurse was pumping the blood pressure gauge again.

Another nurse came in. "How did it go?"

"Fine, she talked the whole time, it was good. I'll be out in a minute."

I was so tired I didn't care. I just wanted to sleep. She checked my blood pressure every fifteen minutes for the next three hours. I slept on, relieved to have the peace and quiet. My mind was at ease. There were no images, just blissful darkness and quiet.

When I awoke about 1:30, she brought me a snack: crackers and ginger ale. I ate them slowly, still so tired with no energy.

Lindsay came and it seemed so strange that I could get up and walk out as if nothing had happened. I was shaky and a little wobbly. But I noticed no one was staring. No, I guess I was doing okay.

Lindsay hadn't eaten, so we went to the Olive Garden. It was her favorite. I told her what I could remember over eggplant parmesan and iced tea.

We talked between my quiet times all the way home. We didn't talk about anything special. It was just an easy conversation with someone with whom I felt safe. It's very easy to talk to Lindsay. I feel I can tell her anything and I know that's because I trust her.

There have been so few people in my life I could trust, and I have mistakenly trusted the wrong people so often.

This distrust was embedded in my early childhood when I was betrayed by the two people who should have been looking out for me. Now, I know I trusted the wrong people in the past because I needed love so desperately. My whole life has been a quest for love and attention. It has been the theme of my life: seek love and find betrayal. But, don't give up. I would tell myself, 'Love is out there somewhere.'

That night I remembered a flashback I had experienced the week before. They were two fleeting images, but very sharp and real. The first was a close-up focus on a man's genitals. They appeared huge and extremely hairy. Immediately after the first, there was an image of myself as a small child swinging from a rope that was tied around my waist. The two images made no sense either separately or together, but they were images from my past. I was sure of that. The images kept reappearing all night, and by morning I was convinced I should tell Dr. Thomas before we got started.

25

THIS TIME I was by myself when I walked up to the two doors and turned to the intercom. "Lesley Owens to see Dr. Thomas."

The lock clicked and I pushed the doors open. They slammed shut again and I heard the same click. That sound always left me with the same sensation. I was locked in and there was no getting around it. I may be able to leave, but for the moment I was still locked in. There were always two thoughts. First, I was safe. In the hospital, I was safe. It was a nice place to be. Second, I couldn't leave because I had a mental illness.

No matter what the public may want to believe, the fact is mental illness is a no-no, regardless of the diagnosis or the cause. People don't want to hear about it, know about it, or be around it. The mentally ill are shunned by almost everyone.

Dr. Thomas was in the nurse's station. The sight of him always made me feel better. He was someone I could trust, or to put it better, I had to trust. If he was going to help me, I had to trust him. I had told myself that for a very long time.

He looked up and came toward me. "Go to the nurse's station on the other side. We'll be using a room over there today. A nurse is waiting for you."

I smiled weakly and walked toward the nurse's station without saying a word. There was no need. They all knew why I was there. On a psychiatric ward, everyone knows everything. There is usually more staff than patients. They know how important attention is to the patients. I wondered if anyone had ever been admitted to a psychiatric ward who didn't desperately need attention. That's something most people never think about. Those with their self-esteem intact, their identity solid and unshakable would never think about it.

A nurse came out carrying a clipboard. "Right this way, Mrs. Owens. We're going to be working down here this morning." I walked past my old room from years ago. I noticed that the old window glass with the pit marks from chair legs crashing into it, and all the long scratch marks made from God knows what had been replaced. All the marks and scratches made by angry, desperate patients were gone. I wondered if someone had finally broken the glass. I had never tried, only looked at it for long periods of time. All the doors were locked–a sure sign of a psychiatric ward. Patients met me in the hall. Few of them returned my smile. I understood why. They were lost in their own troubles and had no time for me.

We went into a room with pretty wallpaper, draperies, and a floor so shiny and clean you could eat off it. I lay down on the bed and looked up. The ceiling was a typical drop ceiling and I noticed immediately that one piece of the fleck board was loose and might fall anytime. It was over the other bed, no danger to any of us in the room now. I spent a great deal of time that morning and the following morning debating whether I should tell the nurse. What would it indicate if I did or didn't tell?

A new nurse came into the room. She spoke with an Irish accent. "Mrs. Owens, a technician is coming up from the lab to do your IV. She'll do a great job. You won't even know you've been stuck."

"That's good."

"Mrs. Owens, why are you crying? It's the stress, isn't it? I understand. It takes a lot out of you when you come in here doesn't it? You go on and cry. Tears are a great release. Here's the technician now. Let's get this needle in as quickly as possible so we will have that over."

The tech set her basket down. It looked like a picnic basket with an overload of utensils and not enough food. She began patting my hand, then the wrist, then the other hand and wrist, and finally up the arm to the elbow. "I'm not going to use a butterfly," she said. "A hitch is much better." She turned to the nurse with a long explanation, while I stared at the panel in the ceiling and wondered why I didn't mention it.

Dr. Thomas came in shortly. "Are we ready?"

I turned toward him. "Dr. Thomas, I remembered something the other day that I think I should tell you."

"Good, but let's wait until we start. Whatever it is, it will be a good place to start." He sat down and the nurse lowered the lights. I had a fistful of tissues beside me, crumpled and used. My breathing slowed and I felt my whole body become heavy.

Dr. Thomas's voice was low. "Now, tell me what you remembered."

"I had a flashback last week about being hung from a rope around my waist in something like a silo. I'm falling headfirst and my arms and legs are stretched out. I am trying so hard to catch myself on something, but I can't."

"Can you see that image now?"

"Yes, I am swinging on the rope and it's tied around my waist."

"How big are you?"

"I am little, real little. But I can run and play. I have long curls and I am wearing a dress. I may be five. I'm embarrassed because the skirt of the dress is falling around my head and I know the men can see my panties."

"Who is holding the rope?"

"A man, but there are several up there with him and they're laughing because I am so scared. They think it looks funny, me hanging from that rope."

"What has happened now?"

"I fell down on the bottom and it's dirty and damp and wet."

"What can you see?"

"I can't see much because it's too dark, but there are other people here. I can hear them laughing and talking. It's all men and they are drinking and joking."

"Do you know any of them?"

"No, I don't know anybody."

"What does this place look like?

"I can't see much, but it is round, and it's made of rock, and then it's wood above the rock. The rock is painted white and the wood is dark, but the rock is all muddy."

"Are there any doors?"

"No, I don't see any."

"Is your father there?"

"Yes, he's here, but I don't see him. I don't know where he is, but he brought me here."

I began to cry again.

"What do you see that's making you cry?"

"There is a huge man standing over there and he's naked, but he's covered with hair. He has lots and lots of hair all over him. The men are pushing him toward me, and I'm scared."

"Do you know him?"

"No."

"What does he look like?"

"He's big and his face is round, and he's dumb. His face is flat with big eyes and a flat sort of nose and a big mouth and he looks fat. The hair is sort of reddish, black." I become more agitated.

"What is happening now?"

"They have pushed me on the floor, and he is bending over me."

"All right now. We are going to quit there. You try to rest and calm down. It's all right. Try to think about those horses of yours. Try not to think about this now. I will see you in the morning."

Dr. Thomas was gone, the needle out, and the nurse was patting my shoulder and trying to soothe me.

"It's all over now, honey, everything's alright. Just try to relax. Nothing is going to hurt you."

I don't know how long I cried or when I went to sleep, but at some point, my mind closed on the overwhelming situation and grotesque creature. I awoke after lunch with a bad headache and completely exhausted. The nurse gave me some Tylenol and ginger ale. The drink eased the burning in my throat, but there was nothing to soothe my eyes. They burned from all the tears. I wanted to cry, but I was able to hold back the tears until Lindsay came for me.

The nurse gave me instructions for the night and squeezed my hand as she wished me luck for the weekend. I left following the footfalls of the morning, and those of another morning ten years before when the world seemed a totally different place to me. My father had forced that world on me without my consent or knowledge. I was handed that world without a key or guide to help me along the way. My parents had used me for their own terrible needs and left me an emotional wreck. As an adult, I found all the tools I had to fix my problems were the wrong ones, and worse than that, I had no idea how to handle the tools given to me.

The ten-year trek through psychotherapy had provided me with many pieces to the puzzle of my life. I could only hope there were more pieces to come. I wanted a full picture of the truth about my childhood. I wanted all the demons and nightmares gone. I wanted to be well. No more depression, anxiety, tantrums.

I couldn't tell Lindsay about the interview until much later that afternoon. I was numb from the scare and felt powerless to combat the memory. The whole scene felt so bizarre, so unreal, but I knew that wasn't right. My mind's eye put me on the end of that rope as a memory does, always in the same position, and I was standing in that pit, whatever else it was, or wherever it was.

I slept a great deal for the next four days. Dr. Thomas had moved my next interview to 9:30 Monday morning instead of Friday. My body felt as though I had been run over by an eighteen-wheeler fully loaded. Every muscle ached. My arms weighed a ton and my chest was so heavy. I wondered how my brain felt. You can feel tiredness in your head, eyes, neck. You can feel pain in your stomach and heart, but how about your brain? How do you know when your brain is tired or hurts? Or does it work like a robot, storing information, solving problems while you are awake, then clicking off spewing out waste in dreams while you are asleep?

The memories of my childhood were taking such a toll on my body. I couldn't help but wonder and be amazed by the brain. I lay in bed trying to understand and accept the consequences of those hideous images. There had to have been a mark around my waist from the rope. Why didn't my mother see it? Where was Daddy while I was in the pit? I knew he was there, but where was he? Was he up above me, somewhere drunk in the truck, on the ground? Had he left with somebody else? How did I get home?

There were no answers that weekend.

26

I WAS PUT in the same room as the Friday before. I looked at the ceiling. Nothing had happened to the tile. It was still in place. I knew it would last through this interview. I didn't think about telling anybody about the loose tile. It was like a good omen for me. As long as the tile lasted, I would be all right. It was my little secret, a bond between me and the unknown. I did wonder if the staff might notice and take bets on when it would fall. Wouldn't that be funny? What if someone found a stash of money in the locker in the nurses' station with a list of bets when it would fall? That morning I couldn't even laugh when I thought about it falling in the night and scaring the poor souls to death in the room. It just wasn't funny and more than that, I didn't care.

The nurse from the first day came in to do the needle. She asked if I had a good weekend. No. I hadn't had a good weekend. My weekend had been awful. What else did she want to know? I was too polite to say that, but it was what I thought. She was chewing gum and kept pressing me.

"Did you do anything over the weekend? "

"No. I didn't feel like it."

"Oh, I'm sorry."

The tears began to slide down my cheeks.

"Mrs. Owens, why are you crying?"

"I don't know. I just cry. I don't want to. I just can't help it. Do you want to know how much I have cried in my lifetime?"

"That's terrible, how much?"

"If you took everything out of this hospital, every piece of equipment, every piece of furniture, cleaned out every closet, and the whole building was standing bare, it wouldn't hold the tears I have shed in a lifetime."

"That's a lot."

"I know, but it's the truth."

Dr. Thomas came in. "Hi, how are you?"

"Not good."

"Bad weekend?"

"Yes."

"Were there any more memories?"

"No."

The nurse broke in. "She was just telling me how much she had cried in her lifetime."

"Yes, we've been working on that depression for a long time, haven't we, Mrs. Owens?"

I nodded, fighting back the tears.

Dr. Thomas pulled up a chair. "Okay. Let's see what today brings."

I lay quiet, waiting for the drug to take effect. At least that would be nice. For a while, the Amytal takes away all the pain, anxiety, and hurt. I am suspended in time until the veil falls away and the memories are exposed.

"Let's go back to where we were the last time. Can you tell me anymore about that?"

"Yes."

"What do you see?"

"I'm standing in the place again. It's dug out in the ground, and it's round with rock walls. Above the rock walls is wood. If I look up, I can see the roof and it has a round hole in the center."

"What else do you see?"

"The floor is dirt, and it's damp. There are people there. All men and they're laughing. There's the man with all the hair. He is naked."

"I wonder why he doesn't have on any clothes?"

"I don't know, but they're taunting him, poking and laughing. There is a big round iron ring hooked to a metal plate on the ground. A man is threading the end of the rope around my waist through this hook. It's pulling me to the ground. My hands are tied behind my back."

"Why is he doing that?"

"I don't know."

"Where is your father?"

"I don't know, but he's there because he brought me, but I don't see him."

"What is happening now?"

"They are pushing the naked man toward me and laughing."

"What does he look like?"

"He is big, with reddish-black hair all over him. Everywhere. And his head is round, but I can't see his face very well. No! No! They are pushing him over me." I was crying now and very restless like I wanted to get away.

"All right, we'll stop there. You rest and I'll see you in the office."

I could hear him go out and the nurse taking the needle out of my arm. When I woke up the nurse came in and sat with me and began talking. She was very comforting.

"Have you been to any support group or incest survivor group?"

"No, Dr. Thomas has never suggested one."

"Maybe you ought to ask him about one."

"Yes, Lindsay has asked me several times to do that."

"Sometimes groups can help you remember things because they'll trigger something that happened to you."

"I know."

"I don't know exactly what happened to you in that place, but whatever it was it scared you nearly to death. Did you know anyone in your community that was retarded?"

"Yes, there were plenty of retarded people, but not like that man."

"Maybe you didn't know him."

"He was familiar, but I don't remember anyone like him, and I didn't know him."

Lindsay came in then. I trusted her with my life. She had been my guardian through this; in fact, for the last ten years, she had been the caregiver, not the other way around as it should have been for mother and daughter.

The nurse gave her explicit instructions for calling the office and setting up an appointment. The nurse squeezed my hand and wished me luck as we left.

Once again, I was walking between the two worlds. The past clouded every thought I had, as well as every face I met. Was it a kind face or one to be frightened of? What did they know about me?

What could they tell about me? What was my face showing?

It was Monday and I had had a week to recover, to a degree, before seeing Dr. Thomas again. It was so strange to go through these treatments because I was walking around doing my daily work, but the thoughts never left my mind. They popped up at any time and I tried to think through the situation. They were a constant distraction.

I struggled between spells of crying and depression over the next week. What had happened to me and why? How could my father let that terrible thing with the bear and the men in the round house happen to me? I was in limbo where I neither wanted to see or talk to anyone. My closest friends and family were all I wanted to see.

The church fundraiser was scheduled for the next Saturday. I was in charge of the yard sale, which meant I had to go to the church to sort through and label things. People came and went bringing things. I saw them, thanked them, answered questions, but my mind was never there. It was back in the pit or trying to identify the hairy man. I could even smell the dampness and feel the wet, cold air. On Friday I helped prepare the vegetables for the Brunswick stew on Saturday. The ladies were their usual playful selves, gentle gossip, old stories retold, new stories just happening. I nodded and smiled but stayed quiet. No one noticed.

When you take away my sisters, who could not deal with what I was doing; my daughter Camille, who couldn't deal with it either; Linc's family, who knew nothing of this and had little or no contact with us; it didn't leave many people for my support system. It left me with two of Linc's cousins, my son and daughter-in-law, their children, and Lindsay and her husband. With this little group I could be myself, wear my real face, whatever it was and simply say I didn't feel good if that was how I felt.

I learned early in childhood to be able to switch those faces in a split second if the circumstances called for it. Anyone who has grown up in an alcoholic family learns this skill quickly. It has to be done in order to keep the family secrets. Maybe not just alcohol but incest as well. No outsider should find out anything about family matters. Denial is taught and learned at a very early age. If I didn't recognize it, or show it or tell it, it had not happened.

The days passed as if I were still drugged. The nights were the same. I'd go to sleep, wake up several times during the night, and think. But there were no bad dreams. There is always something good in everything.

I prayed for God's help. He didn't help, because he couldn't. I was asking God's world to help me when it was Caesar's world that was causing the problem. I feel now I understand so clearly what Christ meant when he said to Pontius Pilate, "Render unto Caesar those things which are Caesar's and unto God those things which are God's." I am not a historian or a very religious person, but I feel I know the true meaning of Christ's words at that moment. We live in Caesar's world and we'd better abide by it. Leave God's world to him. God's world is the world within us, not the one we live in every day. God's world is the one we answer to for ourselves and it doesn't have a damn thing to do with Caesar's world.

Anyway, the stars were out, and I was glad. The fundraiser came and went, and I was glad. I felt good about it. I fed the hungry, gave to the poor, and today, Sunday, I was a better person. But only in

God's world am I a better person, not Caesar's. In Caesar's I am angry and alone for the same reason.

I went to church that morning when I was so exhausted and tired I could hardly move. But so was everyone else who helped with the yard sale and the stew. We were all exhausted and should have been at home in bed, or at least resting, but we weren't. We got up, went to church, sang in the choir, played the organ, sat in the pews; we did our duty. Just as always, we rendered unto Caesar what was his. God was in our hearts.

Now I was home and I was angry. My sister was not there yesterday or today. She was there Friday. She brought us yard sale workers lunch, which was much appreciated, and she brought us lots of stuff to sell, but she wasn't there to help at the church yesterday or for the service today. And the reason wasn't important. The important thing was I was mad. I felt that it was not so much at her as at myself and my circumstances.

So, I couldn't make either of my sisters love me, now or ever. It was too late for all of us. It was too late the day we were all born, but it must stop here. I would get well somehow, sometime. My getting well was the only thing that would stop the awful hurt that affected my immediate family and my extended family.

A short time later I had a dream which dealt with my real anger. I stirred under the bed covers, trying to escape, but from what? I couldn't remember, but my body hurt all over and my heart was racing. I opened my eyes and shut them immediately. I couldn't bear the feeling of terror, of being hopelessly trapped. My head weighed a ton. I could hear Linc snoring and I felt Kina, my Saluki, at the foot of the bed. I told myself, 'It was a dream, Lesley, a nightmare. It's all right now. It was only a nightmare, not real.'

I opened my eyes and tried to lie still. 'Oh God', I thought, 'when is this ever going to end?' I turned my head to look out the window and noticed the sheer curtains were waving in a cool breeze and the sun was shining. All last week had been dull and unbearably humid and hot. It was summer in Virginia. My first thought was, 'At least the sun is shining and it is cooler.' The hand-phone was on my night table. I reached for it and dialed Lindsay's number. Thank God for her. The phone clicked and she said, "Hello". I hadn't bothered to see what time it was, but I knew it was very early on Sunday morning. Her voice sounded groggy. It made me twinge with regret for calling so early, but I couldn't help it now.

"Lindsay, I had a horrible dream."

"I am sorry, what is it?"

"I don't know if I can straighten it out or not, it was so long and complicated, but so real."

"I am sure, tell me what happened."

"Well, you know the Amytal dream about the round ice house and the chicken fights."

"Yes,"

"I am sure it is somehow connected to that one. Anyway, it was like it happened a long time ago because Mama and Daddy were there, and Cile and Logan and Brian and their families, and Grandma Trimball, and Sarah and Lynne. And it was Christmas. Everyone had come to our house for Christmas. There were too many people, so some of us stayed in a house, but there was no real house in the yard, just in my dream.

"I had worked hard to get everything ready, put up all the decorations, and cooked lots of things. But when everyone got there, I was very depressed, and I couldn't enjoy it. I tried to avoid them because I felt so bad, but I couldn't hide my depression. Finally, Logan asked me what was wrong, and I couldn't tell him."

Lindsay broke in. "Did you tell him?"

"Yes. I didn't want to, but I did. I told him that I had tried to talk to Mama and Daddy about the whipping and the awful things–incest–Daddy did to me at Belmead during the war, but they wouldn't listen. Neither one of them would talk to me. I felt so rejected."

At this point, I began to cry over the phone. I couldn't help it, I was thinking about the rest of the dream and it just overwhelmed me. "Lindsay, I can't talk anymore, I'll call you back."

"Okay."

I went into the kitchen and cried, while I tried to fix a cup of coffee. My feelings of rejection and lack of love were more than I could deal with at the moment, even though I have learned so much about control of emotion.

I dialed the phone again.

"Lindsay?"

"Yes."

"I will try to finish. That night when we went in the house in the yard to sleep, it was full of people I didn't know. I said to them, 'You all have got to get out of here, this is not your house.'"

"'Who's going to make us?'"

"I said, 'I am.'"

"They were all drunk and I thought they were drug dealers, bringing drugs up from Miami. There were men and women and even a baby. They were all over the house, having a party, drinking, and having sex.

"One of them looked at me. 'You're not going to do anything. We're going to show you something, bitch.' I knew I couldn't control them, but I had to protect the rest, my sisters and the others.

"So I said, 'All right. We'll draw a line. This part of the house is for you and on the other side is ours and you can't come over the line.'

"They laughed. 'No, honey,' they said, 'it doesn't work that way. We won't go over the line, but you are staying with us. We are going to teach you something about sex.'

"They all laughed and pushed and grabbed at me. Then they said, 'Yes, get the big one out here, he will show her something.' There was more laughing and joking as they forced me to the floor on my back and held me down. 'Get in here,' –I can't remember what they called him. This huge glob of a man came in, his head was down so I couldn't see his face, but he was naked. He knelt over me and all I could see was his penis. At this point I was a child again, and his penis seemed to be longer than I was tall and as big around as I was. He pushed against me and I must have passed out with the searing pain because the next thing in the dream I was still lying there, but he was gone. Now, I know this man was a symbol of my father."

Lindsay's voice came over the phone. "That's scary, Mom."

"Yes, but really the worst part was what happened next."

"What was it?"

"I saw this couple in front of me having sex and the woman was holding a baby. The man pulled out from her and put his penis in the baby's mouth saying. 'Eat this' and he ejaculated. The baby gagged and the semen streamed out of her mouth. The man and woman were laughing and having great fun. Again, the baby is symbolic of me."

"That's horrible, Mom."

At this point, I was sobbing again over the phone. "Yes, and the baby looked exactly like my baby pictures."

"I had guessed that. The baby was you. Was there any more to the dream?"

"The next thing I remember, it was the next day and everybody had gone. I went over to the house in the yard again to clean up. It was a wreck. I had to hurry and clean up because the people who rented it were coming back that day. While I was there, this man came to the door and said the drug people wanted to rent it from us as a permanent stopover. I said I would have to ask Daddy, but I was sure they couldn't do that. But I did go to find him."

"And what did he say?"

"He said, 'How much will they pay?'"

Lindsay laughed. "Yes, that's what he would say."

"Anyway, I was so depressed when I went to church to practice for the Christmas program. I didn't want to face anyone, but two women told me they had called Daddy to ask him what was wrong with me. I knew them, but I can't remember now who it was. And that's about all I can remember."

"Mom, I know you're upset. That is a very disturbing dream."

"What do you think about it?"

"Like you said, it's confusing, but I think there's a lot of memory mixed in with the dream."

"I think so, too. I just wish I could remember who the women were."

"That would be good because I would bet they really did ask him what was wrong with you. Probably a lot of people in the community knew about you, just like you knew about the other girl in school who was involved with incest. People always know these things in a small community even if they don't admit it."

"Yes."

"If I were you, I would try to think really hard about who the big man really was too."

"I know in the dream he was no one I knew. He was just big and maybe kind of stupid. But I think now he was my father even though he looked more like a wrestler. I will try to think about it. I have to get off the phone now. My head is splitting, and I ache all over."

"I'm sure. I'll see you later today."

I hung up the phone and crawled back in bed. I couldn't believe how bad I felt, just from a dream. I tried to go back to sleep, but it was no use. It was going to be a bad day.

About 9:30 Sarah called. I was glad to hear from her, but I felt so bad it was hard to talk to her. I loved my sisters dearly, but it was so hard to talk to Sarah because I couldn't really tell her how I felt. She couldn't stand to hear anything bad and it always made it difficult for both of us. We talked about a few things and she asked if I was going to church. I said no, because I was having a bad hair day and I didn't have to play the organ, so I wasn't going.

She didn't ask what was wrong and I didn't tell her. I just said, "Sarah, you and Lynne, both are very lucky."

She didn't answer me, so I said, "Thanks for calling, but I have to go now. Bye," and that was the end of the conversation. I cried again after she hung up. It always hurts when I realize she doesn't want to have anything to do with my hurt. The strange thing is, I know this, and I know it's simply that she doesn't want to face her own hurts. So, we both suffer in silence. I wish we could face it all together and be real friends as well as sisters. The sad thing for all three of us as sisters is we had nothing to do with the cause.

Alcohol, and incest for me–and maybe for them, but I didn't know. I could only hope nothing happened to them and they hadn't suffered the torture as I had.

At lunch, I asked Linc, "How many days of our married life of forty-two years do you think have been ruined for me and for us all by my nightmares, rejections that bring up old memories, and depression?"

"At least half, maybe more."

"That's a big price to pay, isn't it?"

"Yes, and I'm sorry."

"I know." The day kept on as it had started. I couldn't shake the depression or feeling of exhaustion. I went to Lindsay's for supper and we sat on the porch at twilight and planned the next day. Monday would be better. Workdays were always better, and I almost never had a nightmare two nights in a row. Not that I could remember, that is.

As the sun faded behind the horizon we walked down to the pond and watched the geese. The old nanny with her brood of weaned billy goats came around and wanted her ears rubbed. She's so happy with her new job of babysitting the newly weaned babies. Now she doesn't have to worry about nursing and protecting. She only has to show them where to go to find the best food and give them the assurance of a protective adult.

We checked on the newly weaned calves next. They were anxious about us, but they had had the protection of their mother throughout what amounted to their childhood, without the abuse of a sick father. Isn't it strange that animals don't abuse sexually unless they are put in situations that cause it?

The day ended peacefully with the absolute assurance that tomorrow would be a better day. Without this hope, I could never have gone.

I had an appointment with Dr. Thomas the next afternoon. I recounted the dream as precisely as I could remember it.

"That's a very vivid dream and has lots of symbolism for you."

"I thought so too."

"In fact, I think it's one of the most direct dreams you've had. I mean all the important characters are there. Symbolically, you are trying to protect your sisters. Your parents won't listen to you, it's a holiday, there is drinking and sex, and you are trying to clean it all up and maintain the household. Isn't that the way it was, almost?"

"Yes, absolutely. In the dream I knew the two women who called my father and asked him what was wrong with me, why was I so depressed. But I can't remember who they were now."

"Isn't it funny how that happens? How the material is just sucked away from us? You may remember later. Maybe these women were forward-thinking women in the community, or maybe you had tried to confide in someone, but you don't have any recollection, do you?"

"No, none."

"Well, it will come."

There are many new days in life, but I count these as the most important ones in my life because in fact, they gave me new life. It is trite to say that without your mind, or your health, you have nothing, but to have been robbed as a child of your birthright of freedom of self is a birthmark that can never be fully erased.

I will live with these memories for the rest of my life. For the last forty-five years, I have been living in a post-traumatic syndrome condition. The condition got its name from the experiences of the Vietnam veterans. Is it a new condition, or an old condition with a new name? Does it matter? The human mind can only deal with things it can handle. If it can't handle it at the moment, it stores it away. These events become memories. The ones you can't recall are traumas. The subconscious stores them and they become our nightmares.

My next memory is a dream. I was back at home, where I was raised, and trying desperately to help my mother and take care of my grandson, John. This great stretch of time didn't seem strange in the dream. I was focused on trying to do as much as I could for everybody there. My mother's mother had come to visit. She was in a wheelchair which added to her care. John was running around and there were many things happening on the farm that demanded my attention. Lynne had come to see Grandma, so I had to fix dinner for her too. My father was away somewhere and would undoubtedly come home drunk. This put a lot of pressure on me and my mother. The final straw for me was I had forgotten to get Lynne a birthday present.

When I realized this, I went running out the back door and ran right into Daddy at the back steps. He was leaning on the railing and was terribly sunburned, but not drunk. I took one look at him and said, "You son of a bitch, I'm going to kill you for molesting me."

He jerked back and said, "I did not."

I began hitting him, saying "You did too, you did, you know you did."

"No, I didn't."

By then my mother and several other people were there and they began to pull Daddy away from me.

"Come on, Judd, we know you didn't do that. She must be crazy. Come on, get away from her."

More people were coming, and I went up to each of them. "He locked me up on this farm and molested me, and I just want him to tell me where. It was some kind of a dugout, some underground place and he locked me in there. It's right here, somewhere on this farm. Don't you understand?" My voice was pleading. Each one turned their back on me and wouldn't say a word.

I knew they would try to lock me up because they thought I would hurt him. I persisted. "Don't you see I am not going to hurt him? I just want him to tell me where he locked me up and molested me."

I was getting weaker and weaker, but I kept trying. I had a fork in my hand with just the tip of the prongs showing.

Someone yelled, "You have a weapon, you're going to hurt him."

Then I saw Daddy had a knife and I knew he would use it. I backed away, still begging for help, but no one came. They all turned their backs on me. Somehow, I ended up under some building on my stomach looking out at this sliver of light. Two black men were on their knees crawling to me with a stretcher. I was too weak to move, I just tried to tell them it was all right for them to take me because I knew they didn't want to. I rubbed the tears off my cheeks then I woke up.

I have forgotten many of my dreams. Most of them involved animals mutilated in some way. My father and mother and other members of the family were usually in every dream. As I have said they began in renewed intensity and frequency after the last Amytal interview. It soon became apparent to Dr. Thomas and to me that the dreams were symbols of what had happened in the abuse. As time progressed, they became more and more direct, almost as if they were true memories.

After several years the dreams lessened dramatically, and the depression became much less severe in intensity and duration. The memories kept coming back, and insight into my childhood and family life increased rapidly. As Lindsay predicted, I am still on medication and still seeing Dr. Thomas. I see little change in this life in the foreseeable future. However, my life is so much more enjoyable. I am more at peace and I can almost think of my parents with compassion. My father and mother both died thinking all was forgiven and forgotten. My sisters almost never mention our child-hood, and my children mention their grandparents even less. What we have all lost is like a pebble thrown into the sea, the ripples continue further than the eye can see.

Horses are still a great part of my life. I have built a breeding business that Lindsay can build on later. I am finally able to see the horse as a magnificent animal as well as an endearing friend forever. There will always be a horse for me.

My journey is over. It began as I fell into an abyss of darkness, filled with murky, black waters caused by the most heinous of crimes. I have emerged on the other side, cleansed but scarred. The grass is green, the sun is bright, the end is worth the means.

AFTERWORD

This is my story as faithfully and truthfully as I can tell it. There are only a few things I want to add as a commentary on my journey.

I would never have been able to make the journey or endure the pain without the association of horses. I poured out my love and devotion on them. In return, a horse has never betrayed me or rejected me. Winston Churchill said, "There is nothing so good for the inside of a man as the outside of a horse." My sisters often said as children and young adults, "What would we have done without the horses?"

Horses have always soothed my soul just by looking at them. Different emotions are raised by the condition and looks of the horse, but the effect is always the same. My mind is on the horse, which is the effect I was looking for as a child when I had to get away from the world around me.

As children, we were taken out of Derbyshire County by horse shows. They gave us a goal, a challenge, a responsibility to share. They also gave us another view of the world. A horse show was a place where we could go and, for one weekend, forget everything at home. They were reprieves that helped us live through our weeks. We escaped to the barn and riding ring to get away from our home and our parents.

Forgiving my mother and father may not be possible, but they are my biological parents and I have to acknowledge them. I also recognize that they sacrificed and worked very hard for the land and money I now enjoy. The things I enjoyed as a child are tainted with the knowledge of what I was forced to pay for them. However, I know my life was made more tolerable because of the money. It would have been much worse had we been dirt poor.

Many people will reject the validity of the recovery of repressed memories, the use of Amytal, and the Stockholm Syndrome as a means of survival. To these people, I can only stand behind what I know happened to me and how I have recovered.

All people have secrets that are never told for one reason or another. I have a secret as well that may have changed my life even with the abuse. It deals with my first love. Had I married my first love, my life might have been different. I will never know the answer. My first love has and will hold my heart forever. But that is another story that deserves another time of its own. I have carried the memory of childhood encounters, one brief date, and what could have been throughout my life. Something we all seem to do. Our destiny and the fate of our partners wait to be played out.

Finally, I brought many bad times to my marriage and my children because of my own childhood. For this, I am so sorry, and I beg their forgiveness. I have loved them all and tried to bring happiness to their lives. Dr. Thomas once said, "Marrying Linc may have been the smartest thing you ever did." I do know I married him because I thought he would never hurt me, that he would never betray me in any way. I put him on a pedestal and forgot he was a human being with weaknesses. This was my fault, not his.

About God, I don't know. I do know there are both good and evil forces in this world. And as humans it is our job to conquer evil at any cost to us, letting good spread over the earth.

Maybe there will come a time when I can forgive the bad, and remember it simply as a series of things that happened. I want to fix the bad in this life and hope my next life will begin with better karma, a new moon, and a brighter sun.

PRAISE FOR CAROLYN BABER

"The trauma of sexual assault and domestic violence reverberates violently through the lives of survivors, their families, and communities. When held in silence, shame perpetuates the fragmentation and destructive damage magnifies. *Recollections: A Journey in Courage and Abuse* gives voice to the shattering experience of sexual trauma within a family. By telling this story, my aunt, Carolyn Baber lifts the gray blanket of a victim's shame and transforms it into the expression of a survivor's journey towards healing."

— REV. LAURA BABER, SPIRITUAL DIRECTOR, AUTHOR OF
RHYTHMS OF RESTORATION *AND A SEXUAL ASSAULT SURVIVOR*

"As I read about Carolyn's life, I went through so many emotions. I wanted so many things to change in her life so she could find the happiness she was searching for. The book also shows how a passion in one's life can allow one to survive trauma. The closer you get to the end of the book the faster you read to find out what happens next. The writing will keep you rooting for Carolyn and the ending will give you hope. I highly recommend this book for anyone who is fighting with depression or is trying to help someone fight depression."

— PAM OTTLEY, HORSE OWNER

ABOUT THE AUTHORS

Carolyn Stonnell Baber was a true native Virginian. Born and raised in Central Virginia, she raised her family here as well. She was married for over fifty years and had three children. A school teacher, she received her master's degree from the local university, Longwood. The constants in her life were her family, her horses, and her farm. She started riding and showing at a young age, and the tradition continued with her grandchildren. Her experiences gave her independence, courage, and a sense of justice for the ones that cannot speak for themselves. She enjoyed writing, teaching, and gardening.

Courtenay Baber, MS, LPC, began showing horses as a child with her mother and sister in Central Virginia. She has combined her love of horses with a passion for helping others. As an outpatient therapist, she provides services for adults, focusing on anxiety and depression, and assisting survivors of sexual trauma. In addition, she manages Gray Horse Farm, which offers clinics hosted by top-recognized trainers, along with shows. She provides equine-assisted therapy at the farm through Gray Horse Counseling. Gray Horse Counseling allows her to help the world see the power of healing from animal-assisted activities and therapy.

Lightning Source UK Ltd.
Milton Keynes UK
UKHW020652220621
385957UK00009B/491